D1616735

The Light Shineth in Darkness

The Light Shineth in Darkness:

An Essay in Christian Ethics and Social Philosophy

By S. L. Frank

Translated by Boris Jakim

OHIO UNIVERSITY PRESS   ATHENS

Ohio University Press books are printed on acid-free paper ∞

Library of Congress Cataloging-in-Publication Data

Frank, S. L. (Semen Liudvigovich), 1877–1950.
    [Svet vo t'me. English]
    The light shineth in darkness : an essay in Christian ethics
and social philosophy / by S. L. Frank ; translated by Boris
Jakim.
      p.   cm.
    Translation of: Svet vo t'me.
    Includes bibliographical references.
    ISBN 0-8214-0938-7
    1. Christian ethics—Orthodox Eastern authors.   2. Chris-
tianity—Philosophy.   I. Title.
  BJ1250.F7313   1989
  241'.0419—dc20   89-9287
                                           CIP

CONTENTS

Translator's Introduction: The Life and Work of S. L. Frank

*T*he key to S. L. Frank's life was in his "detached contemplativeness": his entire life was a "blissful dream" or contemplation of that Divine Total-Unity which he felt so deeply. This was Victor Frank's view of his father[1].

Nevertheless, Frank, in his contemplation, could not escape the political and social calamities of his time: he too walked the *via dolorosa* of the Russian intelligentsia of the first half of the 20th century. Victor Frank says[2] that his father, in some way difficult to evaluate now, defined the spiritual character of a whole generation of Russians, especially in the emigration.

S. L. Frank was born in 1877 in Moscow. His father was a physician, who moved to Moscow from western Russia during the Polish rebellion of 1863. Frank's father died in 1882. After her husband's death, Frank's mother moved with her father, M. M. Rossianski, one of the founders of the Moscow Jewish community in the 1860s. Frank's first teacher was his grandfather, who forced the boy

---

1. Frank, Victor. "Semyon Liudvigovich Frank 1877–1950." In *Izbrannive stat'i* [*Selected Articles*]. London 1974. 155–174. The biographical data on S. L. Frank are taken primarily from this essay. Also taken from it are excerpts from S. L. Frank's diary.

2. Ibid. 156

to learn Hebrew and to read the Bible in this language. He would take Frank to the synagogue, where the boy received his first religious impressions, retaining them his entire life. Frank always considered his Christianity as resting on an Old Testament foundation, as the natural development of the religious life of his childhood.[3]

The other major influence on Frank during his early youth was his father-in-law, V. I. Zak. Zak, who passed his youth in an environment of revolutionary populism, introduced Frank to the ideological world of Russian socialism and political radicalism. Frank notes that the influence of these ideas on him was superficial; what influenced him was the general atmosphere of ideological search, which reinforced the necessity of having a "world-view."[4]

In 1892, Frank's family moved to Nizhnii-Novgorod. As an upper classman at the gymnasium there, Frank joined a Marxist study group and became involved with a group of radical intelligentsia. Frank was still under the influence of this atmosphere when he enrolled in the Law Faculty of Moscow University as a 17-year-old in 1894. He became a member then of the newly formed Social Democrats (the forerunners of the Bolsheviks). In 1896, at the age of 19, Frank broke with his fellow conspirators and renounced radical political activity. He could not tolerate the categorical judgments and the shallowness and ignorance of his fellows, and he became indifferent to the revolution and practical revolutionary activity. Remaining a socialist, Frank began a serious study of political economy, which lead him to understand the shakiness and inconsistency of Marx's economic theory.

Student disturbances occurred in most Russian universities during the spring of 1899. Although Frank did not participate actively in them, he composed a proclamation. For this, Frank was arrested and exiled for two years without the right to live in university cities. In the autumn of 1899 he left for Berlin, where he listened to lectures in political economy and philosophy at the university. In Berlin he also wrote his first book: *Marx's Theory of Value and Its Significance* (Moscow 1900).[5]

Frank returned to Russia in 1901 to resume his studies; he was awarded the degree of *kandidat* in Kazan. 1901 marked the awaken-

---

3. Ibid. 158
4. Ibid. 159
5. Ibid. 160–162

ing of Frank's philosophical thought. In the winter of 1901–1902, Frank read Nietzsche's *Also Sprach Zarathustra*. Frank says: "From this moment I felt the reality of the spirit, the reality of the depths of my own soul; and without any specific decisions, my inner fate was defined. I became an 'idealist,' not in the Kantian sense but an idealist-metaphysician, a bearer of a certain spiritual experience, which gave access to the invisible inner reality of being."[6]

Frank's inner crisis was not an isolated phenomenon. It was repeated in many representatives of the new philosophical culture: P. B. Struve, who called for a return to metaphysics in his foreword to Nicholas Berdiaev's book, *Subjectivism and Individualism in the Social Philosophy of Mikhailovsky* (1900); Berdiaev himself, who documented the passage from Marxism to "idealism" in this his first book; the political-economist Sergei Bulgakov (later to become a great Russian Orthodox theologian) whose essay on Ivan Karamazov heralded a similar spiritual crisis. Frank comments: "Without any definite or definable influence of individual thinkers, the current of 'idealism' somehow came spontaneously into being. Intersecting the current coming from Vladimir Solovyov and the Moscow metaphysicians as well as from the symbolist poets, this current flowed into the large religio-philosophical movement of the first several decades of the 20th century—a movement that overcame the traditional spiritual type of the 19th century world-view of the intelligentsia, and gave very remarkable spiritual fruits."[7]

The first decade of this century constituted what Frank called his *Lehr-und Wanderjahre*. He supported himself by the translation of German philosophical works, and participated in a number of politico-cultural journals founded by his close friend the economist P. B. Struve, former leader of the Social Democrats, who was one of those to move from "Marxism to idealism."

In 1909 Frank was one of the participants in the celebrated compilation *Landmarks* (*Vekhi*). In *Landmarks* seven philosphers (besides Frank, the participants were Struve, Berdiaev, Bulgakov, M. O. Gershenzon, A. S. Izgoev, and B. A. Kistiakovsky) united to criticize the radical world-view of the intelligentsia. To quote Frank: "*Landmarks* expressed the spiritual-social tendency whose first harbinger was P. B. Struve. This tendency was composed of two

---

6. Ibid. 163
7. Ibid. 164

fundamental themes: the assertion—against the reigning positivism and materialism of the intelligentsia—of the necessity of a religio-metaphysically grounded world-view; and, on the other hand, a sharp principled critique of the revolutionary maximalistic strivings of the Russian radical intelligentsia."[8]

Landmarks caused a furor; they were received as a brazen betrayal of the sacred tradition of the Russian intelligentsia, a betrayal of the testament of the great social prophets: Belinsky, Granovsky, and Chernyshevsky. Despite the outcry they raised, *Landmarks* were not without influence on a chosen minority of the intelligentsia. The influence of *Landmarks* could be seen in the opposition of the public opinion of the intelligentsia to the Bolshevik revolution and in the appearance of symptoms of religious repentance and rebirth after the revolution.[9]

In 1911–12, Frank passed his master's examination, and in the fall of 1912 became a privat-docent at Petersburg University. He converted to Russian Orthodoxy in 1912. From the spring of 1913 to the summer of 1914 Frank took a sabbatical leave to Germany, where he wrote his first important philosophical work *The Object of Knowledge*, published in 1915 and defended in 1916 as a Master's dissertation.

In *The Object of Knowledge*, Frank sets for himself the goal of revealing the ontological conditions of the possibility of intuition as an immediate knowing of being independent of our acts of knowing.[10] The possibility of intuition as knowledge of being independent of consciousness is explained by the fact that individual being is rooted in the Absolute as Total Unity. Owing to this rootedness in the Absolute, every object before all knowledge of it is close to us in complete immediacy, since we are "fused with it not through our consciousness but in our very being." All logical abstract knowledge is possible not otherwise than on the background

8. Ibid. 166

9. Ibid. 167

10. Lossky, Nikolai. "*Ocherk filosofii S. L. Franka*" ["A Sketch of S. L. Frank's Philosophy"]. In *Vestnik Russkogo Khristianskogo Dvizheniia*. No. 121 (1977). 132–161. The review of Frank's philosophy as presented in the Translator's Introduction basically follows Lossky's analysis of *The Object of Knowledge, The Soul of Man, The Unknowable, The Spiritual Foundations of Society*, and *God-with-us*. In many cases, for the sake of technical precision, I use Lossky's exact wording (translated, of course, into English).

of the intuition of the Total Unity. Logical knowledge is possible only on the basis of metalogical knowledge, on the basis of an intuition of integral being. This integrality is absolute unity or Total Unity, and is not correlative with multiplicity but contains multiplicity; it is the unity of unity and multiplicity.

Logical knowledge, since it deals with elements that are isolated from the whole, always has an abstract character and refers to the lower stratum of being, discontinuous and bereft of life. On the other hand, all of living being, unfolding in time in the form of continuous creative becoming, refers to the metalogical domain. To know this being, what is required is not knowledge-thought, but living knowledge, knowledge-life, attainable at those moments when our "I" not only apprehends an object, i.e., has it extratemporally, but also lives this object."[11]

Frank passed the years of the First World War in Petersburg. In 1916 he wrote and in 1917 he published his book *The Soul of Man* which was to have been his doctoral dissertation, but because of the revolution it was never defended.

Frank considered *The Soul of Man* to be a complement to *The Object of Knowledge*. The reform of gnoseology into "first philosophy" or general ontology outlined in *The Object of Knowledge* necessitates the development of a philosophical psychology as a doctrine of the nature of the individual "soul" and the relation of the "soul" to superindividual objective being.[12] According to Lossky, this work of philosophical psychology explores the element of the soul as a being permeated with subjectivity; investigates the changes that occur in this being when we become conscious of it as an object; distinguishes the spheres of the spiritual and the psychical; and—tracing the interconnectedness between human psychical life and the world in its entirety—shows that the human soul is a microcosm.[13]

From the summer of 1917 to the fall of 1921 Frank served as the dean of the historico-philosophical department of Saratov University. He would have preferred to stay in Petrograd, but the supply difficulties caused by the war and the revolution made it

---

11. Ibid. 132–133

12. Frank, S. L., *Dusha cheloveka* [*The Soul of Man*]. Petrograd 1917. Foreword.

13. Lossky, 133

impossible for him to feed his family (his wife and his three children). Frank arrived in Moscow in 1921 at the beginning of the New Economic Plan, which was accompanied by a short-lived cultural liberalization. Non-communist and even anti-communist intellectuals were allowed to function as academicians and take part in literary and cultural groups. Frank was elected as a member of the Moscow Philosophical Institute and, along with Berdiaev, founded the Academy of Spiritual Culture. The activity of this Academy consisted in the organization of a series of public lectures on philosophical, religious, and general cultural themes, attended by various strata of the public, including students, workers, and Red Army soldiers.[14]

However, this liberalization ended quickly. The Politburo realized what was going on, and arrested and then expelled from the Soviet Union a large number of important scholars and writers, including Frank.[15]

Frank's exile started in September 1922. He lived in Germany until 1937, then he moved to France where he lived until 1945; finally, he went to England, where he lived until his death in 1950.

The years of exile were extremely productive. Frank's great work of this period was *The Unknowable: A Philosophical Introduction to the Ontology of Religion* (Paris, 1938). In this work,[16] the domain of the knowable is said to cover everything that is rational, i.e., everything that is subordinate to the laws of identity, contradiction, and the excluded middle; everything in which one can find repeating elements that therefore can be seen as belonging to the domain of the familiar and can be expressed in concepts. This domain confronts us as objective being. Knowledge of this domain in concepts is abstract, rational knowledge. Objective knowledge does not exhaust the structure of the world; mystical experience reveals to us a deeper domain of the world, something not expressible in concepts, something "unknowable," about which one can have knowl-

---

14. Frank, Victor, 168–169

15. The list of those expelled reads like a hall of fame of 20th-century Russian philoshers: N. Berdiaev, S. Bulgakov, Nikolai Lossky, I. Lapshin, F. Stepun, A. Izgoev, I. Il'in, L. Karsavin, and S. Trubetskoi, among others.—Translator.

16. In this summary of *The Unknowable*, I rely heavily on Lossky, 133–142. This summary is heavily sprinkled with quotations from various places in *The Unknowable*. They are too numerous to footnote.

edge only in the form of "wise ignorance" (Nicholas of Cusa's *docta ignorantia*). Frank explores this domain in three strata of being: (1) in objective being; (2) in our own being; and (3) "in that stratum of reality which, as the primordial ground and total unity, unites and grounds in some way both of these different and heterogenous worlds."

The unknowable turns out to be immediate self-being, a reality which reveals itself to itself and to us insofar as we participate in it. Immediate self-being has the character of "I" only in connection with "thou" who really enters into us, e.g., in the experience of love. True unity of "I" and "thou" is "we," a distinctive element of reality lying at the base of society and more profound than "I." Christianity has in view this reality when it accepts the doctrine of Apostle Paul about the Church as a living body whose members are individual persons while the head is Jesus Christ. Every "I" is rooted in the total unity of "being-for-itself," which is the "kingdom of spirits or concrete bearers of immediate self-being.

Despite the sharp distinction between objective being and immediate self-being, they both belong to one world and for this reason there must exist a unity that encompasses both of them, a common primordial source. This primordial ground can be found by submerging oneself in the world of inner life. Having attained this primordial ground, we transcend being to enter into the domain of the unity of opposites, the domain of the essentially unknowable. This primordial reality can be called Holiness or Divinity, which is distinguished from "God" as a definite form of the "revelation" of Holiness.

Divinity turns to us that side from which He is a person. Like love, He infinitely enriches us with self-giving and creates life as "the being of I with God," contradicting everything that has certitude for logical thought. Like a stream of love, God creates and grounds me, "He contains me in Himself from the very beginning." "He is true God precisely as God-man." "Whence the primordial idea of the Eternal or Heavenly Man encountered in all the more profound religions."

Besides the problem of God-and-I, there is also the problem of God-and-the-world. Frank arrives at the thought that "the calling of the world to being" by God is "the giving of value, the illuminating with meaning"; "the world has its real ground and its ideal foundation in God, and this is precisely the createdness, the creatureliness of the world." The essence of the world consists in the fact that it is a distant likeness of God, and this is felt when we perceive the world's beauty. The world is God's self-disclosure, a theopany. In this way, along with Godmanhood, we have revealed to us God-worldness, the theocosmism of the world.

Since, however, the empirical world contains not only good but also evil, this leads to the problem of theodicy. The presence of evil does not shake the truth of God's being, for God's reality "possesses a greater self-evidence than the self-evidence of a fact." It follows that the connection between God and the "bad" empirical world is "an antinomian-transrational connection and evident only in this its unknowableness."

The only correct attitude toward evil is to reject it, remove it, not to explain it. Not a hypothesis about evil but only a description of evil is possible. When evil is considered, the total unity becomes a "cracked unity." Evil is there where reality itself "desires to be groundless and makes itself such, affirms itself precisely in its groundlessness." Hence, reality has a measureless depth that is dark for us in which "absolutely everything is possible—even what is logically-metaphysically inconceivable."

According to Frank, "evil is born in an ineffable abyss, which lies, as it were, at the threshold between God and not-God." "In living experience, this bottomless place is given as I myself, as a bottomless depth, connecting me with God and separating me from Him." Therefore I am conscious of myself as guilty in evil and sin; this consciousness leads to the overcoming and extinguishing of evil through the restoration of the violated unity with God. "Outside of suffering there is no perfection." Suffering occurs also in God Himself, in the God-man. But "the falling from being, i.e., from God," and the crack in the total unity exist "only in our human aspect." In the Divine aspect, the total unity "remains eternally whole, because all of its cracks are immediately filled from the Primordial Principle with positive being." In the aspect of His eternity, God is "all in all. The world, despite the whole problematic of evil, is—in its ultimate ground and truth—transfigured being—the Kingdom of God."

The other major work published by Frank around this time was *The Spiritual Foundations of Society* (1930). This work is an attempt to define and explore the spiritual nature of society, to investigate society as a type of being, i.e., to develop an ontology of society. Frank finds the presence of two strata in society: inner and outer. The inner layer consists in the unity of "we," while the outer layer consists in the fact that "this unit falls apart into the separateness, opposition, and antagonism of many "I's." Frank calls the inner layer *sobornost'* and the outer layer *obshchestvennost'*. This duality leads to the opposition of the inner organicity and the outer mechanicity of society, the dualities of morality and law, grace and the law, the Church and the world.

Frank defines the goal of social progress to be "the as-complete-as-possible incarnation of the whole fullness of Divine truth in communal human life," "the realization of life itself in the all-embracing fullness, depth, harmony, and freedom of its Divine primordial ground." Frank sees a hierarchical structure of the principles of social life, the foremost of which are the principles of service, solidarity, and individual freedom as the primary obligation, for without freedom service of God is impossible.[17]

In 1933, when the Nazis came to power, Frank lost the ability to earn a living in Germany. Furthermore, when the Gestapo began to take an interest in him, he emigrated to France. When the Second World War started in 1939, Frank, his wife, and one son were cut off from the rest of the family—the remaining children who were living in England. The war years were very hard for Frank: hunger and mortal danger from the Germans in Pétain's government, anxiety about his children, and the consciousness that Europe had fallen under the power of the unleashed force of evil—this was the shadow under which Frank lived and worked during 1939–1945.[18]

The two major works of this period were religious ones: *God-With-Us* and *The Light Shineth in Darkness*. In *God-with-us*, Frank expounds the principles of Christianity and shows that the entire substantial content of Christianity is founded on religious experience, on "the meeting between man's heart and God," "on living communion with God." God is love, and Christianity educates man to carry out the sacrifice of love and to enter onto the way of the Cross, like the God-man Jesus Christ. Frank points out the difference between the mystical Church, which knows no divisions into confessions and which has the the fullness of perfection, and the empirical Church, in which there are many defects. Frank asserts

---

17. Lossky, 146
18. Frank, Victor, 171–172

that our epoch is not a pagan but a demonic one. The union of the churches is necessary for a successful battle against evil.[19]

In *The Light Shineth in Darkness*, Frank attempts to combine "the neglected truth of the mysterious power of sin in the world" with "faith in the positive value of the world as a creation of God and as an expression, in its primordial foundation, of the holy essence of God." This combination leads to a clear discrimination between Christ's absolute truth and its always imperfect embodiment in the world—between the essential salvation of the world and its protection from evil. On the other hand it leads to a perception of the nature of moral creativity as a dramatic Divine-human process of the healing of the world through the imbedding in it of its Divine primordial ground and the battle against dark human wilfullness.[20]

Insofar as man has come to believe in the good news of the Kingdom, and has surrendered himself to the action of the Divine gracious powers that pour down on him together with this news, he is a participant in Divine-human and therefore blessed and gracious being; and his participation in this being forms the foundation and true essence of his entire human existence. This is that truth of his being which is the "way and the life," and this life is that Divine "life," which, according to the Gospel of John, is "the light of men."[21]

---

19. Lossky, 144

20. Frank, S. L. *The Light Shineth in Darkness* [present volume]. Athens, Ohio, 1989, xxiii.

21. Ibid. 74.

Preface

*T*his work was conceived before the war*, and the first version was written in the first year of the war, when it was still impossible to foresee the scale and significance of the demonic forces that were unleashed. Recent events have in no way altered my ideas, but only strengthened and deepened them. But after all that was experienced in those terrible years, it was necessary to express my ideas in wholly different words; hence, the manuscript was rather radically reworked after the end of the war.

Outwardly, the work resembles a theological treatise. I wish to warn the reader that, for good or ill, this outer aspect does not fully correspond to the inner essence of my thought. It is true that my entire intellectual and spiritual development has led me not only to put a high value on traditional Christian thought but to accept Christ's revelation as absolute truth. And I have come to the conclusion that all the woes of mankind have their ultimate source in its old and ever-widening break with the Christian tradition, and that the best and highest hopes of mankind are, reasonably understood, only expressions of the age-old demands of the Christian conscience.

But, on the other hand, I am afraid to be and do not wish to be a theologian—not only because by my education and spiritual cast I am not a theologian, but a free philosopher, but also because I cannot overcome the feeling that all abstract dogmatic theology is

---

* The Second World War.—Translator.

xix

prone to sinful idle talk. According to Goethe's profound, truly religious comment, "Strictly, one can speak about God only with God." The reality of God and of God's truth is revealed to us only in the spiritual experience of the prayerful turning to God, and when God Himself speaks to us through the depths of our spirit, we can only fall silent in the trepidation of penitence or we can prophesy, but we cannot reason discursively. Although the character of our minds is such that we have to interpret this experience logically, every attempt to express this experience in a system of abstract concepts risks tearing the content of religious truth from its living experiential roots, replacing genuine faith by a purely mental construction. Furthermore, religious experience cannot be separated from life-experience, from *fate*, from the personal fate of each of us and from the fate of a generation or epoch in all its tragedy and imperfection, in all its fragmentariness and obscurity. God is known only in tragic struggle and through the torments of human existence; this was expressed well by such solitary thinkers of the modern age as Pascal and Kierkegaard. But this is sharply contradicted by the self-assurance, the pretension to completeness, of all objective theological systems. And although we understand that the experience of all of mankind (for the Christian this means the experience of the Christian church) is richer and deeper than our personal experience, and that we can and must learn from this deeper experience, nevertheless the truths that we glean from this experience become significant for us only when they are compared to and verified by our own experience. Not for a moment must we stop paying attention to what God tells us directly *here and now*. Otherwise, our faith will easily degenerate into a theological pseudo-faith, a purely intellectual or even verbal affirmation of not what we believe, but what we wish to believe. With all due respect for the religious wisdom of the past, for the "faith of our fathers," we must beware lest this respect entice us to worship God not with our hearts, but with our lips, to replace the truth of God with "the commandments of men" (Matthew 15:9).

In all ages, faith has fought with unfaith in the human heart—with open unfaith and with pharisaical unfaith, concealed behind traditional, official theology. The danger from both kinds of unfaith and the necessity to defend the true faith against them have never been so great as they are for contemporary man, educated and formed in a culture that for centuries has been antireligious. "Lord, I believe, help thou mine unbelief" (Mark 9:24)—this eternal cry of the human soul resounds more intensely and tragically now than in past ages. In our age, an almost insuperable abyss separates the vital struggle of the human spirit to find a way out of the woe of unfaith, to find a religious understanding of life in the midst of the soulless world of modern science and in the midst of human willfullness justified by modern morality—from the fixed, closed world of traditional theology. Theological doctrines usually hover outside of life, which contemptuously passes them by; vital encounters between theological doctrines and life are rare exceptions. In essence, it is not a question of the falsity or obsolescence of the content of these doctrines. And the last thing our age needs is a "reformation," an effort to correct the dogmas and canons of the church. Rather, the fact is that modern thought no longer understands why it needs and how it can be helped by the general orientation, the general spiritual style, of these doctrines, and feels that they are anachronistic in the face of our real suffering and agonized search. It is possible to admire the grandiosity and harmony of Aquinas' theological-philosophical system, the highest expression of medieval Christian wisdom, but, though individual ideas in this system remain true and necessary for us, it is impossible to use the system as a whole in our life, as impossible as it would be to substitute Gothic cathedrals for our modern dwellings and factories. But where will we find a new Aquinas? It appears that his time has not yet come.

In our present religious poverty, the only path we have to the saving truth of the Christian faith is not the doctrines of old books, but the lessons of our unhappy lives. The only doctrines we need are those which can help to save us, point us to the true path of life. Even as a hungry man needs bread, even as a drowning man needs solid ground beneath his feet, so we need *religiously contemporary* "dogmas," however elementary, that could give us solid moral support in life. All else, all the luxury of old dogmatic doctrines and debates, has meaning only for individual subtle minds, while for most people these doctrines and debates are only an intellectual pastime in the face of our universal needs.

Thus, the present work aims to be not an abstract theological treatise, but a modest attempt at a religious interpretation of the intellectual experience and the life-experience of the author. Above all, this experience is sociohistorical experience. Like most Russian intellectuals of my generation, in my youth I took as my point of departure the socialistic faith in the salvation of mankind through a radical social revolution. But a long time ago, at the beginning of this century, a group of Russian thinkers, to which I belonged, came to recognize more and more clearly that the unfaith which lies at the base of this dream of a radiant future is unsatisfactory and destructive. We began to realize that this nihilism, contemptuous of absolute values and rejecting the spiritual foundations of being, must lead to a despotism that stifles and cripples the individual. This realization determined our "conversion" from Marxism—first to a rather foggy "idealism," and then to a positive Christian faith. All that has happened during the past forty years, first in Russia and then in Europe, has, unfortunately, confirmed our fears on a scale that no one could have foreseen then. The Bolshevik revolution and the order established by it were a grandiose experiment *in corpore vili* that far surpassed one's worst fears. And then we witnessed the impotence and blindness of the nonreligious humanism of the Western democracies, and the appearance in Europe of a new form of atheism, a titanism that openly preached the demonic cult of violence and predatory love of power, a fundamental denial of all the moral principles of life. One who has understood the spiritual nature of Russian Bolshevism cannot fail to see that Nazism or Fascism is its spiritual brother, only a new version of atheistic demonism. Now that this demonism has flooded the world with a sea of blood, the entire world has understood its deadly threat. However, the true meaning of what has happened is still not understood by many, because of a fact that is accidental from the fundamentally ideological point of view: the fact that two powers, kindred in their spirit of titanism, collided, and Soviet atheism became the temporary ally of Western democracy, which, despite its secularization, is based on Christian moral principles. But now that the war has ended, this misunderstanding has been dissipated to a significant degree.

Historical events can be interpreted in different ways, depending upon to which of their many general and particular causes we give attention. But it appears that many people are now becoming aware that the primary cause of historical movement lies in the change of the structure of spiritual life and of the ideas that guide this life. If this is so, not even the most successful military and political actions can by themselves save mankind, for, as the Apostle says, "we wrestle not against flesh and blood but against . . . the rulers of the darkness of this world" (Ephesians 6:12). The path to salvation lies only in the deepening of spiritual self-conscious-ness, in the re-examination of prevailing ideas.

The present religious meditation aims to serve as this kind of re-examination. In this meditation, I aim to combine an interpreta-tion of my life-experience in the light of Christian faith with my overall philosophical intuition of metaphysical *realism* (in contrast not only to materialism and positivism, but also to abstract ideal-ism), and with religious *panentheism*, according to which God is not only transcendent in relation to His creation, but is also imma-nently present in His creation as its eternal foundation and life-giving principle. The basic premise of my book follows from this. Affirmation of the long-forgotten and rejected truth of the myste-rious power of sin in the world is combined with faith in the posi-tive value of the world as a creation of God and as an expression — in its primordial foundation — of the holy essence of God. On the one hand, this combination leads to a clear distinction between Christ's absolute truth, surpassing all earthly institutions and ac-cessible only to the superworldly depths of the human spirit, and the always-imperfect earthly incarnation of this truth — that is, to a distinction between the essential salvation of the world and the defense of the world against evil. And on the other hand it leads to the perception of the nature of moral creativity as the dramatic Divine-human process of the healing of the world through the em-bedding in it of its Divine primordial-foundation and through the battle against the dark self-willfullness of man. I see a clear, humble, and responsible recognition of these truths as the only way out of the woes that afflict contemporary mankind.

Let all that is one-sided, subjective, and false in my meditation be blown away like smoke, without tempting anyone. But let all that is genuine, Divine truth help others as it has helped me.

London. November 1945.

Introduction:
"The Light Shineth
in Darkness"

*I*n the mysterious prologue to the Gospel of St. John, there is a verse that, being difficult to interpret in general, also has an unclear literal meaning, the explanation of which has long been a problem for scholars. Moreover, this verse is of essential significance, for it is part of the symbolic description of the metaphysical meaning of Christian revelation. This verse — John 1:5 — speaks about the relation between the light of the Divine Logos and the world. In Greek the verse reads: καά τὸ φῶς ἐν τῇ σκοτία φαί νει, καὶ ἡ σκοτία αὐτὸ οὐ κατελαβεν.*

As near as one can say, the riddle of this verse is due to the ambiguity of the word κατέλαβεν. The verb κατελάμβανω usually means to "receive," "apprehend," "assimilate" (in the physical or spiritual sense), but it can also mean to "grab," "seize," "overtake" (in a chase), and, hence, in the final analysis, to "overcome," "defeat." What did the Evangelist wish to say after the words "And the light shineth in darkness"? According to one interpretation, that of Origen, it is a question of the *invincibleness* of the light in its battle with the darkness: once the light shines in the world, it cannot be overcome by the darkness — "the darkness comprehended

---

* "And the light shineth in darkness; and the darkness comprehended it not."

1

it not." The spiritual sun that shines on the world does not know eclipse and cannot go out; it shines eternally, remaining inaccessible to the power of darkness.

But this verse admits another interpretation, to some extent opposite to the first. If the Greek word in question is taken to mean "receive" or "assimilate" (this is how the Vulgate, the oldest Latin translation of the Bible, interprets it), then the verse expresses not the joyous consciousness that the light cannot be overcome by the darkness, but the tragic, bitter consciousness that the darkness is resistant, that it cannot be overcome by the light. The light has entered the world and shines, but (in contrast to what happens in the physical world and what one would naturally expect), it does not overcome, does not dissipate, the darkness. On the contrary, the Evangelist records a terrifying, incomprehensible, evidently unnatural phenomenon. The light shines, but remains surrounded by the impenetrable darkness, which does not receive the light, does not assimilate it, and therefore is not dissipated by it. And the world remains the kingdom of darkness, even though the Eternal Unfading Light shines in its depths.

The very fact that the disagreement between these opposing interpretations started with the most ancient interpreters of the Gospel and has lasted to our own day, indicates that neither interpretation can be demonstrated to be absolutely, objectively true or absolutely, objectively false.* We do not consider ourselves competent to find new arguments that could fully clarify this disagreement which has lasted for nearly two millennia. What is important for us is to point out something else. Regardless of what the Evangelist really had in mind when he wrote this verse, regardless of what he meant when he used the ambiguous word $\kappa\alpha\tau\acute{\epsilon}\lambda\alpha\beta\epsilon\nu$, both of the aforementioned interpretations of this word agree with the general teaching and spirit of the Gospel of St. John. Furthermore, regardless of what the Evangelist really meant in this verse, we must affirm about his religious teaching as a whole that it is determined

---

* It is interesting to note that the first of these interpretations, that of Origen, is expressed in Slavonic translations of the New Testament, while the second interpretation, through the influence of the Vulgate, has become part of the Western Christian (Catholic and Protestant) understanding of this passage. In general, Eastern Christianity understands this verse as the affirmation of the invincibleness of the light, while the Western church understands it as the affirmation of the resistance of the darkness.

precisely by the combination, the joint affirmation of the two ideas that emanate from the two interpretations. There is no doubt that the religious teaching expressed in the Gospel of St. John contains both faith in the invincibleness of the Divine, superworldly light that shines on the world and the bitter recognition of the unnatural resistance of the darkness, which is not dissipated by the light, but surrounds it like an impenetrable wall. Some parts of this Gospel may stress one of these ideas, while other parts may stress the other idea. It is important to understand, however, that only their combination, their joint affirmation, adequately expresses the religious vision of the Evangelist.

But this assumes that these two ideas, and the corresponding different interpretations of the verse in question, do not contradict each other. It is necessary to point out something highly significant with regard to the two possible meanings of this verse, something that is wholly unquestionable, but usually ignored for some reason: namely, that the distinction between the two possible meanings is *not so great* as it seems at first glance and is often held to be.

An inattentive reading of the text might make it appear that it is a question of a *radical* distinction between the joyous affirmation of the triumph of the light over the darkness and the sorrowful consciousness of the powerlessness of the light in the face of the resistance of the darkness—a question of the opposition between the absolutely "optimistic" and absolutely "pessimistic" points of view, as it were. But things are evidently not so simple if the two views can be in harmony, as we pointed out above. If we agree to call these two views "optimistic" and "pessimistic" (in essence, this is inaccurate), it is essential to recognize that even in the optimistic interpretation the verse in question does not contain an affirmation of the absolute, explicit *triumph of the light*, its obvious all-powerfulness and conclusive victory over the darkness (in the plane of the world's being). This verse says only that the light cannot be defeated, cannot be overcome by the darkness that attempts to put it out—which of course is something wholly different. If, generally speaking, the Evangelist undoubtedly believes in the all-powerfulness of the Divine light in the superworldly plane of being (we shall discuss this later), nevertheless in the plane of earthly being the joyous, comforting fact that he proclaims is only that the light is successfully *defending* itself against the attack of the darkness, that the invincibleness of the light against the hostile powers of darkness is assured. Therefore, precisely this so-called optimistic interpretation conceives the light as the principle that, in the plane of worldly being, is attacked by the darkness, and the darkness as the principle that takes the initiative of attack. And the only certainty is that the besieged fortress will never surrender, will never submit to the enemy—because of the superworldly, gracious*, Divine source of its power. Thus, this comforting fact presupposes that the fate of the light in the world is a tragic fate, full of danger. Precisely for this reason this "optimistic" interpretation does not contradict the "pessimistic" one, but easily and naturally agrees with the latter. Furthermore, only in agreement with the pessimistic interpretation is the optimistic one adequate to the general religious idea of the Gospel of St. John. Thus, if we attempt to understand the verse in question in the spirit of this general religious idea, we have the right (leaving aside what the Evangelist may actually have wanted to say) to combine both interpretations and to formulate the Evangelist's general view in the proposition: *The light shines in darkness, and the darkness resists the light; the darkness cannot absorb the light, but the light cannot dissipate the darkness.*

Whether the Evangelist wished to emphasize that the darkness is powerless to put out the light once it has shined in the world or whether he wished to sorrowfully disclose that the darkness is resistant, does not receive the light, and thus is not dissipated by it—in both cases he takes as his point of departure the *dualistic* and therefore *tragic* idea of the opposition between the light and the darkness as the fundamental fact of the world's being. This irreconcilable opposition is revealed both in the invincibleness of the light in the face of the attack of the darkness and in the unnatural resistance of the darkness in the face of the light that should illuminate and dissipate it.† I think that this synthetic interpretation is justi-

---

* The word "gracious" (*blagodatnyi* in Russian) will always be used in this translation in its rather archaic sense of having or being marked by Divine grace.—Translator.

† In regard to the question of the authentic meaning of the word καταλαμβάνειν in this verse, let me offer an opinion that appears paradoxical at first glance, but that seems to me completely justified and capable of resolving the argument. If we take into consideration the fact that the Evangelist John is not an abstract thinker, but an inspired believer and preacher, whose every word is a kind of hint at a mystery unfathomable for the mind, at a concrete fullness of being that *in its very essence cannot be determined with precision*, then it is permissible to admit

fied already by the first half of the verse: "and the light shineth in darkness."

We have become so used to reading the Bible carelessly, to skimming the text without thinking deeply about its real meaning, to accepting the text as a familiar verbal formula, that few people consider the true meaning of these words (i.e., "the light shineth in darkness"). It appears that most people tend to consider these words as nothing more than a rhetorical device, something like a poetic phrase (similar to "a nightingale sings in the stillness"). But one can hardly be satisfied with such a simple and superficial explanation, which is already contradicted by the fact that the verse has a second part, which we examined above. Whatever the true meaning of the second part, it is clear that the darkness is not mentioned by chance, for the darkness is opposed to the light as a real power that is hostile to the light. But in this case, what does the phrase "the light shineth in darkness" mean?

If the past tense were used, "the light *hath shined* in *darkness*," everything would be simple and understandable: a source of light appeared in the darkness; where once darkness was, there is now light. Another Evangelist, in reporting Jesus' stay and sermons "in Capernaum, which is upon the sea coast, in the borders of Zabulon and Nephthalim," remembers what "was spoken by Esaias the prophet": "The people that walked in darkness have seen a great light; they that dwell in the land of the shadow of death, upon them

---

that the Evangelist does not have in mind *either* of the two possible senses of $\kappa\alpha\tau\alpha\lambda\alpha\mu\beta\acute{\alpha}\nu\epsilon\iota\nu$, but uses this word precisely in *the vital linguistic fullness of its meaning*, simultaneously encompassing both senses. This can appear paradoxical only because we no longer feel Greek as a living language, and thus only with difficulty can we apprehend the genuine, living mystical-poetic—and not abstract-logical—meaning of the Evangelist's verse. We might approximately gain a genuine understanding of this passage by translating it as "the darkness did not take it," the living, indefinite and ambiguous meaning of the word "take" expressing precisely the whole fullness of that mysterious relation of dual unity wherein the darkness neither receives and assimilates nor overcomes and defeats the light. As an analogy, consider, *toutes proportions gardées*, Hegel's *intentionally ambiguous* use of the word *"aufheben"* (which means both to "remove," "eliminate," and to "conserve," "preserve") to express the basic idea of his philosophy: namely, the spirit in its development simultaneously overcomes every separate stage of being and conserves in itself that which it has overcome and removed.

hath the light shined" (Isaiah 9:2; Matthew 4: 13, 16). But the Evangelist John wishes to say something else: he does not speak about an event that once occurred in time; he does not say that the light "hath shined" in darkness. Rather, he speaks about a certain eternal (or enduring, to put it more modestly) metaphysical state or relation of light and darkness, which he expresses in the words "the light shineth in darkness." But how can this be? Insofar as we are guided by an analogy to physical light, we must say that where light is, there is no darkness; and where darkness is, there is no light. One state excludes the other. It is natural to think that, once it has shined, the light illuminates, expels, replaces the darkness. On the other hand, it is possible to imagine in some figurative sense that a light lit in the darkness, for instance a candle lit in a dark and stormy autumn night, can go out, as if submitting to the overwhelming onslaught of the darkness.

There remains one possibility (apparently the only possibility) of rationally and distinctly conceiving of a state in which "the light shineth in darkness." In a dark, moonless, but starry sky, stars shine "in darkness" like points of light. Lamps lit in a dark night are visible from a distance as points of light. And even from up close, a faint light, for instance the light from a small lantern, can shine without illuminating anything except an insignificantly small portion of the nearby space, while the light itself is surrounded by a profound darkness which it is not able to dissipate.

But in speaking about the light that shines in darkness and thereby excluding the first two states, i.e., the light that illuminates and dissipates the darkness and the darkness that puts out the light, the Evangelist has something wholly different in mind from the first possibility just mentioned. Let us remember that the light he speaks about is the "true light" ($\varphi\tilde{\omega}\varsigma\ \hat{\alpha}\lambda\eta\theta\iota\nu\acute{o}\nu$: the "genuine light"), the light emanating from God, that light of the Divine Logos through which the world itself came into being. Therefore, it is impossible to claim that this light glowed faintly and that, precisely because of its own inner faintness, it could not dissipate the darkness and illuminate the world. Nevertheless this light—inextinguishable, infinitely powerful in its immanent metaphysical essence, all-powerful (because it is Divine)—is condemned in the world to shine *in darkness*.

Before clarifying this relation in all its paradoxicality, determined by the opposition between the relative empirical "faintness" of the light and its metaphysical all-powerfulness, we must first

6

become aware of the living meaning of the ideas that the Evangelist uses. If we take as our point of departure the conception of modern physics according to which darkness is nothing else but the absence of light, then the Evangelist's words, pointing to the opposition between light and darkness, appear to be meaningless. But we must not forget that it is a question not of physics but of mysterious metaphysics, which is only symbolized in the concepts of "light" and "darkness." More precisely, it is a question *not of concepts but of images* of light and darkness, which only hint at the abstractly unknowable mystery of being. The *image* of light and darkness is given to us immediately (as it was given primordially to the human spirit) in the phenomenon of *day and night*. The "day," the time when the sun rises and shines, is of course triumphant over the darkness of the night, but the night returns in its time and replaces the day. According to the Book of Genesis, God's creation of the light was His first creative act after the creation of "the heaven and the earth," the first act of *the ordering of the world's being*. In place of the earth that "was without form, and void," in which "darkness was upon the face of the deep," there appeared, as the first form of being, the duality between light and darkness. "And God divided the light from the darkness. And God called the light Day, and the darkness he called Night" (Genesis 1: 4–5). Thus begins the first *day* of creation; this relation has endured until now and will endure until the end of the world.

In this perspective (i.e., within the limits of the world's being) light and darkness, like day and night, are opposite, antagonistic principles. The paradoxicality of this situation consists in the fact that the light in its inner, metaphysical essence is the Divine light, the light of God Himself, and thus it is a higher, all-powerful principle. The same John in one of his epistles proclaims the following that "our joy may be full": "God is light, and in him is no darkness at all" (1 John 1:5). This "good news" takes its place alongside other testimony, which we already find in the Old Testament, and which, affirming the identity of God and the light, urges us to believe confidently in the triumph of the light and the powerlessness of the darkness. The Psalmist, righteous Job, and the prophet Isaiah speak of God as the perfect and all-powerful Light. "For with thee is the fountain of life; in thy light shall we see light" (Psalm 36:9). God as light is so all-powerful that before Him "even the night shall be light," and "the night shineth as the day" (Psalm 139: 11–12). God "discovereth deep things out of darkness, and bringeth out to light the shadow of death" (Job 12: 22). The prophet Isaiah teaches man that if he follows the truth commanded by God, "thy darkness [will] be as the noon day" (Isaiah 58:10). Thus, in these intuitions of the Old Testament and even more emphatically in the "good news" of the New Testament, the light—coinciding with the nature of God Himself as it were—is the highest principle, all-powerful, all-triumphant, salvational. And this idea contains something immeasurably greater than the aforementioned conception of modern physics according to which light "automatically" overcomes or dissipates the darkness—simply because the latter does not exist in its own right, but is only the absence of light. No, here it is a question of something else: the darkness as a real force, opposite and hostile to the light, is genuinely overcome, defeated, by the all-powerfulness of the Divine light.

Only now can we understand in all their paradoxicality the Evangelist's words: "the light shineth in darkness." They describe the abnormal, unnatural state of the world's being. Metaphysically all-powerful and triumphant in its essence, the perfect light, which is the revelation of God Himself and therefore "lights" every man, finds itself empirically, in the world, in a state of irreconcilable conflict with the darkness. The darkness cannot overcome the superworldly Divine light (and this is completely natural). And the light cannot dissipate the darkness (and this also is completely natural). The darkness does not receive the light, but resists it, rejects it. This is a great paradox, which cannot be essentially understood or explained, but which can only be affirmed precisely in its unexplainableness and unnaturalness. "The true light," the perfect light, the light that is so powerful that "the world was made by him" —this light "was in the world," but "the world knew him not" (John 1: 10–11).

In seeking rational understanding, rational explanation, we must not attempt to shake or weaken the paradoxicality of this situation. How can an all-powerful, Divine principle find itself in the world in the position of an unrecognized, persecuted, outwardly powerless principle, without losing its dignity and its force of a Divine principle? How can the light of God Himself, this light in the face of which (in its metaphysical nature) even "the night shineth as the day," be a light that empirically, in the being of the world, "shineth in darkness"? How can our perfect joy from the fact that "God is light, and in him is no darkness at all," that is to say, our perfect joy arising from the awareness of the Divine, creative all-powerfulness of the light—how can this joy be combined, without being lessened, with the sorrowful awareness that the world does not receive the light, that the darkness is not dissipated by the light?

If we wish to "philosophize" about this character of being in the sense of attempting to explain it in terms of abstract concepts, we shall only become confused and find ourselves at a dead end. Those who have not the dimmest intuition of the primordial mystery of being, which surpasses the fundamental structure of our "reason," should not reflect on such things. Being in its very essence is *antinomian*, contains the mystery of the unity and coincidence of opposites. From the first words of his good news, the Evangelist reveals to us this *coincidentia oppositorum* as the fundamental tragic situation of the world's being.

To explain logically the mystery of this contradictory situation, to explain it in such a way that it stops being a mystery, is impossible, for to find the rational "cause" or "ground" of this fact of the unnatural resistance of the darkness and its opposition to the light would be to recognize it as natural and legitimate, that is, to *justify* the resistance of the darkness. But precisely this is impermissible. All rational theodicy, any attempt logically and without contradiction to reconcile the fact of the world's evil with the all-powerfulness and all-goodness of God, is not only logically impossible and inconsistent, but in essence is religiously inadmissible, for it conceals, to a certain degree, a justification of evil. The only possible "explanation" of the unnatural state we are discussing is an explanation that does not justify but *exposes* and *condemns*. In other words, a logical or cosmological explanation of the resistance of the darkness is impossible; only a spiritual penetration into its religious mystery, only the exposure of its illegitimate, anti-Divine essence, is possible. "And this is the condemnation, that light is come into the world, and men loved darkness rather than light, because their deeds were evil. For every one that doeth evil hateth the light, lest his deeds should be reproved" (John 3: 18-19).

We must not forget that the image of the darkness symbolizes both evil and the state of invisibility, concealment, hiddenness, whereas the image of the light symbolizes both the good and clarity, visibility, truthful self-disclosure—the "truth." This makes it possible for the Evangelist to "explain" (not in an abstract-logical, but in a concrete-symbolic manner) the resistance of the darkness, its impenetrability for the light. As evil, the darkness is afraid of the

9

light, of the good that is also the light of revelation, making visible what is invisible and hidden. But precisely this resistance of the darkness, in this its self-concealment from the light, contains the exposure and condemnation of the darkness precisely as darkness, indeed its immanent *self-condemnation*. If the darkness did not oppose the light, but went out to meet it and allowed itself to be illuminated, this meeting with the light would signify its disappearance as darkness, its illumination. But the essence of the darkness resists this meeting as a criminal resists the exposure of his evil deeds; the darkness hides from the light as if covering itself with an impenetrable cloak. But in affirming itself in its own being, *hidden from the light*, the darkness discloses that it is clearly distinct from the light, exposes itself as darkness, "condemns" itself.

We shall not examine all that remains incomprehensible and raises further questions concerning the content of this symbolic disclosure of the mystery of the resistance of the darkness. Only one thing is essential for us here. Without logically "explaining" what in its essence is unexplainable (for it is anti-rational and dark), the Evangelist nonetheless lets us somehow understand how the darkness can resist the light even though it is inwardly powerless before it. The darkness exists because evil will hides from, avoids the light. *The all-powerful, Divine light turns out to be not all-powerful in the empirical being of the world insofar as it is opposed by evil human will.* The metaphysically impossible, i.e., the limitation of the power of the Divine principle of light in the world, turns out to be empirically real.

The fifth verse of the prologue of the Gospel of St. John, consisting of just a few words, expressively and profoundly outlines a great theme: the mysterious truth that the all-powerful light of Divine reason, Divine grace, is fated in the world to suffer the opposition of the darkness, though, owing to its all-powerfulness, it cannot be put out by the darkness even in the world. This truth is a concentrated form, as it were, of the entire essence of Christian revelation, Christian faith.

CHAPTER ONE

The Spiritual Problematic
of our Time

What is the practical meaning, the life-meaning, of what we have just discussed? My intent is not self-centered, abstract, theological speculation. Theological truth is always truth as *the way and the life.* Everything else is unnecessary "literature."

I think that the theological (i.e., at bottom the purely religious) problem of the light and the darkness, to which verse 1:5 of the Gospel of St. John offers a profound and mysterious solution, is perhaps the most agonizing, but also the most essential problem of human life. And, as such, this problem takes on an especially acute significance precisely in our time. In the problem of the light and the darkness, the problem of the light that shines in darkness, i.e., in the combination of two fundamental ideas, the incomprehensible, unnatural but factually evident resistance of the darkness to the light, and the possibility of faith in the light despite this resistance of the darkness—are concentrated all the thoughts and doubts, all the hopes, to which the European consciousness has come as a result of the experience of the first four-and-one-half decades of the 20th century, and particularly the horrific experience of the Second World War. In this problem is concentrated all that makes *our* faith, *our* convictions, differ fundamentally—as a result of this experience—from the dominant views of the 18th and 19th centuries. People whose first moral convictions were formed under the influence of the ideas of the 19th century cannot but be aware—

insofar as they have at all preserved the ability to learn from the experience of life—that they have received and are receiving a lesson of the first importance, a lesson that exposes many of their former convictions (indeed the most essential of these convictions) as illusions and sets before them new, tormenting problems. Furthermore, the political events of the 20th century, the fact that, starting roughly with 1914, European mankind has embarked on a long period of destructive wars and great internal cataclysms, culminating in the wild apocalyptic orgy of evil of the past few years, and changes in the conceptions and convictions (partly determined by these events, partly independent of them) of the European world—these events and changes leave the undeniable impression that the 20th century marks the beginning of a completely new historical epoch. When we look back and compare our tragic epoch with the relatively peaceful and successful second half of the 19th century, we find the differences in the style of life and thought of the two epochs to be immediately apparent. And I think we must admit that the essence of this difference is significantly determined by a new experience of the resistance and power of evil in the world.

1. The Power of Darkness

When the chief priests and the elders of the Jewish people came with a crowd of servants to the Garden of Gethsemane to arrest Jesus Christ, He told them: "This is your hour, and the power of darkness" (Luke 22:53). I think that many people, if they wish to sum up the bitter life-experience of the present time, could not find a better expression than these words. The main, decisive impression left by all that it has been the lot of European mankind to experience in recent times is the impression of *the power of darkness in the world.* The forces of evil and destruction are triumphant over the forces of good; as a general rule, error is more powerful than truth; the blind play of irrational forces, in personal and historical life, sets limits to all the hopes of the human heart. This is the dominant impression that we receive from life. This impression leads to the conviction that all that is good, rational, beautiful, noble in the world is a rare exception, extremely weak and fragile, always crushed by and drowning in the forces of evil. The general background and fundamental, dominant essence of the world's being appear to consist in the blind, elemental passions of greed, hate, lust for power, and even meaningless, vicious sadism. That which forty years ago (to some extent even ten years ago) seemed absolutely impossible in European mankind, formed by principles of classical culture, Christian consciousness, and the great humanitarian movement of modern history, has happened with astonishing ease: slavery that surpasses all its ancient forms in cruelty, the mass destruction of whole peoples, the treatment of men like animals, cynical contempt for the most elementary principles of law and truth. The so-called man of culture suddenly became an illusion; in reality he exposed himself as an unprecedentedly cruel, morally blind savage, whose entire culture consists in one thing: the sophistication and improvement of the means of torturing and killing his neighbors. One hundred years ago, Alexander Herzen predicted the invasion of "Genghis Khan with telegraphy." This paradoxical prediction has been justified on a scale Herzen could not have foreseen. Born in the very heart of Europe, the new Genghis Khan unleashed aerial bombardments against Europe, destroyed entire cities, made gas chambers for the mass destruction of people, and now threatens to sweep mankind off the face of the earth with atomic bombs.

Of course, it is easy to lessen the horror and fundamental significance of this consciousness by claiming that the responsibility lies with individual nations or with individual moral-political doctrines that have possessed these nations. This pharisaical tendency, so common to man, especially when he is possessed by enmity, is not only morally false, but is theoretically based on a pitiful inconsistency of thought. It cannot be denied of course that moral and spiritual principles turned out to be stronger and stabler among some of the European peoples than among others. But this does not explain why in the depths of European mankind, one in race and historical culture, a new barbarism could arise and take hold. One for whom the idea of a Christian European mankind, the Christian world, is not an empty word cannot suppress in himself the penitent awareness that this Christian world as a whole is responsible for the moral catastrophe that has befallen it. The German nation was not less a bearer of Christian culture than the other European nations: the writings of its great mystics were one of the profoundest expressions of the Christian spirit; it produced the Reformation, which, despite its later errors, assisted the revival of the Church; and among its great thinkers and poets, it had not very long ago such universally recognized representatives of European humanism and teachers of mankind as Kant and Goethe. The sudden fall of the German nation into an unprecedented barbarism must therefore be considered a manifestation of the spiritual sickness of European mankind as a whole. This was confirmed by the infectiousness of the sickness. Before the war, Nazism, like Fascism before it, was viewed with unexpected tolerance and even favor, and acquired convinced followers almost everywhere in Europe. Furthermore, during the war, in all the occupied and vassal states of Europe it was easy to train whole cadres of people to apply this barbaric doctrine with not less inhumanity than the Germans. The popular conception that the German nation has an innate tendency to cruelty and to contempt for the human person is exposed in the face of these facts as hypocrisy or stupidity. The facts incontrovertibly show that under certain conditions it is easy in a short period of time to transform many Europeans, who are thought to be permeated by Christian humanitarian culture, into barbarians and monsters.

Furthermore, it is just as nearsighted to view a specific doctrine as the ultimate source of the evil. A doctrine here is only the outer shell and ideological justification of the instinct of evil that slumbers in the soul of mankind; and the whole success of the doctrine consists in the fact that it approves the unleashing of this instinct. When the spirit of evil becomes active and seeks to reveal itself, it will easily find justification in any doctrine that happens to be around. Anyone who, spiritually, still has eyes to see knows, for instance, that the triumphant foe of Nazism and Fascism—Russian Communism—is only another form of the same cult of evil and inhumanity, and that after the military defeat of Nazism the danger of the destruction of the moral foundations of society and of all human life has only changed its form, but remains just as threatening. But let us go further. If Nazism and Communism can and must be viewed only as two forms of one and the same evil of "totalitarianism," the suppression of the human person by the inhuman machine of the absolute state, it must also be admitted that totalitarianism itself, in all its variants, is not the essence but only a form of immorality and inhumanity. The spirit of hate, cynicism, and contempt for human life is much wider and more widespread than any doctrine. During the war this spirit naturally made enormous, horrible conquests when it possessed the souls of the fundamental enemies of totalitarianism. During those years, who among us did not encounter kind, cultured people who preached the mass annihilation or enslavement of the German nation? And whatever the military arguments in favor of using the atomic bomb, world history will record to the everlasting shame of mankind that a method of war which uses an artificial earthquake to cause the sudden death of hundreds of thousands of innocent people was first employed by the Anglo-Saxon world, the generally recognized bearer of the principles of law and respect for man.

No, we must have the courage to look truth in the eyes. All that we experienced during the war and all that we dimly felt even before this catastrophe bear witness to this. The spirit of evil is not concentrated in particular individual carriers of evil, and to conquer these carriers by militarily defeating them does not mean to defeat and annihilate the spirit of evil itself. This spirit has the mysterious ability to jump from one soul to another like the sparks of a fire. Like the phoenix, this spirit rises from ashes in unexpected new forms. For this spirit is primordially concealed in the soul of mankind; it is a superhuman force that cannot be overcome by any purely human efforts and external measures. This spirit is truly "the prince of the world"; and thus the world is in "the power of darkness."

The contemporary German philosopher Nicolai Hartmann expresses his pessimistic view of the world in the general metaphysical affirmation that the *level* of being is inversely proportional to the *force* of being, that the higher—being a derivative superstructure above the lower—is always weaker than the lower. Spiritual forces are weaker than animal forces, the forces of the organic world are weaker than the forces of the inorganic world. But one can recognize the power of darkness over the world even without accepting this formula. It is sufficient to limit oneself to the modest and unquestionable recognition that nothing in the world's being guarantees the triumph of reason and the good. In other words, it is not possible to establish a direct proportionality between the *value level* of a manifestation of the world's being and the *real force* or *influence* of this manifestation. Nature, the structure of the world's being—including history, i.e., the fate of man—appears to be indifferent to good and evil, truth and untruth, reason and foolishness. In this sense the "kingdom of this world" is very clearly "the power of darkness."

Of course, this idea of the power of darkness in the world, just like the idea of the light that shines in darkness, is a truth that is as old as life-experience or as old as the human heart that believes boldly in opposition to all the evident facts of the empirical world.

On the other hand, the heart that believes or seeks to believe has, from time immemorial, been tormented by doubts, unable to harmonize its faith, its search for the truth, with the meaninglessness and injustice of the fate of man in the world. It is sufficient to remember the Book of Job, the pessimism of Ecclesiastes, the sorrowful uncertainty about life of the ancient Greek poets, beginning with Homer.

But if in all ages there has existed a disharmony between the content of faith and the objective order of things as it is affirmed by experience and rational knowledge, if in all ages those who are innocent yet suffer ask themselves Job's question and the human heart is tormented by the fact that evil so often triumphs in the world and good perishes—nevertheless, general ideas about the order and progress of the world's being, different in different periods, have given completely different answers to the question of the relation between the content of faith and the content of life-experience or scientific knowledge. Thus, for example, the ancient Jews conceived the all-powerful God, the creator of heaven and earth, as not only their political protector, the immediate master of their destiny, but also as the "God of war," who gave Israel victory over its enemies and assured its political ascendancy. In other words, the content of religious faith and the content of historical knowledge and political wisdom appeared then simply to coincide. On the other hand, the ancient Greeks saw the world, the "cosmos," as the direct incarnation of divine reason and divine harmony: the content of religious faith (at least of philosophically purified faith) was in complete harmony with the data of astronomy, physics, and biology, and were confirmed by them. But perhaps the greatest harmony between faith and knowledge was achieved in the medieval world-view, which combined the Christian religious consciousness with the natural science and metaphysics of antiquity. If we take the world-picture expressed, for instance, in the philosophy of Thomas Aquinas or in the *Divine Comedy*, we will receive the strongest impression that the best minds of that age were convinced—despite the age-old experience of the endless triumph of evil and unreason in the world—that the structure of the world and the progress of worldly life were determined by religious principles. Religious morality, eschatology, the dream of the kingdom of heaven, fit harmoniously into the world-picture painted by scientific cosmology. God as love—this loftiest, most "unearthly," most improbable (from the point of view of objective knowledge) Christian idea—was for Dante the cosmic force that moves the sun and all the stars ("*l'amor che muove il sol e l'altre stelle*"). This was the time when people not only thought sincerely that, despite all evidence to the contrary, everything in the world, the growth of every leaf of grass and the motion of celestial bodies, the fate of every individual man and the historical fate of mankind, occurs rationally, in harmony with Divine Providence, but also that this harmony, affirmed by faith, can be objectively disclosed by all life-experience and scientific knowledge. It seemed that the world-picture revealed by scientific and philosophical thought, as well as historical experience, directly confirmed the religious hopes of the human heart. The truths of the Gospels seemed to be in harmony with the truths of astronomy, physics, history, and political philosophy.

There is no need here to describe how the history of human thought has refuted these ideas and to explain why they are no longer possible. It is clear that an insuperable abyss separates the modern perception of life and the world from ideas of this kind. The difference is so great that a comparison is almost impossible and of little use.

Leaving aside for this reason this mode of thought, so removed from us, let us consider only that contrast which is instructive for determining the peculiar character of the ideas of the 20th century. As we pointed out, the ideas of our age are substantially different from the ideas of the recent past, and even from the ideas that constituted the convictions of the most advanced, scientifically educated circles of European society. We refer to possibly the most characteristic feature of the spiritual crisis of our time: namely, the collapse of faith in the so-called progress of mankind. Dimly felt since the Renaissance, the idea of progress, i.e., the predetermined intellectual, moral, and social improvement of human life, was formulated in the last third of the 18th century in the intellectual constructions of Turgot, Lessing, and Condorcet. The combination of faith in the higher calling of man, a faith that grew from the seed of Christianity (the philosophers of the idea being unaware that this was its source), with naive rationalism produced *historical optimism*, which was the basis of the world-view of the best, most enlightened, and noblest people of the end of the 18th century and the beginning of the 19th century. This historical optimism, this faith in progress, was faith in the predeterminedness and imminence of the attainment of the absolute good, the "kingdom of God," on earth. In this age (the end of which is still so close to us, and in the echoes of which so many uncritical minds of our time still live) mankind lived by faith in the easy, pre-assured victory of good and reason over evil and unreason. It appeared to mankind that it was following a straight path, unencumbered by serious obstacles, to the attainment of the ideal state of man's being. Both liberalism and the socialism that replaced it were only different variants of this faith in the assured imminent attainment on earth of the entire fullness of the truth. Mankind lived by the confidence that its loftiest, ultimate dream would be realized. Faith, as the bold profoundest hope of the human heart, appeared to coincide with the objective, rational knowledge of reality, with the achievements of strict, exact science.

Faith in progress could be faith in "evolution," i.e., faith in the continuous, gradual, organic, and thus peaceful perfecting of human nature and the conditions of human life. Or it could be, according to Marx's celebrated formula, faith in the sudden "leap" of mankind from "the kingdom of necessity to the kingdom of freedom," from the kingdom of evil and meaninglessness to the kingdom of the good and reason. But in both cases it was utopianism: faith in the *attainability and predetermined attainment of absolute good in the world*. It was characteristic of this world-view that it considered "the power of darkness" to be either a random (and essentially incomprehensible) misunderstanding in the history of mankind (in view of the accepted innate rationality and goodness of human nature) or, in any case, a temporary and unnatural state of human life. And on the other hand "the power of light" was conceived as the normal, natural state, whose attainment was therefore considered to be easy and assured. This point of view was largely developed in opposition to religion, not only to faith as it was professed and propagated by the Christian churches, but also to religious faith in general. The adherents of this view usually considered themselves to be non-believers, but in essence this view consisted in the conviction that the *objectively known* nature of the world and of man accords with the hope of the human heart, namely, with faith in the ultimate triumph of the "light" (i.e., the good and reason), and even directly confirms this faith, gives it the character of reliable knowledge.

But in our age this faith appears to the thinking man, that is to say, to the man who has consciously experienced the historical and spiritual events of the past few decades, as literally "antediluvian," as preceding the historical "deluge" of the 20th century and as having shown its inconsistency in the face of this deluge. There is no need to explore in detail the meaning, arguable in many respects, of the historical events of our time. One thing, at least, is clear: the historical experience of the past few decades has delivered a fatal blow to the faith in progress, the faith in the continuous and linear material, intellectual, and moral perfecting of mankind. Now our thought is occupied not with the idea of progress, but with that which people of the recent past strangely forgot: the historical phenomenon of the collapse of great civilizations and their replacement by long ages of barbarism lasting many centuries. We can no longer believe that the power of darkness is only an accidental, temporary state of the world and that it is continuously dispelled, defeated by the power of light.

We are concerned here neither with politics nor with history as such. Of course it would be frivolous and unwise to attempt to construct a general philosophical-historical world-view on the basis of the political experience of the last two or three decades, to attempt to demonstrate general truths on the basis of facts referring to a short period of time. We mention these basic features of the epoch we are experiencing not as sufficient grounds for general philosophical conclusions but only partly as occasions for the appearance of a new world-view and partly as the natural illustrations of this world-view.

Whether under the influence of these historical events or even perhaps independently of them and partly even prior to them (on account of some unexplainable inner evolution of spiritual life), something has occurred that we must simply affirm as an undeniable fact: the collapse of faith in progress (having until recently the significance of axiomatic certainty), in the ceaseless perfecting of man, in the continuous triumph of the light over the darkness predetermined by the very structure of man and the world. This faith has now been replaced if not by the substantiated conviction that darkness has power over the world and man, then at least by an indefinite but acute consciousness of this power of darkness. The words "the whole world lies in evil" (written by the same John who wrote the enigmatic words "the light shineth in darkness") have now ceased to be a habitual, ecclesiastical formula and have become a serious, bitter truth. If there is a life-conviction that dominates all of us it is the involuntary, bitter, but indelible impression—diametrically opposed to the recent faith in predetermined progress—that *the world is characterized by its stubbornness in evil*, that evil is an enormous terrible force that dominates the world and is somehow immanently characteristic of the world. Under this impression, not only is the naive, optimistic faith in the predetermined, easy, immanent triumph of good over evil exposed as a fatal error, but the diametrically opposed conviction is formed that the battle between good and evil is, within the limits of the world's being, an *everlasting battle*. Not only is the task of overcoming the world's evil not easy, it is excruciatingly difficult. Not only is victory in this battle not predetermined, but the very understanding of the meaning and essence of the battle is changed.

Since "the whole world lies in evil" and evil is immanently present in the world and in human nature, *the battle has a meaning that is wholly independent of the belief that evil can be defeated*. Furthermore, the battle has the meaning that the ultimate triumph of good is impossible within the limits of the world's being. This is not defeatism, bitter resignation in the face of evil. Rather, since it becomes clear that the triumph of evil means simply the end of life (it is sufficient to recall the threat of atomic war), the duty and necessity of waging an intense, indefatigable battle against evil are felt with maximal acuteness. The deeper the roots of evil, the more intense must be the battle against evil. The fact that this battle must continue eternally within the limits of the world's being does not lessen the significance and necessity of the battle. The fact that every individual man must defend himself and that mankind as a whole must defend itself against the destructive forces of evil does not mean that the battle is meaningless and must cease. Life that is full of excruciating difficulties and tragedy is better than death, decay, decomposition. And courage combined with a sober perception of things is more meaningful and reasonable than courage nourished by illusions. The need for optimistic illusions only shows that man is inwardly not ready for the difficult trials of battle; and to be nourished by these illusions is to risk capitulating in the face of the real difficulties of battle, to risk not being able to bear the *heroic* significance of human life. The acuteness and distinctness of the impression of the everlastingness of the battle between light and darkness, and the impossibility and inconsistency of any views, scientific or theological, that are founded upon the neglect of this battle constitute the spiritual character peculiar to our time.

2. The Crisis of Humanism

This conviction affirming the power of darkness in the world, so characteristic of the spiritual state of our time, has another aspect that merits the closest attention. In comparison with the world-view of the recent past that was described above, this aspect can be defined as *the crisis of the faith in man, the crisis of humanism.*

Faith in progress, faith in the predetermined perfecting of man, as well as the utopian faith in the realization of the fullness of truth and good on earth, was based on faith in the dignity of man and his high calling on earth, that is, *faith in man.* The origination of this faith in man was connected with a profound misunderstanding, which determined the character of its typical justification and had a fateful influence upon it. There can be no doubt that, in essence, this faith has a Christian origin. In the Christian revelation, the Old Testament idea of man as the "image and likeness of God," as a privileged being who enjoys the special protection of God and is called to reign over the rest of creation, was focused in the idea of the *Godsonhood of man,* in the idea of man as the bearer of spirit and thus a being born "from above," "from God." But owing to a strange misunderstanding, the meaning and causes of which we shall discuss in detail below in another connection, it was not understood that the Christian revelation was the source of the faith in man and that the "humanism" of the modern age arose *in direct opposition* to the Christian world-view; and precisely in this form humanism determined the character of the faith in man until our age. Man's faith in himself and in his great calling on earth, a faith which possessed man from the beginning of the epoch that is called the modern age, was experienced by him as a wholly new consciousness, as a spiritual revolution against the general style of the medieval life-understanding, sanctified by the church. The birth of humanism in the modern period was a proud revolt against forces that had enslaved and humiliated man. One of the first and most influential harbingers of humanism, Giordano Bruno, defined this new human self-awareness as "heroic fury" ("*heroice furore*"). Despite its sharp opposition to the medieval Christian world-view, this faith in man was initially permeated by a general religious atmosphere. During the Renaissance, humanism was associated with pantheistic tendencies, with the rejection of a fundamental distinction between "earth" and "heaven," with the Platonic idea of the heavenly homeland of the human soul. Likewise, Descartes' faith in human reason was faith in *lumière naturelle*: the superiority and infallibility of human reason were founded upon the fact that, in his rational knowledge, in his "clear and distinct ideas," man is the bearer of *lumière naturelle*, the divine "light." Descartes' follower Malebranche could even combine this view with the pious mysticism of Augustinianism. Moreover, the Puritans who settled in America and first proclaimed the "eternal rights of men and citizens" founded these rights upon the sanctity of the personal relation to God. And this association of faith in man with faith in God is present in Rousseau; in the form of "natural religion." But in general it is precisely in the 18th century, the age of the French "enlightenment," that the final rupture between these two faiths occurs: the faith in man comes to stand in opposition (characteristic of the humanism of the modern age) to all religious faith in general and becomes combined with religious unfaith, with the naturalistic and materialistic world-view. This combination constitutes the essence of that view that dominated human thought during the past two centuries and which can be called "secular humanism."

But in this form humanism contained a profound and irreconcilable contradiction. The cult of man, the optimistic faith in his great calling to rule the world and to affirm the dominance of reason and the good in the world, is combined in secular humanism with a theoretical view of man as a being who belongs to the kingdom of nature and is wholly subordinate to its blind forces. Already the French materialists of the 18th century drew from this a conclusion which was essentially incompatible with faith in man: they affirmed that the universal motive of human conduct is egoism and even that man is nothing but a special machine (*l'homme machine*). If, in spite of this, in the 18th century and the first half of the 19th century it was still possible to believe that man has a special, high place in the hierarchy of the universe, this belief was based on the idea of man as a being of a special, higher order, fundamentally different from the rest of the animal world. It was possible to believe, for example, that man's distinguishing feature is his reason (*homo sapiens*) or his moral consciousness. Rather obscure from the very beginning, the theoretical foundations of these propositions were destroyed by Darwinism. Darwinism destroyed the ancient assumption that man is fundamentally different from the rest of the natural world and replaced this assumption with the idea that man is simply part of the animal world, a close relative of the ape, the descendant of an ape-like creature. The anthropological theme of Darwinism, i.e., the scientific exposure of the arrogance of human self-awareness, found new confirmation in the teaching of psychoanalysis (Freud himself underscores this significance of psychoanalysis). It is not enough that man has turned out to be an ape-like being; from now on he is recognized to be a lump of living flesh, all of whose psychic life and ideas are determined by the blind mechanism of sexual desire; not rational consciousness, not spirit and conscience, but blind, chaotic, subconscious forces rule human life.

These crushing blows to all the ideas upon which faith in the high dignity and calling of man could objectively be founded (blows that in essence were inevitable owing to the fundamental naturalistic tendency of secular humanism) strangely could not destroy for a long time (and for epigons they have not destroyed it yet) the purely irrational power of this faith over the human heart. In other words, despite its conscious aim, secular humanism became more and more a pseudo-religious faith with the passage of time.

A paradoxical, excruciating, dangerous situation gradually arose. In its initial practical achievements, secular humanism was not only an exceptionally influential and powerful point of view, but also a deeply beneficial one. Secular humanism was the object of the selfless enthusiastic faith of the best people of the 18th and 19th centuries. It was the doctrine that was responsible for the greatest achievements of European mankind: the emancipation of the slaves, political freedom, the rights of the individual, social and humanitarian reforms. But in its traditional form it was clearly contradictory and inconsistent. This is so evident now that we can remember only with disbelief and touching sadness the ease with which the human heart believed in secular humanism. One of the most subtle and advanced minds of the 19th century, a thinker who was well ahead of his time and who was perhaps the first to acutely experience the crisis of secular humanism, the Russian writer Alexander Herzen, wrote in his confession *From the Other Shore* under the direct impression of the collapse of the ideals of the movement of 1848: "Finally explain to me why one cannot believe in God, but is obliged to believe in man. Why it is stupid to believe in the kingdom of God in heaven, but not stupid to believe in the kingdom of God on earth." And at the end of the 19th century the Russian thinker Vladimir Solovyov summed up the world-view of naturalistic humanism (the teaching according to which man, as the product of blind animal forces of nature is called to realize on earth the kingdom of the good, reason, and justice) in the deadly ironic formula: "Man is an ape and therefore must lay down his soul for his neighbor." If such a half-educated epigon of secular humanism as Maksim Gorky could not too long ago write a hymn in praise of man and naively exclaim, "Man—what a proud sound this has," then it is natural for an educated, thinking man to ask why does the name of a creature who does not essentially differ from the ape, a creature who is nothing but the product and instrument of the blind forces of nature, why does the name of this creature have a "proud sound"?

However strongly European thought continued to affirm blindly a faith whose objective foundation had been destroyed, this contradictory spiritual state could not remain stable and last indefinitely. In the final analysis this contradiction was destined to destroy from within the very world-view of humanism. As long ago as the 1840s, the time when the faith in secular humanism was most intense, a solitary German thinker, Max Stirner, boldly and cynically affirmed the natural right of man, following his true nature, to reject all service of higher ideals and to be openly and unabashedly an egoist. This was a natural, logical conclusion from Feuerbach's humanist doctrine, which proclaimed man to be a self-sufficient absolute and affirmed that in religion, in the idea of God, man only illusorily separates from himself and hypostasizes his faith in himself, in his absolute superiority. But Stirner's nihilistic theory was only the first attack, in practice ineffectual, on the "rock" of the humanistic faith.

Soon another disciple of Feuerbach came to a doctrine that was destined to produce great cataclysms in the world and to destroy the very foundations of the humanistic faith. It is a significant coincidence that 1859 saw the appearance of both Darwin's *Origin of the Species* and Karl Marx's *Critique of Political Economy*, in the foreword to which the doctrine of economic materialism, fatal to secular humanism, was systematically formulated. As faith in the predetermined, imminent realization of socialism as the absolute triumph of reason and the good in human life (a faith which here takes the form of a precise scientific prediction), Marxism continues the tradition of the optimistic faith in progress, this fundamental theme of secular humanism. But in Marxism human nature is defined not as good and rational, but as evil and greedy. The funda-

24

mental factor of history is recognized to be *greed*, the struggle between classes for the possession of earthly goods, hatred between rich and poor. The greatest characteristic paradox of Marxism, which discloses the already evident degeneration of humanism, is the doctrine that the unleashing of the class struggle, the unleashing of the evil instincts of man, is the only path that leads to the kingdom of socialism, to the kingdom of the good and reason. In Marxism, faith in man and his great future is based on faith in the *creative power of evil*. It is not by chance that this is combined with the replacement of man as an individual by the cult of the "class" or "collective." For if all that is higher, good, spiritual is realized in man as an individual person (for the person is the image of God in man), then the elemental force of evil is incarnated more adequately in man as an impersonal particle of a collective, mass, mob. Thus, it is natural that Marxism is already something other than secular, non-religious humanism: it is a "humanism" that is consciously *anti-religious* and *anti-moral*. In Marxism, humanism is conceived as *titanism*, as faith in the triumph of the element of *revolt* in man, realized through the unleashing of the forces of evil. The contradiction between the idea of man's purpose and future and the idea of man's true nature, or the contradiction between the *end* of human progress and the *means* to its attainment, reaches such intensity here that it is possible to speak of the inner degeneration of the humanistic idea in Marxism.

The end of the 19th century witnessed yet another significant phenomenon of the degeneration of secular humanism, a phenomenon expressed in the ideas of Nietzsche. Nietzsche's greatest achievement is the fact that in his person human thought came to the distinct awareness that the secularized conception of man is incompatible with the humanistic cult of man. Despite Nietzsche's anti-religious and anti-Christian pathos, his refusal to worship man in man's empirical, natural, ordinary ("human, all-too human") being reveals a genuine religious striving of Nietzsche's spirit and contains a recollection of a forgotten fundamental truth. His lapidary formula "Man is something that must be overcome" sums up the inner collapse of secular humanism and pronounces its death sentence. This terrifying formula contains the dim intuition that man in his purely natural being is a deviation from a certain higher *idea* of man, that what is truly human in man is his higher, "superhuman," precisely *Divine-human* essence; and that in this sense the natural-human element must really be overcome and illuminated.

25

But this forgotten saving truth is only dimly seen by Nietzsche and undergoes a terrifying distortion in his thought. The demand that man must be overcome also signifies the overthrow of the very *idea* of man. That reality, rightly or wrongly understood, which for ages has been perceived as the incarnation on earth of the higher, life-illuminating, Divine principle—the reality of man in his distinction from all other, purely natural, creatures—is cast into the abyss.

What replaces it? Inasmuch as Nietzsche remained enslaved by the traditional anti-Christian and anti-religious tendency of secular humanism, the idea of the "superman" not only had to take the form of *antitheistic titanism*, but could only be grounded *biologically*. The fundamentally correct tendency to remind man of his higher, aristocratic, "superhuman" origin and purpose is unnaturally distorted into the glorification of the superman as an *animal of a higher breed or race*, with the measure of high breeding being the element of power, cruelty, contemptuous amoralism. The incarnation of the superman is the Renaissance villain Caesar Borgia or the ancient German, the "blond beast." Thus, a fateful, terrifying event occurs in the world of ideas: secular humanism is overcome by the proclamation of *bestialism*.

Until recently this strange and terrifying mixture of spiritual intuitions of genius and delirious moral errors could have seemed to be an exotic flower of a solitary aristocratic thought; it seemed that fashionable Nietzscheanism, relatively harmless for life, would remain an intellectual hobby for circles of snobs. But now after vulgarized Nietzscheanism first became the basis of the doctrine of German militarism and then, in unnatural combination with demagogy and the cult of the "masses," degenerated into the theory and practice of Nazism—the cult of pitiless cruelty, the horrors of total war, and the annihilation of the "lower races" in gas chambers have shown the true meaning of the degeneration of humanism and its transformation into bestialism.

Marxism and Nietzscheanism heralded the inner collapse of secular humanism. Thus, the inevitable and completely legitimate exposure of the illusoriness and contradictoriness of secular humanism led to a fateful, terrifying result. The condemnation of the deification of man as a natural being as idolatry took the form of the rejection of faith in the very idea of man, in the holiness of man as the image of God. Expressing this in terms of the basic theme of our work, we can say that the perception of the inconsistency of the

26

idea that the natural, unilluminated being of man can be the creator and bearer of the higher light leads paradoxically to the cult of darkness as the element that has the capacity *to generate the light out of itself.*

Completely opposite to each other in other respects, Marxism and Nietzscheanism achieved solidarity in this cult, in the faith that the higher state of mankind can be achieved through the unleashing and sanctioning of the lower, animalistic, evil forces of man's being. This new, distorted faith can be called *demonic utopianism*. Demonic utopianism replaces the contradiction of secular humanism by an even more glaring contradiction. The end to which this contradiction leads in practice has been demonstrated by recent history. In Russian Bolshevism, Marxism has transformed old humanitarianism socialism into the evil tyranny of despotism; dark, evil means to the realization of the kingdom of good and truth turned out to be ends in themselves: evil did not give rise to good, but cynically affirmed itself, enthroned itself on earth. Meanwhile, the amoral biological aristocratism of Nietzsche's doctrine, combined with revolutionary demagogy, degenerated into the doctrine of the creative role of violence, the practical fruits of which mankind has gathered in all the horror that it has lived through. The collapse of secular humanism has led to the domination of the world by the mind-set and life-practice of a gang of criminals, has before our eyes drowned the world in a sea of blood and tears.

The historical fate of secular humanism was determined by the inner contradiction that ate at it from the very beginning. Faith in the greatness and high calling of man, the cult of man as a holy being, ends with the blasphemous rejection of all that is holy in man, with the cynical glorification of the evil, animalistic element in man, with the loss of man as the image and likeness of God. Such blasphemy and cynicism could not be borne by the human heart. By some instinct beyond all rational argument, by some innate organ of spiritual knowledge, the human heart began to sense long ago that the historical fate of secular humanism was leading human thought on a false path and must lead it to the abyss. The horrific experience of our time has confirmed this feeling with final certainty—at least with regard to the mass application of vulgarized Nietzscheanism, while that part of European mankind which is not yet blind is beginning to see that vulgarized Marxism leads in practice to the same result.

This consciousness is a characteristic constituent of the spiritual crisis of our time. What can human thought oppose to this terrifying result at which it has arrived?

3. On Sorrowful Unfaith and Modern Gnosticism

Before attempting to answer this question, let us juxtapose the themes and conclusions of the two preceding discussions. At first glance it could appear that the bitter, pessimistic consciousness of the power of darkness in the world and that cult of darkness as a creative force which issued from the degeneration of humanism are kindred spiritual tendencies. This supposition contains a grain of truth in that both of these tendencies oppose the naive, optimistic faith in the real power and triumph of the principles of good and reason in human life. Compared to this naive faith, based on the idealization of the real structure of the world's being and particularly on the idealization of the real nature of man, both of these spiritual tendencies of our time can be defined as *unfaith*. Both are the result of a bitter life-experience which exposes previous optimistic ideas as illusions. Marx was undeniably right when, in opposition to the naive glorification of the innate goodness of man, he demonstrated the power of greed and class egoism. And Nietzsche was right when he exposed the spiritual degeneration of secular humanism, the insufferable self-love of man in all the insignificance and banality of his natural, "all-too-human" being.

But this is the only resemblance that exists between these two forms of the degeneration of humanism and the consciousness of the power of darkness in the world. Taken as a whole or in their basic theme, these two spiritual tendencies not only are not kindred, but are even sharply opposed to each other. Indeed, the conviction that the world is dominated by the power of darkness has as its determining feature the rejection of utopianism, the rejection of faith in the realization of the ideal state of the life of man and the world. On the contrary, the view that is based on the cult of darkness, and that we have called demonic utopianism, unnaturally, contradictorily combines the denial of the power of the good and faith in the power of darkness with a special *utopianism*, i.e., with the faith that darkness is a creative force which is destined to realize the ideal state of worldy and human being. The two tendencies contradict each other as skepticism and fanaticism, as wisdom and demonic possession. The true destructiveness of the spiritual tendency that has taken hold as a result of the collapse of humanism lies not in the fact that it is unfaith, but in the fact that it is frenzied idolatry—a mad, evil faith that demands the mass sacrifice of human lives. A blind and blinding faith, it powerfully stimulates human activity, driving it to a false, deadly goal. Demonic utopianism is a *revolutionary* doctrine in the deepest, most fundamental sense of this word: it preaches the necessity (and believes in the possibility) of overturning the very foundation of the world's being, of constructing the world anew, using the dark, evil elements of man's being as creative forces for this purpose. Whether the creative force is greed and class hatred as in Marxism or love of power and mercilessness toward the weak as in Nietzscheanism, in both cases man is educated in the deification of evil passions, in the faith that by means of these passions mankind will advance to a new, radiant, beautiful state, to "heaven on earth." If at one time faith in God was unnaturally replaced by the blind faith in man, now the collapse of humanism leads to an even greater blindness and madness: faith in man as the bearer of the good and reason is in turn replaced by faith in the creative power of the evil that possesses man. Anthropolatry, the worship of man, is replaced by *satanolatry*, the worship of Satan, the true "prince of this world."

On the other hand, this overcoming of humanism preserves traces of its origin from the deification of man and is only a further stage of the degeneration of this deification, for the concrete bearer of this demonism is the autonomous will of man. Salvation is expected from the revolt of man in his dark, chaotic being against God, and not only against God as a higher principle above man, but also against that which is immanently divine or God-like in man himself, against the principles of the good and morality. This demonic bestialism can in no sense be called *humanism*. But as faith in the saving and creative force of human self-willfulness and the anarchy of spiritually void human nature, it remains "hominism." And as such it is the most perverted and contradictory form of utopianism, the unnatural combination of extreme unfaith and completely blind faith.

Diametrically opposed to this tendency is the bitter, sobering conviction we described above: the consciousness of the fundamental, permanent imperfection of the world's being; and the weakness, if not the impotence, the lack of ontological assurance in the world—in the face of the power of darkness—of human dreams, of human efforts to establish the principles of good and truth in the world. But the opposition of these two tendencies becomes most intense when the cult of darkness as the creative force that is designated to realize the ideal state of the world degenerates into pure *cynicism*, into satanical possession by the forces of evil as such. This degeneration is wholly inevitable because of the glaring inner contradiction (of which we spoke above) that eats at this tendency from within like a worm.

Cynicism or cynical unfaith is the rejection of the very principle of holiness and the necessity to worship holiness. This is the spiritual tendency which deserves the name of *nihilism* in the precise sense of this word. In a certain sense one cay say that secular humanism—faith in man that lacks religious or metaphysical ground and is based on the replacement of faith in objective, absolute values by service of purely subjective-human values—from the very beginning contains the seeds of nihilism. Secular humanism therefore has the immanent tendency to become consistent nihilism. Apostles of the vain deification of man, adepts of faith in the easy and imminent realization of the kingdom of God on earth (but without God)—by purely external, human means—have the general tendency to pass from this vain, idolatrous faith to cynical unfaith, because of the inner ungroundedness of their faith and the inevitable disillusionment brought about by life-experience. They easily experience the collapse of their faith as the collapse of all faith in general; the inevitable "twilight of the idols" assumes the character of the dethroning of holiness in general. Since it is not possible to establish the kingdom of the good and happiness for all of mankind, it appears that nothing is left but to reject all service of the ideal in general and to live as comfortably as possible on earth. It appears that this is the psychological tendency of all revolutions that are based on the dream of realizing an ideal state by human powers: the initial fanaticism is replaced, as a result of the inevitable disillusionment, by a mood of cynical unfaith.

This tendency is manifested to an extreme degree in the faith of degenerate humanism, which is based on the cult of evil and strives to the ideal of the unchaining of the forces of evil in demonic utopianism. The practical consequences of this faith are such that man begins to drown in the forces of evil he has unchained. Since, contrary to expectation, these forces of evil do not lead to the desired "salvation," and since they must be continually unchained in the hope of achieving the desired result, people are gradually habituated to evil as an end in itself; evil begins to seem an ordinary, natural state. Under such conditions it is especially easy to lose faith in the ultimate goal of this unchaining of evil, and even the taste for this ultimate goal. On this path there easily arises the firm belief that the triumph of evil as such in human life is not only natural, but also legitimate. Initially understood and practiced as a means to the attainment, if not of the moral good, at least of some higher, ideal, objectively legitimate state—evil now becomes an end in itself. Satan gains genuine power over human hearts, in which the faith that gives life to the soul dies. Entire nations give themselves to the service of the black mass. Rapacious lovers of power and money cynically mock the people's masses, whom they have tricked by preaching the service of some higher, noble goal; and whom in practice they have forced to serve only them, the leaders. They have transformed the people into an obedient herd, which can be freely milked and slaughtered so that the leaders can lead a dissipated life. This is the real result of the unlimited despotism to which demonic utopianism leads.

Now we return to our question: What can human thought oppose to this terrifying result at which it has arrived?

Not only the moral degeneration which is the incarnation of cynical unfaith, and not only the unnatural demonic utopianism which leads to pure cynicism, but even the source of these errors, secular humanism itself, with the associated utopianism—provokes (owing to the contradiction that lies at its base) an immediate healthy reaction of common sense and conscience. Precisely this combination of common sense and the voice of conscience leads to a spiritual tendency that is extremely popular among the best minds of our time, to a tendency that can be called *sorrowful unfaith*. In contrast to cynical unfaith and in sharp opposition to the latter, sorrowful unfaith is the bitter consciousness of the actual power of darkness in the world. Sorrowful unfaith is a lack of faith in the real power of ideal principles that is combined with "faith" in the principles themselves, that is to say, with reverence for their holiness and the awareness that they must be served. Sorrowful unfaith is the combination of *naturalism* or consistent theoretical unfaith (i.e., the fundamental view that the world is universally dominated by blind, meaningless forces of nature indifferent to the hopes of the human heart) with the sense of the chivalrous, heroic service of an unattainable ideal. One of its philosophical precursors,

Bertrand Russell, defines this tendency as the defense of our ideals against a hostile universe.

Sorrowful unfaith is one of the most characteristic and touching phenomena of the spiritual life of our time. Man has become disillusioned not only with the vain faith of utopianism, but even with the possibility of realizing higher values in the world. He has come to the conviction that not only is the victory of good and reason not guaranteed in the world, but even that they are probably fated to be defeated, for evil and madness triumph in the world as a general rule. I shall never forget a sad, brief formula of this pessimism which I once heard: "To be a prophet, it is enough to be a pessimist." But this pessimism in regard to the world's order and the progress of the world's life, this metaphysical "defeatism," so to speak, does not destroy in the human heart the very worship of good and reason, the holiness of the human person. Holiness turns out to be weak and powerless in the world, *but it does not therefore stop being holiness.* This spiritual tendency leads to the moral demand *to defend the hopeless position of good against the triumphant, all-powerful force of evil.* The meaning of human life consists here in defending the dignity of the ideal without any hope of realizing it in life; it consists in the heroic deed of perishing while defending the doomed enterprise of good and truth. This is reminiscent of the sad, proud formula which expresses the spirit of ancient honor of the dying Roman republic: "The cause of victory pleases the gods, the cause of defeat pleases Cato" ("*Causa victrix deis placuit, sed victa Catoni*").

This spiritual tendency which we call "sorrowful unfaith" is, of course, first and foremost, *unfaith* in the generally accepted sense. In a certain sense, this unfaith is directly opposed to that naive, massive faith which gives man the feeling that his life is fully assured by the unlimited, all-encompassing power of good and wise Providence over the world. In contrast to this massive faith, sorrowful unfaith mercilessly rejects all trust in forces that control reality and affirms all hopes of the human heart to be illusory, affirms the hopeless loneliness and despair of man in his love of holiness, which alone is the true ideal foundation of his being.

Nevertheless, insofar as this unfaith is *sorrowful* unfaith, insofar as the human heart experiences sorrow from the awareness of the triumph of evil in the world, rises against this triumph, considers itself obliged to be true and to hopelessly serve good and truth— this spiritual state is akin to faith in some sense. It contains that

32

element of faith owing to which faith is the selfless reverence of the holy, the worship of holiness. This openness of the soul to the action of holiness, this firm refusal (unjustified and even absurd from the rational point of view) to submit to the evil forces of the world, this readiness for selfless heroism, is undeniably of great value before that supreme judge who judges not thoughts but the heart.

It would be a great misunderstanding to classify (as it is often done) both sorrowful unfaith and cynical unfaith under the common name *unfaith*. Rather, the distinction between them is precisely the dividing line between faith and unfaith in the primordial and practically most essential and fundamental meaning of these concepts. However great the significance of the distinction between the acceptance of Providence or the existence of a personal God and the rejection of Providence or the existence of a personal God (that is, the distinction between faith and unfaith in the usual, popular sense), this distinction is inessential compared to the distinction between the presence of the sense of holiness, the consciousness of the obligation to serve good and truth, and the loss or rejection of this consciousness. The abstract acceptance of God's existence is worthless if it is not based on immediate worship; on the other hand, if immediate worship is present, the living core of the primordial essence of faith is present. The simple fact must never be forgotten that faith is a state of the heart, not an idea of the mind.

But it is possible to go even further. It is possible to affirm that if we disclose the hidden premises of sorrowful unfaith, premises that are not explicit but that are in essence necessary for the explanation of this unfaith, this spiritual state of sorrowful unfaith will be revealed to us as a special religious faith, even in the sense of the theoretical acceptance of the reality of a superworldly, absolute principle. Indeed, if (as sorrowful unfaith consciously affirms) holiness, good, and reason do not have any ontological roots in being, any objective reality; if they are nothing else but a purely subjective product of the human heart, then one could not in essence understand what is the ground of the obligation to worship and serve holiness. The objection might be raised that the question of ground is irrelevant here; the human heart is completely free, that is to say, the heart is drawn to holiness without any ground, simply because holiness is inwardly attractive; like the attraction to pure beauty, such a selfless love does not require ground and does not need it.

33

Expressing the same thing in the language of abstract philosophical thought, we can say: holiness preserves its significance of value, of that which is dear to the human heart—completely independently of the degree to which it has objective ontological force and is capable of being realized.

This objection neglects one very significant thing: the distinction between *value in the subjective sense*, i.e., value as a simple expression of the factual predilection of the human heart, and *objective value*, i.e., value that is experienced as belonging to reality itself, that is completely independent of its actual human acceptance, and that is therefore recognized as something the worship of which is *obligatory*. Insofar as it is the product of the human heart, value can only be value in the subjective sense. In other words, its meaning is exhausted by the fact that it is an actual human feeling. Wherever this feeling is present, the value that arises from it is also present; where this feeling is absent, the value is also absent. No fundamental valuation, no approval or disapproval that pretends to objective validity is possible here. Subjective value is just as arbitrary and capricious as the human love that produces it. It is clear that pure subjectivism in the interpretation of that which is worshipped as holiness is incompatible with the objective validity of the moral judgments that are necessarily part of that spiritual tendency which we call sorrowful unfaith. Pure subjectivism is adequate only to pure, consistent nihilism, which denies all objectively obligatory values and affirms the unlimited arbitrariness of human valuations and desires. In other words, whatever the skeptical content of sorrowful unfaith, this kind of unfaith—as a "world-view" or conviction—pretends to be a guiding principle of human life, or the foundation, the point of reference, of human life. But that by which we are guided, that which defines the path of our life, that which is the foundation of our life, must in any case be something other and greater than only our subjective mood. We can find a solid foundation only in the soil that bears us up, not in ourselves; we can be guided only by the stars, not by our own ideas.

Thus, the very worship of holiness, as it is contained in sorrowful unfaith, silently and unconsciously involves the recognition of holiness as a *higher, unearthly principle*, which in some sense surpasses all earthy actuality and, even more so, the derivative, "creatural" nature of the human "heart." That this higher principle turns out to be powerless or insufficiently powerful in the plane of *the world's being* does not lessen its absolute ontological dignity, its immanent validity that belongs to it in some other, superempirical, superworldly plane.

Since it is the worship of objective, superempirical holiness, sorrowful unfaith is not ordinary unfaith. It is not exhausted by the element of unfaith, for its unfaith refers not to the very princple of superworldly, absolute holiness but only to the power of this principle within the limits of the world's being. However powerless the principle of holiness is in the world, the recognition and worship of holiness are in some sense faith in the *existence* of holiness. If we keep from confusing the world's being, empirical reality, with being in general—we can say that in essence sorrowful unfaith is based on faith in a higher being of holiness, though it considers this being to be wholly other than the world's being and therefore powerless in the face of the latter. The sense of the tragic solitude and powerlessness of man on earth in his profoundest, holiest hope involves the awareness that in this hope he represents on earth a higher, unearthly entity.

In essence, this is a kind of "Platonic" faith in any extraworldly, superworldly sphere of ideal being; and a faith in the kinship of the human soul with this "heavenly homeland," which alone explains the excruciating exile of the human soul on earth, this vale of sorrow and evil. But this is also a kind of dualistic faith of the gnostic type: faith in a distant God, alien to the world, faith in a God who is the bearer of all-goodness but who lacks allpowerfulness and even immediate power over the world. Since the time John Stuart Mill in the mid-nineteenth century made his famous profession of faith, where he said that he believes in the allgoodness of God but not in His all-powerfulness, this gnostic faith has been assimilated—consciously and more often unconsciously—by many of the best, most independent minds of our time. This faith, which once, at the end of antiquity, attracted human hearts with such force, permeates the spiritual atmosphere of our time, though the majority of its adepts are not fully conscious of this.

This kind of faith contains the only true ground of that spiritual tendency which we call sorrowful unfaith. However, here too, consistency and the correct theoretical grounding are not intellectual luxuries, but have an essential practical value. Therefore it is highly significant to know whether or not adherents of sorrowful unfaith are conscious of its underlying premise. Insofar as these adherents remain unconscious of its ontological (and, in the final analysis, religious) premise, insofar as they are not aware that the

35

value in which they believe is a reality, *a genuinely existent entity*—the spiritual state of sorrowful unfaith is a state of proud, individualistic heroism: Man proudly opposes himself, the hidden depths of his own soul, to the universe. In essence, this leads to the idolatrous cult of man, and the exposure of the inconsistency of utopian, secular humanism (the exposure that precisely gives rise to sorrowful unfaith) stops midway as it were, does not attain its goal. On the contrary, insofar as man becomes conscious of the higher, superworldly reality of holiness, he becomes conscious that he must *humbly serve* the principle that is infinitely above him. It is true that the distinction between the two states, conscious and unconscious, is in practice often not so sharp as it might appear in the abstract formulation of their theoretical content. The transition is often gradual, barely noticeable: for on the one hand the heroic consciousness already essentially contains the element of the service of holiness; and on the other hand the consciousness of the humble service of the higher principle is connected nonetheless with the consciousness of the higher, aristocratic dignity of man, conditioned by the consciousness of this humble service. A clear consciousness of the genuine premises of this unfaith has an essential practical significance: like all clarity of thought, this consciousness facilitates the exposure of possible errors and makes it easier to follow the right path.

But this contemporary gnosticism, though it contains an element of religious faith, remains *damaged, imperfect faith*. If according to the classic definition of the Epistle to the Hebrews, "faith is the substance of things hoped for, the evidence of things not seen" (Hebrews 11:1), contemporary gnosticism contains the latter feature ("the evidence of things not seen") but does not contain and decisively rejects the former feature: It is a *faith without hope*, the faith of the inwardly broken human heart, incapable of giving comfort, spiritual peace, or joy. It is a peculiar amalgam of faith and unfaith.

4. The Tragic Nature of Life, and Faith

Is this defective faith—faith in the reality of holiness combined with the bitter consciousness of the powerlessness of holiness in the world and thus the solitude, the desolation, of man in the world—the ultimate that can be attained in our time by the human soul that seeks God and opens itself to holiness? Or does

36

the soul of contemporary man still hope to attain a fuller, deeper religious satisfaction, without falling into pious falsehood and abandoning intellectual and moral honesty?

When we speak of the "spirit" or mood of "our age," we must not hypostasize such notions or attribute to them the significance of a universal, all-determining force. Goethe's Mephistopheles says that the so-called spirit of the age is nothing but the "spirit of the masters" in whom the age is reflected. This ironic remark is wholly just. The bearer and creator of ideas is not some "spirit of the age," but the living human soul with its needs and urges, which are always fundamentally the same. And since such needs include the thirst for religious faith, since St. Augustine's words of genius are always valid in regard to human nature: "Thou created us for Thyself, and our heart is not calm until it finds peace in Thee"—it follows that "our age," like all ages, seeks, and is therefore capable of finding, a positive religious faith.

We set aside those cases where contemporary man, tired of doubts, succeeds in simply stepping over the abyss that separates him from the traditional content of ecclesiastical faith and in finding comfort and peace in the simple acquisition of this content without its independent inner verification. For our purposes, only that spiritual path is instructive and interesting on which contemporary man, having passed through a "crucible of doubts" (to use Dostoevsky's phrase), seeks and finds within his own personal spiritual situation a faith that meaningfully overcomes these doubts. We ask: is there a path on which, starting from the defective, bitter faith of contemporary gnosticism, and not rejecting the element of truth that this faith contains, it is possible to acquire spiritual experience that leads to the fullness of joyous, comforting faith?

Such a path not only exists, but even coincides with the path which leads to the bitter faith of contemporary gnosticism. As we attain a greater depth of spiritual experience and a greater subtlety of religious thought that corresponds to this depth, on this path we shall necessarily overcome this bitter faith, which is only a preliminary state of religious knowledge, and attain a greater and more joyous fullness of faith. It will then become clear to us that the defective "gnostic" faith is only the fruit of a too rationalistic and therefore schematically simplified argumentation which is not adequate to the genuine depth of reality. A conclusive clarification of this situation, i.e., a genuine, sufficiently deep-penetrating justification of faith, should be the result of our book as a whole. However, here we can and must present some preliminary, general considerations that will help us to overcome the bitter gnostic faith and to see the horizons of another faith, fuller and more joyous.

First of all, we must recall the simple fact that *we are not the first* in the history of mankind to experience a tragic age of catastrophes, the collapse of the rational, intelligible foundations of being, and the triumph of the forces of evil over the forces of good. On its historical path mankind has experienced more than one such age. But mankind has not lost its religious faith; it has known how to combine the bitter lessons of empirical reality with the joy of religious hope. Furthermore, precisely ages of this sort have often been ages of the appearance or intensification and blossoming of religious faith; the best example is the appearance and propagation of the Christian faith. The Christian faith was born in the midst of the Jewish nation precisely in the bitterest and most arduous epoch of the national-historical existence of this nation; and this faith took firm hold in the ancient world precisely in the most arduous epoch of the collapse of the ancient culture, the destruction of the whole glorious past, in the midst of the horrors of anarchy that accompanied this collapse. Although this age tended to the pessimism of the gnostic faith, this pessimism was overcome by the hopeful, joyous faith preached by the Christian church.

Moreover, we must not exaggerate the significance of historical epochs in general and the tragic nature of the present historical epoch in particular. In the final analysis, the collapse of hopes, the power of evil in the world, the absurdity of life, are the immanent eternal characteristics of *all* human life in its empirical aspect. Neither our epoch nor any epoch in general is responsible for such things as the instability and shortness of human life, the domination of life by blind chance and the "indifferent" forces of nature, the incompatibility between the dearest hopes of the human heart and the real character of the empirical world, the incompatibility between empirical forces and the forces of good, and, finally, the tragedy that lies in the very fact of death, the death of those we love and our own death. Historical ages of collapse, such as our age, only emphasize, make more distinct, the eternal tragic nature of human life—the tragic nature that only nearsighted minds do not see in happier and more peaceful ages. But was it only blindness, was it only spiritual cowardice seeking comfort in illusions, that was the source of faith in previous ages, that helped people combine the consciousness of life's tragic nature with genuine religious faith?

Turning now to the essence of the problem, we must first point out that the mere recognition and worship of holiness as such, i.e., as a kind of absolute value or a kind of ideal "kingdom of values" (a favorite concept of certain German philosophers), do not exhaust the living experience of holiness. The element of "value" or "holiness" in living experience is experienced only as an abstract feature of some concrete spiritual reality. The very experience of the worship of holiness, precisely in the consciousness of its obligatoriness for us, in the perception of its nature as a kind of unconditional command (the "categorical imperative"), contains a perception of the living reality of holiness as a directing and determining spiritual *force*, as something analogous to our own will. Holiness is perceived as being organically inwardly kindred to the mysterious, superworldly being of that which I call "I," my person. We can debate to what extent the analogy is valid: to what extent we are right to identify holiness with the essence of the human person and to what extent we must distinguish between the two. Both theological thought and philosophical thought are full of this endless, perhaps unresolvable, debate. But it cannot be denied that in the broad, general sense the calling of holiness by the ancient, primordial name "God" (or "Divinity")—the name of the superworldly being who to some degree is analogous to a person—is the only form in which religious experience can be adequately understood. What we experience here is the living contact with a reality that has an inner kinship with the intimate depths of our soul and infinitely surpasses us only in its ontological significance and value. As the German mystic Angelus Silesius says, "the abyss of the soul is drawn to the abyss of God."

Despite the indefiniteness of this concept of Divinity, the perception of its legitimacy and necessity radically changes our inner self-awareness, creates for us a wholly new spiritual situation. The sense of the metaphysical solitude, desolation, instability of my person is replaced by the sense of its metaphysical security, its possession of an eternal refuge inside this higher reality. The sense of danger, the sense of fear in the face of being is replaced by a sense of inviolable peace, based on inner trust of this higher being. If the contemporary German theoretician of tragic unfaith, Heidegger, proclaims "fear" to be the metaphysical essence of human life, this is opposed by the testament, grand in its simplicity, of Socrates, the founder of rational religious thought: nothing bad can happen in this world or the next to a man who is devoted to the good. The positive expression of this feeling is given in the Christian revelation of God as the "Father" or as "love" ("God is love"—1 John 4:8). In his tragic fate on earth, man gains courage and the meaning of life not only from the worship of holiness and the selfless service of holiness. The ultimate and stablest foundation of his life is the consoling, comforting, blissful feeling that he belongs to the heavenly homeland, to the house of God as His Father, the feeling of inviolable security and assuredness in God. Man is conscious of himself as not only the servant of God; the most complete expression of his religious sense is that he is a *child of God.* If, historically, mankind owes this fullness and depth of religious consciousness, this consoling and strengthening self-consciousness, to a Christian education, i.e., to the revelation of Christ—this revelation is also given with complete self-evident certainty in immediate inner experience and is therefore revealed to sufficiently deep-penetrating thought, directed at the understanding of Holiness.

Of course, there is still a great distance between this and the massive, traditional faith in the all-powerfulness of God. It must be confessed candidly that a man of our age—precisely if his religious feeling is intense and true, if his consciousness of the tragic nature of life, the power of sin and absurdity in life, is acute—succeeds only with great difficulty in believing in the all-powerfulness of God, in the absolute superiority of Divine Providence over the entire world. The torments of doubt presented in the Old Testament in the immortal Book of Job have long dominated modern thought. It is sufficient to compare the tragic struggle of the greatest religious genius of the modern period, Pascal, with the untested calm and rational simplicity of Thomas Aquinas. And one of the most religious minds of the twentieth century, Charles Péguy, confessed that, often and for long periods of time, he was unable to say the words "Thy will be done." It is necessary to have the courage to say that this concept of the all-powerfulness of God has become inadmissible in its usual, naive, massive, traditional form; that precisely for the most profoundly believing consciousness this concept has to be supplemented by the Christian revelation, not yet fully disclosed in all its profundity, of the *suffering* God who takes part in the agony of the world. It is not so easy to believe, without all kinds of qualifications and clarifications, that the all-good God, with the dispassionateness of an all-powerful Lord, confident beforehand in the wisdom and beneficence of His acts, chose Hitler as the instrument of His will to lead mankind—through the torments of innocent women and children murdered in gas chambers—on a path predetermined by Him. Religious thought, guided by the moral consciousness, cannot fail to be tormented (especially in the face of the suffering of others) by the question of how the fact of the world's suffering and evil can be harmonized with the all-powerfulness of the all-good God.*

But in some deeper, more mysterious, ineffable, superrational sense, this idea of the all-powerfulness of God cannot be rejected by the religious consciousness. And this is not at all because (as unfaith usually maintains) we tend for our self-consolation to arbitrarily postulate the reality of the objects of our hopes and desires, or because, according to the German expression, wish is the father of thought. No, in some sense, the idea of the all-powerfulness of God is given wholly immediately and with utter self-evidence in religious experience. First of all, the consciousness of our kinship with God as our loving Father, i.e., the immediate feeling that the holiness we serve is also the solid ground upon which we stand, or that the force that draws us to serve holiness is inwardly akin to what is holy and illuminated in our own will—this consciousness is associated with the certainty for us of the general idea of Divine

---

* The usual explanation that evil originates from the freedom of will that God gave to man, though He inevitably risked that man would depart from the good (while Divine Providence transforms even the evil caused by people into a means to good)—this explanation does not withstand criticism. Even leaving aside Bergson's decisive argument against the conception of the freedom of the will as the freedom of choice between several different possibilities, there remains one absolutely unresolvable doubt. Like all people, saints possess free will and are subject to temptation; but either by an innate tendency to saintliness or by a special sanctifying grace, they overcome temptations and attain saintliness. Why could not God create all people as saints? Or why does he give people only that grace which (according to Pascal's deadly ironic comment) "is called sufficient because it is insufficient" to overcome temptation? There can be no rational answer to these questions. According to human understanding, God is just as responsible for the evil that emanates from the freedom of the will as a parent is responsible for the freedom that he gives his children who are too weak or insufficiently wise to use it.

Providence, the Divine protection under which we stand and which guides our life. A loving father or mother is a being full of constant concern for us; in our human service of the good and truth, we feel—in the case of a sufficiently distinct and complete consciousness of what the good and truth really are—the vital support of the principle we serve. We are led and strengthened; we are guided by a higher, superhuman, superworldly force. Such is the immediate experience of every courageous, heroic warrior for the truth, even when he does not take clear mental account of his situation and considers himself an unbeliever. If a heroic warrior is alone in the world; if he takes sober account of the enormous, crushing force of evil against which he has risen; even if he is sadly conscious that he has few true allies in the world, that everywhere he is surrounded by human mediocrity, villainy, and cowardice —nevertheless in his metaphysical self-consciousness (and contrary to what is affirmed by sorrowful unfaith) he does not feel himself alone. The experience of holiness is directly linked to the experience of a great kingdom of holiness as a reality to which he belongs, a powerful unearthly force that protects and supports him. This is the essence of the great eternal and immediately self-evident truth of the idea of God as the unshakeable ground, the powerful, invincible ally and guide of man.

The primordial root and meaning of the idea of the all-powerfulness of God are revealed precisely in this connection. The "all-powerfulness" of God is only another aspect of the *absolute supremacy* (immediately evident in religious experience) of Holiness in relation to our will. God is all-powerful not in the sense that He is a kind of immeasurable crude physical force that externally and immediately suppresses everything else, or a kind of all-powerful tyrant, before whose terrible unlimited power everyone must bow. Rather, God is all-powerful by that irrepressible force of attraction with which He draws the human heart and conquers it from within by His absolute authoritativeness and persuasiveness. When, aware of the moral and religious necessity of the struggle against the abuses of the Church and his calling to this struggle, Luther challenged all the powers in the world with the words *"Hier stehe ich— ich kann nicht anders,"* he gave a classic expression of the certainty of the all-powerfulness of God in this sense for religious experience. All righteous men who undergo torture and death in carrying out God's will, God's truth (this was manifested even before the Christian saints in the deed of Sophocles' Antigone), are living wit-

42

nesses of this inwardly experienced all-powerfulness of God. In modern philosophy Kant expressed this experience in the teaching of the all-conquering ideal force of the absolute moral law: the "categorical imperative."

Thus, religious experience, bearing its certainty in itself, comes to the awareness of the immanent ideal all-powerfulness of the all-good Divine will, *despite* the lordship of evil and the meaninglessness of life. We saw above that, going contrary to all experience of empirical life, the dualistic-gnostic understanding of life believes in holiness, i.e., in the *reality* of holiness, while asserting that holiness is powerless in the world. Now we see that a fuller and deeper religious experience contains the consciousness of the *absolute power* of this holiness, despite its empirically limited force. The makeup of religious experience, i.e., the perception of the reality of Holiness, also includes the *immediate experience* that this Holiness is an invincible, all-conquering force, i.e., that its *supremacy* signifies its inner, *immanent* all-powerfulness. This experience is so immediate, so self-evident to our "heart" that, insofar as we really have this experience, it cannot be shaken by any "facts," by any empirical truths. Let the problem of theodicy remain unsolved, let it be the case that we are unable to understand how the metaphysical all-powerfulness of holiness is compatible with the empirical lordship of evil—this contradiction shakes the certainty of religious experience as little as the certainty of any empirical fact is shaken by our intellectual inability to harmonize it with other known facts. The history of scientific thought is full of such tormenting doubts, which nonetheless never give one the right to deny that which is established with certainty in experience. And if for an unbeliever experience is limited beforehand to the domain of sense perception, the meaning of that which is called "faith" consists in the possession of *experience*, i.e., in the ability to apprehend something with certainty in the spiritual (i.e., nonsensuous) domain.

The soul that has faith (in the broad sense of faith as the consciousness and worship of holiness) simultaneously lives in two worlds and recognizes the reality of both worlds: it sees the "world," that world which "lies in evil"; and it has direct experience of another, higher or deeper, world—the world of Holiness, through which it acquires the unique meaning of its existence. This is the spiritual tendency that we have called sorrowful unfaith, understood as gnostic faith. But despite this gnostic faith, despite the certainty of the distinction and, in this sense, the dualism between

43

the two worlds—experience does not allow us to postulate an insuperable abyss between the two worlds. Rather, experience points to the fact of the direct intrusion of higher forces into our life—an intrusion which alone illuminates and saves our life.

The conviction that the empirical world is completely self-contained, that it is closed to the ideal powers of another, higher world, is only a naturalistic prejudice, which is scientifically and philosophically unjustified, and contradicts the immediate experience of human life. From all that has been said above, it is wholly evident that there is at least one domain of reality in which these two worlds are present together and closely linked, and in which powers of a higher order flow into the sphere of empirical being; this domain is the *human heart*. In all moral and religious experience, a higher power flows into and acts in the world through the invisible depths of the human heart; and in some sense, this power is all-powerful, i.e., it reveals its inner, immanent superiority over all the powers of this world. The human heart—that is, the dualistic, spiritual-empirical or psychic-corporeal essence of man—is the only place we know of where these two worlds meet, the only opening through which the gracious powers of another, higher world can flow into the empirical world. The very fact of the existence of such a boundary region indicates that the empirical world is not an absolutely closed system, inaccessible to influence from outside, or, more precisely, from another, superworldly dimension. This fact is in complete harmony with the theoretical tendency of recent positive science. If there is a view that can be considered shaken by the contemporary development of scientific knowledge, it is unquestionably the simplified naturalism of the nineteenth century, in which the system of natural forces was represented as self-contained and exhausted all of being. But at the present time even positive scientific knowledge considers the world to be much more changeable and plastic than could have been allowed previously. A whole series of fundamental conceptions was shaken which expressed the conviction that the system of the world's being was closed, self-contained, finished (e.g., the laws of the conversation of matter and of energy, as well as the general notion of the unchanging and unalterable "laws of nature"). Without examining these ideas of contemporary science in greater detail, we can limit ourselves to one unquestionable conclusion: the barrier in the naturalistic world-view that but recently separated the immanent kingdom of the unchanging forces of nature from any conceivable spheres of another order has fallen. It is sufficient for us that we again "know nothing" in this domain; at least we have once again learned, like Socrates, to *know* that we know nothing, and that what previously appeared to be unshakeably grounded knowledge is again open to question. For us the essential achievement of this contemporary intellectual tendency is that scientific thought has become more modest in its rejections and has begun to say the word "impossible" less frequently and with less self-confidence. More than ever we can now prize the wisdom of the French physicist Arago's saying: "Outside of the domain of pure mathematics, I would hesitate to use the word 'impossible'."

Thus, we have no scientific or experiential ground to deny the objective validity of that which is immediately known to us from inner religious-moral experience: the possibility of the intrusion of higher gracegiving powers into the empirical world, and the active participation of these powers in the world's life. In brief, we do not have any objective ground to deny the possibility of the *miraculous*; and if our religious consciousness tells us of the *reality* of such an intrusion of higher powers into the empirical world, this consciousness cannot be convincingly refuted. It is necessary to guard against two equally natural errors. One must not exaggerate the empirical might of these powers or attribute to them external all-powerfulness in the empirical plane. One must not forget the paradoxical fact that, despite all its metaphysical superiority and all-powerfulness, absolute Holiness appears *in the makeup of the world* as only one of the powers that must struggle against other powers. *In the makeup of the world*, God struggles against the "prince of this world"; the power of grace struggles against the opposing power of evil will. In the empirical world, the powers of good are opposed by the powers of evil, the "power of darkness." The confusion of the self-evident metaphysical all-powerfulness of Holiness with its supposed all-powerfulness in the empirical world, with its supposedly predetermined triumphalness in the empirical plane is an error of naive optimism. On the contrary, we must recognize that, in entering the world and acting in it, the higher powers of grace must in some sense adopt the appearance of powers of this world and adapt to the categorial conditions of empirical being. Here a kind of *kenosis* occurs, a kind of outer self-abasement of the higher powers, the appearance and action of Divinity in an earthly form, in the form of a "slave." In taking such a form, the higher powers of grace submit to the basic conditions of the being of this world: in the world they are fated not only to participate actively, but also to suffer; not only to overcome, but to be overcome.

On the other hand, neither should one underrate the influence of the higher powers of Holiness in the empirical world. The fundamental pessimism that bemoans the utter powerlessness of good and truth on earth and the all-powerfulness of the powers of evil which is incomprehensible to the human heart—this pessimism or metaphysical defeatism is a nearsighted view and completely untrue in a wider perspective. On the contrary, *the superworldly, metaphysical all-powerfulness of Holiness must somehow flow into the world and be reflected in the world.* Holiness is invincible in the world and has, despite all the ascendancy of evil, a certain mysterious attraction and infectiousness for human hearts. If we add to this the fact that the powers of evil are, in essence, destructive powers which therefore, in a wider perspective, destroy themselves, then—without simplifying the rationalistically unfathomable paths of God's action and without falling into naive optimism—we acquire the right to combine a sober, responsible recognition of the powers of evil in the world with an indestructible belief in the power of Good and Holiness.

Thus, for a sufficiently broad religious understanding of life, a sober, truthful recognition of the lordship of evil in the world is not satisfied with the rationalistically simplified scheme of gnostic faith in a Holiness that is powerless to help us in our fate in this dark world. Instead, this truthful recognition comes to the awareness of a more complex, though problematic, situation in which the immanent all-powerfulness of Holiness is combined with the tragic struggle between good and evil in the empirical world.

Here we finally come to the experiential ground of faith in the absolute, unlimited superiority and all-conquering all-powerfulness of Divine Providence. Psychologically it is very easy to define this ground: it is absolute trust (the trust of a child) in the wisdom of the all-good will of Holiness which surpasses all our human conceptions. Human reason, including the rational moral consciousness, tends to consider itself the highest, absolute measure of all that is good and all that is evil, of what should be and what should not be. Human reason passes judgment on Providence, demands to know why Providence tolerates evil, and tends to think that only its powerlessness can justify Providence. From this point of view the unreasoning, absolute trust (the trust of a child) in God appears to be a "blind" faith, i.e., a kind of lower, imperfect tendency, which is impossible for and unworthy of a thinking consciousness. But what, strictly speaking, is "reason," and what is the basis of the belief in the unappealable authoritativeness of its judgment? "Reason" is nothing else but the clear, distinct, uncontradictory description or affirmation of the content of our *experience*. The only source of the *material content* of our knowledge is experience. But our experience is always limited; more precisely, the basic structure of our experiential knowledge consists in the self-evident awareness that the experiential content which is expressed in distinctly perceived concepts, and in this sense is "understood," is only a small and dependent *part* of some infinite fullness of reality, accessible to us precisely as an unknown, unattained, unclarified reality. And since reality in its fullness is a kind of unity that determines the nature and properties of all its partial contents, it is the case that together with experiential knowledge of all that has been revealed to us there is also immediately given to us the self-evident awareness of the limitation and inadequacy of all our knowledge. Therefore, the first and absolutely universal axiom of experiential knowledge is: *all reality is something greater and other than all that we know about it, and even than all that we can ever know about it.* Thus, the makeup of rational knowledge necessarily includes knowledge of the limitation and inadequacy of rational knowledge, that "knowing ignorance" (*docta ignorantia*) which was first and for ever affirmed by the founder of rational thought, Socrates.*

This general thesis is evidently also applicable to evaluations of all that occurs in life, to judgments about that which should be and that which should not be, that which is good for us and that which is bad, that which—in the fate of each of us individually and in the fate of mankind and the world as a whole—serves our good and that which causes us harm. It is true that we are given the ability to clearly distinguish between good and evil, that we unerringly know that love, justice, respect for the holiness of a person are good, and that hate, egotism, inhumanity are evil. To put it in religious terms, we are given the ability to distinguish with certainty light from darkness, holiness from that which is hostile to holiness. But in everything else, in our judgments about that which is good and that which is evil *for us*, in our evaluation of the significance *for*

---

* My book *The Unknowable*, 1938 is devoted to a detailed substantiation of this thesis.

us of suffering and earthly joys, health and sickness, riches and poverty, life and death—we are evidently guided only by our limited, inadequate ideas, to which with utterly unjustified self-confidence we attribute the significance of absolute truth. As Winston Churchill once said with characteristic moral force in the tragic days of the war: "Man knows only his duty, he does not know what is good for him."* In this sense, precisely our rational positive or negative judgments about that which occurs in the world, our complaints about the meaningfulness and inadmissibility of events and the structure of the world's life, are expressions of a blind, objectively unfounded *faith*, namely, faith in our own infallibility, in the certainty of our conceptions. In the face of this self-assured human blindness, unreasoning "childish" trust in the all-good Providence is revealed to be not blind faith, but the only genuinely *reasonable* attitude. It is reasonable because it emanates with immediate persuasiveness from the very experience of Holiness. Even as no facts of empirical reality can refute faith in the reality of holiness, so no facts of empirical reality can refute faith in the unfathomable *wisdom* of Divine Providence. Instead of wilfully, unlawfully, and unnaturally subjecting this higher, absolute power to the judgment of *our* conceptions, *our* ideas about that which should be and that which should not be, our ideas about good and evil (as is the case with the posing of the problem of theodicy), we, in awareness of our ignorance, affirm our trust in the unfathomable absolutely higher will, the holiness and infallibility of which are self-evidently revealed to us in religious experience.

Religious experience (even in its most defective form) is knowledge that, besides the visible layer of being which is accessible to us (i.e., empirical reality), there exists a deeper layer, another dimension as it were, the content of which is not immediately accessible to us. Outside of a relation to this deeper layer, we cannot survey being as a whole, we cannot understand and evaluate the general meaning of being. Therefore that which immediately appears to us as evil or absurdity can, from the point of view of "heaven," turn out to be the instrument of wise Providence. God says in Isaiah: " . . . my thoughts are not your thoughts, neither are your ways my ways . . . For as the heavens are higher than the earth, so are my ways higher than your ways, and my thoughts than

---

* A back translation from the Russian.—Translator.

your thoughts" (Isaiah 55: 8, 9). The *visible* triumph of evil and unreason can be, in an unfathomable way, the instrument and path of the triumph of God's mysterious intention, that is to say, the triumph of the all-powerful all-goodness and wisdom of God. And insofar as we have authentically religious experience, i.e., insofar as we know in inner experience the immanent absolute superiority of Holiness—this possibility becomes an experientially given, though rationally unfathomable, reality.

If it is naive, and completely illegitimate, to view the all-power-fulness of God as an external, physically all-powerful force that crushes all else in the empirical plane, nothing prevents us from recognizing that in the higher, invisible plane of being there operates some higher power that directs the obscure play of earthly powers in accordance with its good intentions. Nevertheless (here we return to the main theme of our work), this comforting conviction could be an illusion, a poisonous inner contradiction, for the sensitive moral consciousness, if we did not also take into account the paradoxical, though indubitable, fact that in the *empirical* world this all-powerful force (which invisibly and unfathomably directs the entire process of the world's life) appears as only *one* of the forces of being and finds itself in a tragic struggle (a struggle that never ends within the limits of the world's being) against the forces of evil and darkness. Precisely the awareness of the real participa-tion of God in the tragic struggle against evil (this struggle which is the fate of good and holiness on earth) and, hence, *His participation in the world's suffering*, gives us the highest and most ultimate reli-gious understanding of life that is accessible to us. The suffering God, the God who shares the agony of creation, who out of love for creation participates in its tragic struggle, who at the price of His own torments extends to man a strengthening and saving hand—the suffering God is the necessary complement to the all-powerful God. If such a combination is rationally unfathomable, the reverse situation—a God passionless in His all-powerfulness, a God who unfathomably has doomed creation to an agony in which He Him-self does not participate—would be religiously and morally incom-prehensible and unacceptable. Reigning over the world and direct-ing the world and each of us to the good in an unfathomable way which yet is mysteriously evident for the human heart full of hope and faith—Divine Providence lowers itself to the level of the world, enters into and is present in the world as a participant in the world's tragedy. Like a loving father or mother, God suffers with the suffering of his children, is full of agonizing care for them, remains with them always at the price of His own suffering, helps them and saves them. Let this be unfathomable—it is the most ultimate truth that is accessible to us, a truth that is in harmony with all the fullness of our being, both in its outer conditions and its inner essence.

The general conclusion of these meditations on the spiritual problems of our time is immediately apparent. We now have a precise answer to the question we posed at the beginning of this chapter: namely, What is the significance for contemporary man of St. John's theme of the light that shines in darkness? In themselves (i.e., independently of all spiritually unverified borrowing from the content of traditional dogmatic thought) the spiritual problems of our time have the tendency to lead the human heart to the perception and affirmation of the mysterious religious truth contained in these words of St. John. In contrast to the age preceding ours, having gained irrefutably certain experience of the power of darkness over the world; having overcome all kinds of naive optimism and utopianism; but also, in the horrific experience of demonism and cynical unfaith, having understood the necessity and legitimacy of religious faith, its genuine meaning in human life—contemporary man, from his own spiritual experience, on the basis of his exposure of the errors of the past, comes to faith in the superworldly *Divine light*, which, in the world, shines "in darkness." He comes to that concrete fullness, combining "pessimism" and "optimism," of the spiritual perception and illumination of life whose profoundest expression is St. John's words: "The light shineth in darkness."

50

CHAPTER TWO

The Good News

1. The Revelation of Christ as the "Good News"

*I*f we ask ourselves what does it mean to have Christian faith or to believe in the revelation given through Christ, then, leaving aside all more concrete definitions of this faith and noting only the most general, but also the most essential, significance of this faith for us—we can give the following answer. To have Christian faith is to acquire, apprehend, see a truth that, illuminating our life, gives us the spiritual strength to calmly and even joyfully bear the tragic nature and meaninglessness of our empirical life. It is to have a source of courage and consolation in the midst of suffering. It is to have fundamental *joyful truth* or *good news* that determines our whole life-feeling.

This consciousness is met halfway as it were by the remarkable fact, giving us hope beforehand, that Christ's revelation was called the "good news." How strange it is that the title of the four tales of the life, sermons, and acts of Jesus Christ that are part of the New Testament and have been translated into all the world's languages, has itself not been translated. The tales are called "evangels"* in all

---

* The only exception is the English language, where the "evangel" is called the "gospel," a word that is derived from the Old-English "godspel," which means "good news." But in English, this old, literal meaning of the word has been lost and is not part of the modern usage.

languages, and people who do not know Greek do not know what this word means—a word which, surrounded by an ecclesiastical halo, evokes in believers only an obscure sense of reverence, but does not say anything their hearts or minds can understand. In this we perhaps have an early example of the transformation of living faith, understandable by and effectively determining the heart, into "theological" faith.

But it is known that the word εὐαγγέλιον means no more and no less than precisely "good news." And how good it would be if this were indeed what we called these holy books, if, in opening the New Testament, we knew at once (just as the first generations of Christians knew) that the tales of the life, words, and acts of Christ as related by His four disciples (or based on the tradition coming down from them) contain the *good news*; in other words, that these tales wish to tell us a *truth that gives joy*. We, contemporary people, children of a dark, arduous, terrifying time, how greedily we await the good news, news that could console us, give us hope, and tell us of joy that has already been attained!

What is the nature of this good news? What is the nature of the joy about which this news tells us? Of course, it would be easy to answer this question by a simple reference to the dogmatic faith-teaching of the Church. According to this teaching, the good news is the news of the *redemption of the world* through the coming to the earth of the only begotten Son of God, Jesus Christ, His taking upon Himself the sins of the world, His death on the cross, and His resurrection from the dead. The world, suffering from the consequences of original sin, was thereby reconciled with God, and the faithful in Christ were promised everlasting bliss after His second coming.

The inadequacy for us (for the majority of contemporary people) of this traditional answer consists in the fact that it contains a theological doctrine that is hallowed by tradition, but poorly understood by us; and therefore this answer is experienced too often in a form we can call theological pseudo-faith. We dimly feel that this teaching is based on certain ancient archaic ideas that are perhaps full of mysterious wisdom, but that are no longer directly accessible to us. However reverently we regard this incomprehensible wisdom, we are not in a position to immediately perceive in this christological and soteriological doctrine the *authentically good news*, i.e., news of the *real good* that will save us. And when contemporary theologians reason about redemption in the traditional ecclesiastical style, the religiously sensitive consciousness involuntarily asks itself whether we need this doctrine and what is its genuine, living meaning for us.

Of course, the acknowledgment that a traditional doctrine is incomprehensible does not signify its critique or, even less, its refutation. But we are clearly aware of one thing: for this theological formulation to have meaning, one must first be able to simply see, perceive, experientially feel the reality to which it refers. In some sense, this reality is utterly simple, that is, it must be immediately evident and certain for the human heart. Fortunately, we remember that in this sense our position is the same as that of the Galilean fishermen who were first told the good news. If the theological doctrine of redemption has become incomprehensible or difficult to comprehend for us, for them it was simply unknown. Fortunately for us, it follows with utter certainty from the very text of the Gospels that the good news as it was first preached to the Galilean fishermen coincides neither with the finished theological doctrine of redemption as it was first distinctly formulated by Apostle Paul nor even with the general premises of this doctrine, i.e., faith in the messianic glory of Jesus and in the religious necessity of His suffering and death. For these truths were revealed, as a great mystery, by Christ to His closest disciples only at Caesarea Philippi at the very end of His earthly life and activity (Matthew 16: 13–21), whereas the same Gospel says that all of Jesus' earthly activity *began* with the "good news of the kingdom." It is utterly evident that the good news preached to the Galilean fishermen has some other content, more direct and simple. And it was precisely this good news which was somehow learned and apprehended by those who heard Jesus' first words, who were religiously astonished by meeting Him, by the immediate effect of His person—long before they learned the news of the mysterious paradox of His fate: His suffering, death on the cross, and resurrection.

This fundamental, primary meaning of the good news is expressed in the words: "And Jesus went about all Galilee, teaching in their synagogues, and preaching the good news of the kingdom" (Matthew 4: 23). That the essence of Christ's revelation is the *good news* can be seen immediately, outside of all theological theories, in the "beatitudes" of the Sermon on the Mount, in which they that mourn are promised that they shall be comforted, and they that are persecuted for righteousness' sake are promised that theirs is the kingdom of heaven, and that they must rejoice and be exceedingly glad; or in Jesus' words: "Come unto me, all ye that labour and are heavy laden, and I will give you rest. Take my yoke upon you, and learn of me . . . and ye shall find rest unto your souls" (Matthew 11: 28-29). The good news is repeatedly explicated by its comparison to the news of some enormous imperishable *treasure* which is in our possession and frees us—in contrast to the harsh Old Testament—from all earthly needs and cares (we shall examine this in greater detail below). The joy brought by Christ is His own joy and is therefore "perfect joy." And when the Apostle teaches the faithful, he does not forget, first of all, to counsel them to "rejoice evermore" (1 Thessalonians 5: 16).

There is not the slightest doubt that the good news brought by Christ was understood as genuine news of some *completely real, vital life-good.* This should be, and for the truly faithful is, its fundamental meaning for us. Insofar as we believe that Jesus' revelation has eternal force and is directed at us too, we must even now be in a position, outside of all theological theories, to understand the *real meaning* of the good news and to feel the joy that it bears. Of course there would be no need for parables and symbols if this news spoke of something that were explicitly revealed to sense perception, and evident in this sense. But the "good" of the good news is not only not given to the senses, it is even ineffable in a certain sense. Despite its reality and distinctness, despite all the stability with which we possess it, the good news is given to us only in a form which reveals itself to the depths of our spirit and is thus immediately *inexpressible.* Despite its essential simplicity, the good news is a kind of infinite, inexhaustible fullness, which we can clarify only approximately by describing some of its attributes. It should not be thought that we thereby depart from the simplicity of content that made the good news accessible and immediately understandable for the Galilean fishermen. For all that is simple and obvious for the heart is inexpressible for abstract thought. The content of Christ's good news is no more abstractly definable than beauty, than the bliss of love. Nevertheless, as is the case with related goods, it is possible to find words that can allow one to apprehend and feel the reality we are discussing.

2. The Good News as News of the Kingdom of God

If, first of all, we attempt to clarify the content of the good news in its purely historical aspect, we would have to say that it was the "good news of the kingdom," that is, good news about the ancient dream of the Jewish nation concerning the "kingdom of God." In its traditional form this dream was religious in terms of the character of its *hope*, but purely political in terms of its *content*. In having concluded an everlasting alliance with the nation of Israel, Jehovah did not abandon this nation in its woes and humiliations; sooner or later He will make manifest His protection of this chosen nation, destroy its foreign enemies who repress it, and restore its political independence, power, and material well-being to an unprecedented degree. This purely political idea of the kingdom of God, the idea of the earthly kingdom of the Jewish nation established by the intrusion and protection of God, was later gradually complemented by moral and religious themes in the religious consciousness of the Prophets. This coming kingdom of Israel was to be a kingdom of good and truth, in which all would be taught by God and have God's law in their hearts; this was to be a kingdom which would reconcile all nations, in which gentiles together with Jews would glorify the name of the one true God and become, like Israel, the "possession of God." Finally, a moral and spiritual transformation was to embrace the entire world: "the wolf shall dwell with the lamb" and God shall work "wonders in heaven and in earth" (Daniel 6: 27). This will be the day of the Lord, great and glorious. This miraculous rebirth of the kingdom of Israel was to be accomplished by a special messenger of God, the Messiah, a descendant of King David. This coming lord and savior of the nation gradually came to assume a more and more unearthly, supernatural form in the nation's consciousness and was finally identified with the mysterious heavenly man—the "son of man" of the prophet Daniel's vision and of the Book of Enoch.

In regard to this traditional dream of the kingdom of God, the good news brought by Christ consisted *first of all* simply in the news of the nearness of the kingdom, in the news that the kingdom could come in a matter of days. Furthermore, the coming of Christ and His miracles meant that the kingdom of God *had already come* in its embryo as it were, had already been attained by the Jewish nation. Although the time of its complete triumph and attainment which would be evident to all is known to no one except the Father in heaven, one must live by the consciousness that the coming of the kingdom is imminent, that its attainment has already begun.

However, if this news of the imminence of the coming of the kingdom of God, this eschatological position, exhausted the meaning of the good news (as a recent school of German Protestant theology attempted to prove), we would have to admit that the good news has no real significance for us and our time. The good news could then be only an object of historical inquiry, a curious example of illusory human hopes. It cannot be denied that this imminence, understood *literally*, i.e., measured in human time, has turned out to be an illusion. Such an interpretation of the good news would be tantamount to precisely a religious denial, to the assertion that we cannot now believe in the good news, that is, that we cannot have Christian faith.

But in reality things are not so at all. The preaching of the nearness of the kingdom of God was only part of more substantial good news about the *means* or *character* of its coming. Thus, the good news brought by Jesus Christ stops being for us an object of idle historical curiosity and skepticism and begins to touch chords that sound in our own hearts.

Let us explain what the case really is. Despite the wide range of variants of the traditional Old Testament idea of the kingdom of God (from the purely national-political hope to the faith in the coming complete transfiguration of the world), this idea remained a dream concerning a more or less miraculous *event in the external world*, the dream of attaining something that transcends all that is in man's possession or forms the permanent ground of his existence. It was a dream concerning something that, like a beautiful fairy tale, opposes bitter objective reality and is to be realized *in opposition to* all the real conditions of human life—something that, miraculously, like a *deus ex machina*, is to intrude into the world and transform it.

The "good news of the kingdom" brought by Jesus Christ, the boundless joy that He proclaimed, consists in the fact that the kingdom of God—this new, ideal state of life, at which all the hopes of the human heart are directed—is not something that must miraculously come, in some unknown future, *intruding into and conquering life*. Rather, the good news proclaimed that the kingdom of God is already embryonically attained in our hearts and must be attained completely by *organically growing into the world and inwardly possessing it*. The organic growth and development of the kingdom of God in the world depends on our own will, on the intensity of our striving to attain the kingdom. The kingdom of God is conquered by us, is won by force: "and the kingdom of heaven suffereth violence, and the violent take it by force" (Matthew 11:

56

12). Whether or not we perceive and genuinely attain the kingdom of God and use its goods depends on us ourselves. *The kingdom of God is not transcendent but immanent in relation to human being.* "The kingdom of God cometh not with observation, Neither shall they say, Lo here! or, lo there! for, behold, the kingdom of God is within you" (Luke 17, 20-21).* Not the idle dream of the external miracle of the coming of the kingdom of God, but the recognition of its reality as something we have already attained leads to the triumph of its genuine, all-encompassing realization. That it has already come, that it is already within us, does not contradict the fact that in another aspect it is yet to come, is only desired, and that we must pray, "Thy kingdom come." For, owing to its immanence in relation to our being, owing to its organic growth into us and through us, we possess it as we possess a mustard seed, which is destined to become an enormous shade-tree, or as we possess a negligible quantity of yeast from which a large quantity of dough can be produced. But in this tiny seedling of the kingdom of God we are already blessed participants in the kingdom, we already possess boundless riches that cannot be taken away from us, we already possess all the goods that we await from the perfect attainment of the kingdom, and can rejoice in our enjoyment of these goods.

Thus understood, the idea of the nearness of the kingdom of God stops being a vain, illusory hope and acquires a profounder meaning, reveals a nature that speaks directly to the human heart. This is determined by the fact that this new understanding of the means or character of the realization of the kingdom of God ultimately presupposes a wholly new understanding of the kingdom of God itself. In Jesus' sermons, the idea of the kingdom of God in its historical form (i.e., as it was apprehended in its various versions by the Jewish religious consciousness) is only the point of departure for a wholly new revelation, wholly "new" news about that which is the kingdom of God, i.e., about the nature of the illuminated, transfigured, perfect state of being.

---

* It makes no difference whether the appropriate Greek word ἐντὸς ὑμῶν means "within us" in the sense of the presence of the kingdom of God in the depths of the human spirit; or (as some translate it) "among us." In both cases the expression implies the *immanence* of the kingdom of God in relation to the sphere of human being.

3. The New Concept of the Kingdom of God

If the coming of the kingdom of God is not a miraculous external revolution, if the kingdom of God is already embryonically present in our hearts and must organically grow into the world, this is determined in the end by the fact that what we mean by the kingdom of God is not some *external order* of life established through the intrusion of the externally ordering good will of God; rather, in its ground the kingdom is an *eternal inner order of being*. In Christ's words, the kingdom of God is prepared for people "from the foundation of the world" (Matthew 25: 34). For this kingdom is nothing else but *the groundedness of human being in the reality of God and His truth*. Or, more precisely, the external attainment of the kingdom of God, the realization of God's good will on earth, is the consequence, external expression, and incarnation of the already existent and everlasting lordship of God's will "in heaven," that is, in the ontological depths of being. If in its external aspect the kingdom of God is to come or is already coming, if it is an event occurring in time, in its deep essence the kingdom of God is an eternally existent order of being; and since this order consists in the immanent rootedness of human being in the reality of God, the kingdom of God in this sense is *man's eternal possession*.

The astonishing and dumbfounding discovery that the kingdom of God (which heretofore has been only the object of the rapturous but timid dream of the miraculous transformation of reality) is *already really and firmly in our possession*, that it has always been in our possession inasmuch as we are the children and heirs of our Father in heaven—this astonishing discovery is the genuine content of the joyful good news brought by Jesus Christ. The kingdom of God must triumph on earth only because—in another, profounder dimension—it has eternal being and is man's homeland to which every human soul can always return if only it is able to see this homeland, believe in it, and if it genuinely desires to abide in it.

Thus, the good news is far more than the news of the kingdom of God as a state that is to come. Rather, in its fundamental meaning the good news is the revelation and proclamation of certain *eternal horizons* of man's being that were heretofore hidden from man's sight, the revelation of the *eternal ground* upon which man stands. The revelation of the essence of the kingdom of God as the eternal homeland and eternal possession of the human soul exposes the

58

inconsistency of that prevalent life-feeling for which tragedy, abandonment, poverty, solitude, humiliation, are the normal, natural, *real* state of man's being on earth. Orienting ourselves in the world, we are conscious of ourselves as homeless wanderers. We can only dream of another life, blessed and peaceful, but we must recognize with profound sorrow that these dreams and hopes turn out to be illusions in the face of merciless reality. In this tragic predicament the good news reaches our hearing: "If you are a homeless, destitute, persecuted wanderer in the world, this is only because you have abandoned and forgotten your homeland. Look about, remember your homeland, return to it, and all that you vainly seek will be in your possession at once. You will stop being a destitute wanderer; you will immediately become the immeasurably rich owner of an enormous treasure. Moreover, the king of this homeland of your soul is your own father, and he is full of love for you."

Precisely *this* content of the good news gives it eternal meaning and validity, makes it actual and essential *for all times and all human existences*. In this its fundamental meaning, the good news is *just as real* for us now as it was for the Galilean fishermen who first heard it. It is possible to boldly go even further and say that for us, people of the present, the good news has an even greater significance, contains an even more joyful revelation, bears even greater comfort, than for the Galilean fishermen. The more unhappy, lonely, and abandoned a man feels himself to be, the more radical the revolt that the good news produces in his whole life-feeling, and the more boundless the joy that this good news brings. Although the Old Testament man, perhaps like all men of antiquity to some extent, was conscious of the powerlessness, instability, transitoriness, of his existence, nevertheless he believed in the existence of a mysterious higher power—God or gods—from whom he could hope to obtain help or support through prayer. Man's unhappiness consisted only in the fact that the relation to this higher power was completely *transcendent*: somewhere beyond man there was a power completely heterogeneous in relation to him, which, if it wished, could help or save him; this power was naturally conceived as a being that inspires terror, like a tyrant that one can only hope to appease. The religious consciousness then was essentially the feeling of a slave toward his all-powerful master. But a more comforting note also sounded in the Old Testament religious consciousness: the relation between God and the Jewish nation was conceived in the form of a *union* based on an *agreement*; and this union was conceived as being analogous to the union of marriage, in which the wife, though she submits out of fear to the autocratic will of her husband, can count nonetheless on his protection and love. Both the Psalmist and the Prophets taught man that God will not reject the penitent sinner, that He loves even though He punishes, and that therefore He will one day pardon and save His people. As we have seen, this faith lay at the base of the hope that God will one day establish His kingdom on earth.

In regard to this religious life-feeling, the good news brought the joyful, comforting revelation that God is not a fearful tyrant, but a loving father, in whose house there is always sanctuary for man, and that thus the kingdom of God is not only the object of a dream concerning that which one day must come, but also, in a more primordial aspect, the already attained (or rather the eternally present) possession of man—namely, the homeland of his soul, to which he can always return. Thus, the purely *transcendent* relation between man and God, based on fear and meek hope, was replaced by an *immanent* relation, by the consciousness of the primordial eternal nearness of God to man, the assuredness of man's existence, which has eternal sanctuary in the home of his loving Father, in the kingdom of God "in heaven," this primordial homeland of the human soul.

But however great and immeasurably joyous this revelation, news of which Jesus brought, for the Old Testament man it was the realization (although in a new form, unexpected in its absoluteness) of his faith in the coming of the kingdom of God, his faith in the salvation that must come from God. The good news in this sense did not violate but fulfilled the ancient law of God, the Old Testament faith.

The good news has another and an immeasurably greater significance for us, contemporary people, who have lost our faith and are conscious of ourselves as defenseless orphans, abandoned in an alien, hostile world. The tragic nature of our contemporary metaphysical feeling based on unfaith consists in the consciousness of our utter desolation, our utter abandonedness, in the world—in the consciousness that we are hanging over an abyss into which we are doomed to fall or that we are the playthings of indifferent forces of nature (including blind human passions and urges). With regard to this life-feeling, the good news of the kingdom as the desired eternal homeland or ground of man's being is an absolute revolution, which replaces fear and despair with the wholly opposite joyful feeling of the complete assuredness and stability of our being. For us, contemporary people, the good news has roughly the same meaning that the unexpected joyful meeting with his father had for the prodigal son, hungry and in agony in his destitute exile; this parable applies directly to us.

For us, who have lost the living feeling of God's being and who thus in our fundamental metaphysical life-feeling are conscious of ourselves as destitute, homeless wanderers in the world's being—the good news is something like the discovery of a hidden treasure, the unexpected stability and security of our being. In this aspect, i.e., as an everlasting, permanent element of man's being, *sub specie aeternitatis* as it were, the good news is news of our permanent possession of immeasurable riches. Precisely in this sense the good news is elucidated by parables of treasure buried in a field and of a precious pearl for which man gives all that he has. What is essential here is the counsel not to collect treasures on earth "where moth and rust doth corrupt, and where thieves can break through and steal," but to collect treasures in heaven where moth and rust cannot corrupt, and thieves cannot steal. "For where your treasure is, there will your heart be also" (Matthew 6: 21). Man cannot exist out of himself alone, by the powers and means that are inherent in his own being; he has need of certain "goods," certain riches, that are outside of his being. "On earth," i.e., in the world, man by himself is destitute and forced to attach himself to perishable external treasures, which can be taken away from him at all times; therefore human life is always full of suffering, need, cares, worries. And here the good news consists in the fact that, in a wholly other dimension of being (called "heaven"), the soul possesses an imperishable, permanent treasure, and is thus freed from all needs and cares. In the light of this metaphor, we finally begin to understand the genuine, real meaning of the good news. The good news is that the human soul is not closed, is not alone, and therefore is not doomed in this its isolation to destitution and need; that, on the contrary, the soul has in its depths a certain forgotten secret passage to an eternal, imperishable treasure—namely, to *the infinite fullness of Divine being*. The good news is the news that the human soul possesses a *deep reality* whose revelation overturns at once the usual tragic situation of our life, truly saves us, giving us the peace and joy of solid, secure being in our Father's house.

Perhaps the objection will be made that, thus understood, the good news preached by Christ is not "new," not the revelation of

61

something that was heretofore unknown; for this good news essentially coincides with Plato's teaching of the ideal world, of heavenly being as the true homeland of the human soul. In itself this statement should not confuse us. Only the spiritually timid, the unfree, those who are not inwardly permeated by the spirit of Christ's truth, can be offended by an apprehension of the resemblance between Christ's revelation and the teaching, i.e., the religious experience, of the "divine" Plato, whom the ancient fathers of the Church called a "Christian before Christ." To be offended by this would be to forget the fundamental Christian truth that the Spirit "bloweth where it listeth" (John 3: 8). The resemblance between Christ's revelation and Plato's perception of the eternal, prototypical, ideal, heavenly world is a fact witnessed by the whole history of church doctrine.

Nevertheless this resemblance is not an identity. The essential and profound distinction between the religious spirit of Platonism and the good news of Christ is that the former has a closed, aristocratic character, whereas the latter is freely accessible to every human soul. For Plato, the recollection of the heavenly homeland, the possibility of returning to it and gaining solid ground in it, is the privilege of wise men, for it demands a capacity for the intense labor of pure thought. In Christ's revelation, on the contrary, the possession of the deep reality of the kingdom of God is given to every human soul that seeks it; here everyone who asks receives, everyone who seeks finds, everyone who knocks is admitted. Here the saving truth has been hidden "from the wise and prudent . . . and revealed . . . unto babes" (Matthew 11: 25). Here every human soul as such finds itself in primordial inviolable nearness to the heavenly Father, is inextricably linked with its Primordial Source, in whose image and likeness it is created and whose stream of boundless love continuously flows into it, fortifies and nourishes it. Here aid, comfort, and stability are given to the human soul precisely to the degree that it needs them. Here the poor in spirit, they that mourn, the meek, they which hunger and thirst for righteousness, they which are persecuted for righteousness' sake, are blessed. Here it is necessary, and sufficient, to be like "babes," i.e., to be conscious of one's own powerlessness, in order to enter into the kingdom of heaven. For here the essence of the heavenly homeland is God as the heavenly Father, God as love. And this all-encompassing, all-forgiving love shines like the sun on the righteous and sinful alike and saves every human soul if only the soul itself seeks to be saved from its usual homelessness and solitude. This solitude is replaced by security, sanctuary, "two-ness" (to use Nietzsche's term, i.e., *Zweisamkeit*).

In this sense, the good news brought by Jesus Christ revealed *for the first time* in the history of the world that our being, the being of every human soul, is not the agony of solitary confinement, not being that is doomed to death, but the joyful, unalterably stable, and blessed *being-with-God*. It is not by chance that He who brought this news was called Emmanuel, "God-with-us."*

4. The Good News as News of God-manhood. The New Dignity of Man

We come now to another, profounder meaning of the good news. The good news is news of *The Godsonhood of man or* (what is the same thing) *of the Divine-human ground of human existence.* We leave aside for the moment the significance of the person of Jesus Christ in this connection; for—in the plane not of theological theory but of our religious experience, our living knowledge—this significance derives from the general meaning of the good news. Utterly transfiguring all of our life-feeling, all of our self-awareness, this meaning consists in the fact that God is our Father or that, inverting the judgment, our true father is God Himself. This means that all of us, even the most sinful and weakest among us, are truly children of God, that we are born "from above," "from God," that, as the Apostle Paul told the Athenians, quoting one of their own poets, "we are . . . his offspring" (Acts 17: 28). This means not only that the ground of the relation of man to God is no longer the relation of fear in the face of a severe tyrant, but is now a relation of love and trust of a loving father. In our contemporary world, the idea of the father has to a significant degree lost the meaning which it had in ancient tribal existence and which is implicit in the Gospel symbol of God as our Father in heaven. God as Father is, in this ancient sense, more than a being of whose love and protection we can be assured. The blood relationship with the father, with the head and incarnation of family and kin, means that God as Father is the

---

* This is discussed in detail in my English-language book *God-with-us,* 1945.

inner foundation of our own being, the ground on which we stand or, more precisely, the ground in which the roots of our own being are buried. Henceforth it is not the case that the ontological ground of our human existence is duality, the total separateness and heterogeneity between God and man, which is only secondarily overcome by their external unity. Rather, henceforth the primordial ground of this relation is *kinship, unity*, the *unbreakable connection* of God and man. Man's desolation, solitude, and powerlessness are not his natural state, not an expression of the primordial ontological order of his being. Rather, this desolation, solitude, and powerlessness are unnatural, signify a violent rupture of that which is primordially one and whole. And, in essence, this rupture is illusory, signifying the powerless, unnatural attempt of man to break apart an everlasting, primordial link. We do not need to seek God, we do not need to take any special measures, in order to secure a ground for our existence *outside* of ourselves. On the contrary, we are not only primordially linked with God, but are so organically and inseparably interwoven with Him that *we are in Him and He is in us*. This eternal, absolutely stable ground is an immanent part of us, belongs to our own being. Our own being is based on our Godsonhood; our human existence as such is permanently rooted in the soil of *Divine-human being*.

This new human self-consciousness on the foundation of the good news not only gives us the sense that our existence is absolutely secure, replacing the sense of solitude and the associated sense of fear and timid hope with a joyful sense of peace, a tranquil consciousness of the unbreakable bond of love. But it also signifies something greater: a complete revolution in *the primary metaphysical life-feeling* of man. Man is conscious of himself as a "person," as that ineffable, incomparable, absolutely valuable individual bearer of life, thought, dreams, hopes, which is the very essence of man's being and which is more valuable to man than everything in the world, for everything in the world has meaning and value only in relation to this center of my being—my person. But it is precisely as a *person* that I am immediately conscious of myself as a homeless wanderer and exile in the world, for the forces of the empirical world are impersonal, indifferent to me as a person. In the world I am not an absolute, irreplaceable principle, but only one of an infinite variety of beings—an insignificant, insubstantial, rapidly perishing particle of the world. If in general the religious feeling is the hope that in this my tragic position I as a person can find for myself a protector in the metaphysical depths of being, then the good news as news of the Divine-human ground of human being is the joyful, incomparable consciousness that I *precisely as a person*—in this my ineffable, incomparable, irreplaceable, absolutely valuable, unique being—am *not alone* in being, but am akin to and have an unbreakable bond with the primordial ground of being. The good news is that my person is not only the "image and likeness" of God, but also what "God hath revealed . . . unto us by his spirit" (1 Cor. 2: 10), the revelation of the Divine principle. Being alone in the world, I as a person am not only not alone in being, namely, in the depth dimension of being, in the primordial essence of being, but I am even an incarnation as it were of this primordial essence. That mysterious principle owing to which I am a person has its absolutely stable ground in the holy primordial source of being, for it is His expression in the world. Man's being is not limited by the fact that he is a natural creature; precisely as a person, he is a *supranatural* being, akin to God and having the ground of his being in God. In essence, historically this revelation, this good news, gave rise to the very *concept* of the person, to man's knowing himself, to his perception of his own inner essence, that ineffable higher principle we call the person. Neither the ancient world nor the Old Testament world knew (or knew clearly) man as a person; this idea was introduced into the world by Christianity, in the good news brought by Christ. But once it came into the world, this human self-consciousness forgot its origin and ground, and precisely for this reason modern man, conscious of himself as a person, began to feel tragically isolated in being. The understanding of this profoundest meaning of the good news signifies for us, people of the modern world, the liberation from the nightmare of error that weighs on our life, the truly saving news of the genuine, ontologically grounded roots of our being as persons.

Moreover, this new self-consciousness of man, given to him by the good news, signifies a wholly new consciousness of his dignity. In this connection, the good news brought about *the greatest spiritual revolution* that has ever occurred in the world, possibly *the only genuine revolution*, for all later revolts that set for themselves the task of raising the level of human existence have consciously or unconsciously drawn their forces from the good news, have realized its meaning in a partial and always distorted form. All the "eternal rights of man" that were proclaimed later originate from the "powers" granted by Christ to people, from the "power to become the sons of God" (John 1: 12). Contrary to ideas widespread in Christian and anti-Christian circles, the good news proclaimed not the insignificance and frailty of man, but his *eternal aristocratic dignity*. This dignity of man, and of every man in the primordial ground of his being, owing to which this aristocratism becomes the foundation, and the *only* legitimate foundation, of "democracy," i.e., the universality of the higher dignity of man, of the innate rights of *all* people—this dignity is determined by his kinship with God, by the Divine-human ground of human being.

The ideals of freedom, equality, brotherhood, have their true primordial source precisely in the good news. The king's children, the children of the heavenly King, are *free* by their very essence; and the New Testament, based on the good news, is full of reminders of "the glorious liberty of the children of God": "You have been called to freedom, brothers" (Galatians 5: 13); and, "where the Spirit of the Lord is, there is freedom" (2 Cor. 3: 17). And the king's children, precisely as such, are *equal* in their dignity; this dignity knows no distinction between Greek or Jew, slave or free man, for they are all the same, all children of God, or, as the Apostle says, "Christ is all, and in all" (Colossians 3: 11). And finally, *brotherhood* is the relation between the children of a common Father; in its essence this brotherhood presupposes a common Godsonhood. All the claims of modern humanism have as their original source and only objective justification the good news of the Godsonhood of man. In this its true essence, the principle of humanism is more than a claim or "right" of man. It is the holy obligation of man to defend his dignity, to remain true to his high origin. All of Christian morality emanates from this new aristocratic self-consciousness of man. It is not, as Nietzsche thought (led astray by the historical distortion of the Christian faith), the "morality of slaves," "the revolt of the masses in morality." On the contrary, it is based, on the one hand, on the aristocratic principle of *noblesse oblige* and, on the other hand, on an acute sense of the *holiness* of man as a being that has a Divine-human ground.

Henceforth, man respects his neighbor and himself, for in the depths of the one and the other he sees the reflection and presence of God Himself. "When thou seest thy brother, thou seest thy Lord," says one of Jesus' "sayings" (*logia*) that has not entered the Gospels but appears for internal reasons to be authentic—a saying that coincides with the New Testament precept that by feeding a hungry man and giving drink to a thirsty man we give aid to Jesus

Himself. And in another direction, in the direction of self-consciousness and self-knowledge, man, conscious of his primordial connection and interwovenness with God, begins to understand that his own being in its ontological depths is something greater than a closed, self-contained, "only-human" existence. In his depths man discovers the presence of God Himself. From this newly acquired point of view, man interprets his usual solitude in the manner of St. Augustine: "If I had only seen myself, I would have seen Thee" (*viderim me—viderim Te*); or: "Thou wast always with me, but I was not with myself."

This content of the good news, which for the first time revealed to man his genuine dignity and thereby affirmed the *holiness* of the principle of humanness, was considerably stifled and pushed aside in the historical tradition of the church by the opposing doctrine of *the insignificance of man* (which in essence does not contradict the faith in the dignity and holiness of man, but only completes it by a relatively different element, having force in regard to the fallen nature of man).* This is the origin of that fateful historical misunderstanding owing to which *humanism* evolved in opposition to the Christian religious consciousness. Here it is our right and duty (precisely in connection with the collapse of the nonreligious humanism we described above) to restore the idea of man that was originally contained in the fundamental meaning of the good news.

We must now examine the relation between the clarified meaning of the good news and the significance of the person of Jesus Christ.

5. The Person of Jesus Christ. The Living Ground of Christology

When in Caesarea Philippi Simon Peter answered Jesus' question "whom say ye that I am" by saying "Thou art the Christ, the

---

* This distortion of the primordial, truly Christian idea of man is much more serious in the Western church (where it emanates from St. Augustine's severe, one-sided doctrine of the slavery of man) than in the Eastern church, which still remembers the original meaning of the kinship between man and God. I consider it my duty to note that I owe this clarification to the remarkable work of the Russian-French student of church doctrine, M. Lot-Borodin.

Son of the living God," Jesus answered in turn: "Blessed art thou, Simon Barjona, for flesh and blood hath not revealed it unto thee, but my Father which is in heaven" (Matthew 16: 15–17). The Divine revelation to Simon Peter, this immediate religious experience that revealed to him the genuine significance of the person of Jesus, is also the experience of every consciousness that perceives the truthfulness and grandeur of the good news brought by Christ. This experience is the living ground of all later christology. It is not sufficient for the heart that thirsts for true faith to accept the dogmatically fixed christological doctrine of the church only out of respect for church tradition (to accept this doctrine "on faith" as it were) if this heart lacks an immediate understanding of this doctrine, if this doctrine lacks inner self-evidence for the heart; such self-evidence can be given only by living religious experience.

As we have seen, the good news in its fundamental and profoundest meaning is the revelation of the Divine-human ground of human being, i.e., the revelation of the groundedness of the human person in God Himself, and thus the revelation of the absolute security and holiness of the person. But in essence this revelation cannot be a simple affirmation, doctrine, or theory, for as such a simple affirmation or doctrine this revelation would not only be an unfounded, unpersuasive assurance, but its form would not even correspond to its content. If the ultimate, absolute truth could be adequately expressed in an idea, judgment, affirmation, etc., i.e., in some *impersonal general relationship*, this would mean that the person would have to be subordinate to this general relationship, that the person as such, in his concreteness and uniqueness, is not the image and incarnation of the absolute, Divine primordial-ground of being. And, contrarily, insofar as the person is the real image and likeness of God, the expression of the absolute Divine primordial-ground of being, the truth of this cannot be simply an affirmation or doctrine. It must be given to us, first of all, in the form of revelation. Revelation (one of those concepts or words the living meaning of which has been obliterated from long use in theological language) is a type of knowing in which reality is revealed in such a form that *it itself reveals itself*, directing itself at us, spiritually penetrating us and acting upon us. Revelation is knowledge of reality not through our mental possession of reality, but through the presence of reality itself, through its active conquest of us, owing to which all doubt in the truth of the knowledge disappears. Insofar as this very reality— God Himself—is a *personal* reality; or, more precisely, insofar as it is a reality about the ineffable nature of which we can judge only through its likeness and incarnation, the human person—this reality can be revealed only in the form that is adequate to it: the form of the *person*. In other words, if the person is genuinely the image and likeness of God, then the person and only the person is the adequate expression of the truth. Therefore, the truth of Godmanhood, which is the profoundest meaning of the good news, could be revealed to people only by a personal being, who in His own person reveals this truth to people and could say of Himself: "I am the way, the truth, and the life" (John 14: 6). This is why faith in the truth of the good news must inevitably be expressed in faith in the person in whom this truth was revealed. This is the *fundamental distinction* between Christ's revelation and all religious or philosophical doctrines, even those that are close to this revelation in their content (among these doctrines is Platonism, whose resemblance to Christianity we discussed above).

The word or concept "truth" has two very different meanings from the purely philosophical point of view. In one sense truth is the coincidence or correspondence of the content of our thought with the reality at which our thought is directed, i.e., with some object. Truth in this sense is useful in that it helps us to orient ourselves and to act correctly in the external world; it underlies the beneficial practical significance of science as the basis of the technological conquest of the world. But to have truth in this sense is not yet enough. First of all, an unavoidable doubt, represented in philosophy by skepticism, constantly undermines this significance for us of the truth in this sense: according to this doubt, this "truth" has something mirage-like about it, something that is not "true" but illusory and imaginary. This point of view is not at all an artificial product of the human mind. Much of the Eastern world still believes that knowledge of the external world not only does not have particular value, but even leads away from the true path; and, in the light of the dire consequences of technological progress based on the scientific knowledge of external reality, the Western world is coming to the same conclusion. Truth that is capable of leading to the destruction of life, truth that undermines the very foundations of our being—such a truth is *not truth at all* in some other, more substantial sense. In its essential, primary sense, truth is not the external disclosure of reality through our thought, but the *self-revelation* of reality in our self-consciousness, *through which we overcome the instability of our being and inwardly commune with genuine reality*. Truth is communion with the Light, the inner illuminated-ness of our consciousness, which reveals to us the meaningful, right, "true" life. Possession of the first kind of truth makes us "learned," "educated," but leaves us powerless; possession of the second kind of truth gives us *wisdom*—a wisdom that is given not in abstract judgment but only in *personal life*.

Furthermore, that which we have just attempted to describe is not an abstract philosophical theory, but the data of living religious experience, that which is given to that concrete sense of truth which tells us that the living person is *truer* than all abstract thought, which tells us that the truth in its ground is not an abstract judgment but *living being* given in the form of a person. We can express the relation between the person of Jesus Christ and the content of His revelation very simply and convincingly outside of all philosophical theories. Jesus Christ was more than a messenger when he brought us news of our Godsonhood, of our primordial belonging to the kingdom of our Father; for if Jesus were only a messenger who himself has no relation to the news, how could we believe in the truth of this news? On the contrary, *Jesus Himself certifies this truth by His person*, for His Person is the most adequate concrete incarnation of this news. It is as if the call to return to our homeland were addressed to us by a man who has just come to us from there. The content of the good news that He has brought is confirmed by His entire aspect, by all His acts, by His voice, which we apprehend as a familiar voice and which awakens in us the dormant memory of our homeland. For according to the parable in John 10: 1-4, the true shepherd enters by the door, i.e., he enters into us through that place of our soul which opens freely to him: "To him the porter openeth; and the sheep hear his voice: and he call-eth his own sheep by name, and leadeth them out . . . And the sheep follow him: for they know his voice."

But this certification or living confirmation of the good news does not exhaust the significance for us of the person of Jesus Christ. Since this Person is Himself the living incarnation of the reality that He proclaims, He possesses the *force* of this reality; for-ces emanate from the Person of Christ that help us not only to apprehend, to hear His news, but also to go out to meet it, to genuinely realize the call that it contains. He who brought us the good news, the call from the homeland, and certified its truth by His Person, had the authority and power to actively draw us to our homeland, to pour into us the spiritual forces that are necessary for this return, for the overcoming of our isolation. Through Jesus Christ, we not only hear the call, directed to us, prodigal children, from our heavenly Father to return to His house; but through Jesus, through His Person, there pours down on us a stream of Divine love that gives us the strength to follow His call. In other words, the content of the good news is not exhausted by the revelation that we have a refuge in our homeland, in our Father's house; this content is complemented by the fact that the loving Father, through Jesus Christ, actively draws us to Himself, helps us to return to our homeland, which we would not be able to do by our own powers (even as an impoverished, destitute, powerless emigrant does not have the power to return to his homeland, despite the call he has heard).

The living reality of this impression from the Person of Jesus Christ, of this perception of Him as the incarnation of Divine love and truth, is the basis of the Christian doctrine that has become the center of the Christian faith. It is necessary to say that this doctrine has become the center of the Christian faith to such a degree that it sometimes even overshadows in our consciousness the content of the good news brought by Christ—a content which is the objective foundation of the doctrine. In this form, christology threatens to degenerate into an abstract doctrine, a degeneration which is especially unnatural for the religous consciousness that emphasizes the *personal* aspect of the Divine truth. A theological interpretation of this doctrine is not part of our task. What we have just clarified is sufficient for us. It follows from what we have said that this new, joyful life of man in inextricable unity with God or in God has become the life with Christ or in Christ. The good news as the revelation of the *Divine-human* essence of human life and thus as the overcoming of the life-feeling of solitude and destitution—this good news has become the living force of our being through the consciousness and very fact of our everlasting inner communion with Christ. In view of the adequacy of Christ's revelation of the reality of God; or (what is the same thing) in view of the fact that Christ's person is the adequate incarnation of the living truth, of God Himself—our life with or in God, our rootedness in the Divine-human ground of being, coincides with the rootedness of our being in the person of Christ. There is no need of later, complex doctrines concerning the person of Christ to directly feel the truth of His words: "The Father is in me, and I in him" (John 10: 38).

71

6. Christ's Church

And, finally, one more thing follows from this. The revelation of the Divine-human ground of human being, the good news that the human soul is rooted in God and is eternally nourished by God's grace, by the bread of life that gives life to the world (John 6: 33, 35) and by the "well of water springing up into everlasting life" (John 4: 14)—this good news, disclosed in the person of Christ, revealing as it were a wholly new dimension, a new horizon, of human being, thereby also affirms a new form of *human communion*.

If we take as our point of departure the purely historical aspect, we will remember that the good news was brought not to separate, isolated, abstract individuals, but to the nation of Israel; and that the good news was the completion and fulfillment of promises made to this nation by God. This does not contradict the fact that this news was also intended for the whole world and for all of mankind, for, according to the prophetic consciousness mentioned above, the rebirth of Israel in the "kingdom of God" was also to be the unification of Israel with all nations into one common family. But in both of these aspects, national and universal, the good news was not news of some new state of individual human souls, but news precisely of the "kingdom" that was to come or be revealed to people, news of the birth or revelation of a new *communion*, a new collective organism. Those who heard and understood the good news of the rootedness of their being in God thereby became members of that holy "nation," sanctified by God Himself, which the chosen nation of Israel had been from the very beginning according to the promise. Hence, the Apostle could apply to Christians the fundamental idea of Israel as a nation chosen by God: "But ye are a chosen generation, a royal priesthood, a holy nation, a peculiar people; that ye should shew forth the praises of him who hath called you out of the darkness into his marvellous light" (1 Peter 2: 9).

This purely historical aspect of the good news, in which it is associated with the Old Testament idea of Israel as the chosen nation of God, is in harmony with the very essence of the good news. The revelation of the infinite fullness of the Divine-human ground of human being signified not only the overcoming of the isolation and desolation of mankind in general, but also the overcoming of the isolation and desolation of man as an individual. The children of one Father who have returned to His house and who dwell together in this house naturally make up one family, a family in the most profound, ancient sense, in which it is one collective organism, one spiritual being that has a common source of nourishment, a common blood-circulation as it were. If God, as we have seen, is not a transcendent entity detached from man, but the immanent source, the immanent ground of man's life, then all the participants in this Divine-human ground are not isolated but inwardly fused to one another. The revelation of this deep infinite Divine-human ground of human being produces a complete change in the structure of human communion: owing to the unity and commonality for all people of this their deep ground, communion is not the external contact of human beings, but the expression of their common rootedness in one living whole. And since the visible, living incarnation of this common Divine-human ground is Jesus Christ; and since this ground pours its forces into us through Him—the unity of the participants in Divine-human life is their unity in Christ, and Christ could reveal to people: "I am the true vine, and my Father is the husbandman. I am the vine, ye are the branches: He that abideth in me, and I in him, the same bringeth forth much fruit" (John 15: 1, 5).*

This is the reality of Christ's church, not as an institution or organization intentionally created by Christ or His disciples at His command, but as a mysterious Divine-human collective organism organically grown from the Divine power that poured into the world through Christ and living by this power. Thus, being news of the Divine-human ground of human being, the good news is also the news of something even greater than the brotherhood of people: namely, news of the inner fusion and solidarity of the participants in Divine communion in one invisible but real living organism. This is not the place, and there is no need to examine the diverse possible meanings of the concept of the church. As is generally the case in the domain of religious life (the domain of living truth, which in essence is the fullness of heterogeneous and opposite determinations), nearly every one of these prevalent widespread divergent interpretations of the church contains an element of truth and is essentially compatible with other interpretations. Let us only note, however, that here we understand the church as an

---

* This meaning of the Christian faith has been superbly clarified in the book *Catholicisme* of the French theologian Lubac.

invisible, externally indefinable, potentially universal "communion of saints": a communion in *holiness* as one fused Divine-human being, embracing all human souls insofar as they have the deep ground sanctified by God and rooted in God. If in the surface layer of being, in the "world" that is not sanctified and permeated by God, every man is an isolated, inwardly solitary being and must bear his burdens and sorrows alone—nevertheless in his inner being, in the Divine-human ground of his being revealed to him through the good news, every man is (to use a marvelous ancient image) like one leaf among many leaves of one tree nourished by common life-giving juices through a common trunk and common roots.

Thus, the good news reveals to man that all his habitual ideas about the nature of life based on sensory perception and the rational understanding of the external structure of his being in the world—are inadequate to the genuine deep essence of his being. Insofar as man has come to believe in the good news, become permeated with it, surrendered himself to the action of its gracious powers, he has become a participant in a wholly special being, which is blessed and full of grace precisely because it is Divine-human; and participation in this being forms the ground and true essence of all human existence. This is that *truth* of human being which is "the way and the life"; and this life is that Divine life which, according to the prologue of the Gospel of St. John, is "the light of men."

The good news is therefore news of the rootedness of human life *in the light of the Divine Logos.* But precisely this light which is Divine, this light which in its inner nature is *all-powerful in its all-goodness* and whose revelation is the content of the truly good news —this light nevertheless shines *in darkness.* This returns us to the basic theme of our work.

CHAPTER THREE

The Kingdom of God and the World

1. The Paradoxicality of the Good News

*T*he foregoing clarifications of the meaning of the good news not only do not exhaust, but do not even distinctly outline all the originality of the good news, all its paradoxicality compared with our habitual ideas about life. Moreover, insofar as we remain within the limits of the above-clarified meaning of the good news, the human soul naturally begins to suspect that what is called the good news is only a pious lie, an illusion or fiction, invented for our consolation. Faith in the good news encounters a fundamental objection, which at first sight appears to be unusually weighty and invincible. The facts of the world appear to testify that, despite the "good" or the "treasure" which has been made accessible (as we are told) by the good news, the world and human life have not changed for the better in their fundamental content. Tragedy, suffering, falsehood, death, factually dominate the Christian world no less than they dominated the non-Christian world, the world before the revelation of the good news. Thus, what is called the good news has evidently not brought man and the world any tangible, empirically demonstrable good—any improvement of the fate of man in the world. True, it would be incorrect to say that the good news brought by Christ has changed nothing at all in the world. On the contrary, even from the purely worldly point of view, in the plane of the world's history, Christ's revelation was possibly the greatest of all historical revolutions, the beginning of a new world epoch. But whatever value we place on the contribution of Christ's revelation and Christianity to the fate of the world, this contribution does not, in any case, consist in a significant decrease of suffering and an increase of the well-being and earthly happiness of man. It is precisely honest, truthful souls, seeking not words but *reality*, who find agonizingly tempting the idea that the salvation of man and the world proclaimed by the good news does not occur at all, remains empty words; and that this exposes the good news itself as a lie. From this point of view, the assistance that man obtains, for instance, from medical science or social reform is much more of a real "salvation" or at least amelioration and improvement of human life than the salvation proclaimed by the good news. Ideas of this sort are a constant source of questions about the meaning of the good news and doubts about its truthfulness.

It would be the sign of a bankrupt faith to consider this doubt as merely a shocking bit of impiety. Rather, the true believer must openly confront this doubt. The fact is that this vulnerability of the good news from the point of view of the rational-moral evaluation of the world and life necessarily belongs to the very essence of the good news in its authentic peculiarity, in its conscious paradoxicality. In its very essence and, hence, for ever, the good news is "unto the Jews a stumblingblock and unto the Greeks foolishness" (1 Cor. 1: 23). This stumblingblock and this foolishness lie precisely in the relation of the good proclaimed by the good news to the real situation and medium of human life which the Holy Scripture calls the "world."

Whether we can believe in the good news, i.e., whether we can accept that it is nonetheless *the authentically real good news*, the news of the salvation of man and the world, news of the assuredness of man's being, of the joy and bliss prepared for people—is our own affair. But simple, objective fairness requires the recognition that Christ's good news never promised that which unbelievers demand or expect from it. Later, in another connection, we shall consider how we should conceive the possibility, contained in Christ's revelation, of *the perfection of the world.* In any event, the good news does not directly say anything about this. Instead, the good news of the salvation of the world promises (and this constitutes its conscious paradoxicality) man a new ground and new

76

horizons of life, proclaims the gift of peace and "perfect joy" to the human soul, but with the preservation of the *habitual*—i.e., *tragic*—situation of man in the world.

The paradoxicality of the good news is most immediately expressed in the words: "My kingdom is not of this world" (John 18: 36). We know of course how hateful these words are to every unbelieving soul. And we admit beforehand that there is real ground for this hatred: in the history of the Christian world the idea expressed in these words has been the source of the greatest abuses, has been often used, and is used even today, for the hypocritical concealment and justification of egotism, indifference to the suffering of our neighbors, moral passivity and indifferentism in regard to the acute problems of human life that trouble the conscience. However, the situation is the same, in essence, for all Christian truth in general, which does not know any external measures, and therefore can easily be distorted, can easily be hypocritically usurped by untruth. This situation is governed by an old principle: *corruptio optimi pessima*. But the believer must always take this risk in affirming and defending Christian truth.

Let us probe the meaning of the words: "My kingdom is not of this world"—a meaning that is no longer clearly perceived by the consciousness, because of the frequent use of these words, which have become a well-worn formula. Not only according to the historical origin of the idea of the kingdom of God, but also according to the content of the *concept* of the "kingdom," it would appear that a kingdom is power over people and things, i.e., power over the world, a real force that makes it possible to dominate and control the world. But, contrary to this elementary logic, Jesus Christ, who refused when the people wanted to make Him a real, earthly king, recognizes Himself to be the King when he stands bound, a beaten and humiliated prisoner before Pilate; and He explains this paradox by the fact that His kingdom is not of this world: "If my kingdom were of this world, then would my servants fight, that I should not be delivered to the Jews" (John 19: 36). His "kingdom" has all the attributes that naturally belong to a ruler, with all his total power and security, with all the kingly elevation of his position, and its "perfect joy"; but His kingdom is such that in the world He is powerless, solitary, persecuted, subjected to mockery, beating, and a shameful, agonizing execution. The Gospels emphasize that the kingly dignity of Christ was first announced to the world in the inscription above His head on the cross on which He was crucified. What a terrible, almost unbearable paradox! Not only the mob, not only the chief priests and scribes, elders, and pharisees, said mockingly: "If he be the King of Israel, let him now come down from the cross, and we will believe him" (Matthew 24: 42), but even for His disciples who loved Him and believed in Him, this paradox was unbearable and shook their faith. The 16th chapter of the Gospel of St. Matthew relates how the Apostle Peter (who was the first to recognize Jesus as the Messiah, the "son of the living God," and who with this earned the blessing of Christ, His confirmation that this was revealed to Peter by the heavenly Father Himself), when Christ began to reveal to His disciples that He will suffer and be killed—how the Apostle Peter did not understand how kingly, messianic dignity could be compatible with death on the cross, and began to rebuke Christ: "Be it far with thee, Lord: this shall not be unto thee"—for which Peter in turn earned an angry rebuke. And even after all the revelations given to them by Christ, His disciples were dejected by His death on the cross; it seemed to them the collapse of their faith in His messianic glory: "But we trusted that it had been he which should have redeemed Israel"—said the disciples who were on their way to Emmaeus to the resurrected Christ. And Christ had to explain once again to these "fools and slow of heart to believe" that it was necessary for Christ to suffer "these things and enter into his glory" (Luke 24: 21–26).

The human spirit has constantly resisted (even among those who wish to be Christ's disciples) this paradoxicality of the good news, according to which the kingdom of God is "not of this world," and the victory over the world not only remains invisible in the world itself, but is necessarily attained only on the path of suffering and humiliation. The human spirit constantly seeks what it thinks is a more understandable, natural, and rational understanding of the "kingdom" or the victory over the world.

Before this natural, almost invincible resistance of the human spirit, incapable of accepting the good news in its conscious paradoxicality, it is necessary, not fearing reproaches and taking upon oneself the risk of distortion which is always possible here, to openly profess and preach this conscious paradoxicality of the good news. The paradoxical revelation of the kingdom that is not of this world contains two closely linked propositions. First of all, this revelation affirms that precisely the disciples of Christ, i.e., those chosen by Christ, those closest to His kingly power and glory, not only do not enjoy any of the privileges of the world, but must even necessarily suffer and be persecuted in the world. Second, this revelation affirms that Christ's victory over the world, the salvation brought by Him to the world, remains invisible in the world itself until the end of the world, so that the world as such continues to exist in all its tragedy and untruth as if Christ's victory had never occurred and no salvation had ever been attained. These two propositions contradict "common sense" and the natural moral understanding to such an extent, they are so much "unto the Jews a stumblingblock and unto the Greeks foolishness" that the genuine truth of Christ's revelation must always remain the greatest paradox; and genuine faith in this revelation is given to man only with great difficulty, and is essentially accessible only to the minority of people.

The first of these elements—the paradoxical necessity precisely for those who have become wholly permeated with Christ's spirit, who have found peace and salvation in Christ, and who truly possess the "treasure" revealed by Him and participate in His kingly power, to experience suffering, persecution, and humiliation in the world—is so well-known, has been preached so many times and so unambiguously by Christ Himself and His Apostles, that there is no need to give it special consideration. It is sufficient to mention it.

The suffering and death on the cross of Jesus Christ are the testament, the everlasting model, for His disciples. "If any man will come after me, let him deny himself, and take up his cross and follow me. For whosoever will save his life shall lose it, and whosoever will lose his life for my sake shall find it" (Matthew 16: 24, 25)—thus unambiguously and categorically is predicted the fate of all those who will believe in the good news and follow the path that it indicates. The good news announces beforehand that it brings to those who believe and follow it not an improvement, but a severe worsening of their earthly fate. "We must through much tribulation enter into the kingdom of God" (Acts 14: 22)—thus, in harmony with the true meaning of the good news, the Apostle taught the believers.

But this testament acquires its true meaning only in relation to the *second* aforementioned paradoxical element in the content of the good news. A superficial understanding might easily suppose that the prescribed necessity for Christ's disciples, the preachers of His revelation, to experience suffering and persecution in the world is nothing else but an expression of the necessity for preachers of any new truth, for adepts of any new plan for the improvement or salvation of human life in the world, to be perse-cuted and to suffer until they overcome the inert majority that is naturally hostile to them. In other words, the necessity of suffering for Christ's disciples might be understood outside of all connection with the *content* of their faith—as a simple consequence of the necessity of struggling for this faith; after all, other plans for the salvation or improvement of life also necessarily demand self-sacrifice from their adepts.

But this view is fundamentally unsound. The suffering of Christ's disciples in the world is determined not by the fact that they struggle with their faith, but by the very content of their faith, by the content and meaning of the good news. The good news brought by Christ is such that the "world" is fundamentally hostile to it. Below we shall attempt to clarify this relation of fundamental *antagonism* between the world and the good news of the kingdom brought by Christ, between the world and Christ's truth. Here we concentrate on only one essential aspect of this antagonism, al-ready mentioned above: namely, that the world *cannot believe* in the truth of the good news and tends to reject it because the good proclaimed by this news is *invisible*, because the kingdom of Christ is a kingdom "not of this world," because Christ's victory over the world does not give visible, palpable fruits in the world itself, in which untruth, evil, and suffering continue to reign.

From the day the good news was proclaimed to the present day, this paradoxicality has given rise not only to disbelief in the good news, but even to open mockery of it. In the face of this para-doxicality, how natural it is to demand a "sign" in order to believe in the reality of the good or salvation that is proclaimed. Nevertheless, this desire to see a sign contains already that unfaith, that spiritual blindness, that resistance of the "worldly" tendency, which contra-dicts the very meaning of the good news. Jesus Christ wrathfully condemns the religious untruth of this position: "This is an evil generation: they seek a sign, and there shall no sign be given it" (Luke 11: 29, 30). Lack of faith and the desire to have a visible, tangible, incarnate confirmation of the good news are a spiritual state that contradicts the very *meaning* of the good news and is evidence of its misunderstanding. Christ had to rebuke even His closest disciples for this, and even today the fundamental objection against the Christian faith is reducible precisely to the unaccept-ableness and incomprehensibility of this its paradoxicality.

Let mockers mock. But the good news *in its intention* is news of

80

a "treasure in the heavens," invisible to the earthly gaze, not given to the senses. It is possible to wonder why precisely the world, i.e., the order of the visible, earthly life of man, appears to remain beyond the limits of the salvation proclaimed and realized by Christ, beyond the limits of new, blessed, joyful life; and why the world turns out to be a sphere of being that *contradicts* and *opposes* the kingdom of God. But it is not possible to deny that the Gospel, the good news, openly recognizes and is directly founded upon the inevitability of this dualism, so that this dualism *is part of the meaning of the good news*. The good news claims to be the true good news, i.e., it proclaims salvation and joy without even hinting at the attainment of that which later came to be known as "progress." The good news summons people to become perfect like their heavenly Father and gives them the real possibility of becoming perfect; but the good news does not at all promise the improvement of the world, but rather even predicts the worsening of the state of the latter. Christ foresees a time when "because iniquity shall abound, the love of many shall wax cold" (Matthew 24: 12). He foresees "great tribulation, such as was not since the beginning of the world" (Matthew 24: 21). And if the good news is to be preached to the whole world, then on the other hand it is predicted that the world *will not receive it*, but will persecute its preachers. And even in regard to the last days and the end of the world there remains a doubt: "when the Son of man cometh, shall he find faith on the earth?" (Luke 18: 8).

2. The Good News and the Salvation of the World

A serious uncertainty or doubt arises here which deserves special consideration, for its source may be not simple unfaith, but an essentially righteous seeking, prescribed by Christ Himself, of the kingdom of God and His truth: namely, the insatiable hunger of the human heart for the realization of this kingdom in all its all-embracing fullness, for God to become truly "all in all."

A teaching that contradicts to such a degree all that is usually conceived as the "kingdom of God," the coming of which seemingly must be identical to the salvation and transfiguration of the world—can this teaching be the "good news of the kingdom," which, as we have seen, is the good news brought by Christ? Is

Christ not the Messiah, that is, *the savior of the world*? The Old Testament dream of the Messiah may have been imperfect, but it contained the promise of the *genuine* salvation of the world in the sense of the genuinely real triumph of God's truth on earth. Can the New Testament, Christian revelation contain less, be poorer than the Old Testament hope?

Of course not. Of course, *in the final analysis* the good news of the kingdom necessarily includes news of the complete salvation and transfiguration of the world, news of a "new heaven and new earth," wholly subordinate to the will of God and permeated by the truth of God. The Lord's Prayer—"Thy kingdom come, Thy will be done on earth as it is in heaven"—already implies the hope that the world will submit to the will of God and enter the kingdom of God. And since it is said, "Ask and ye shall receive," the good news contains the promise that this hope will be realized one day. This means an unconditional acceptance of the truth contained in the Old Testament dream of the realization of the kingdom of God in the world, its incarnation on earth. Jesus of Nazareth recognized Himself to be "Christ," the Messiah, a being sent by God (as it was predicted by Moses and the Prophets) to save Israel and, through Israel, the whole world: a being sent to genuinely realize the kingdom of God, the kingdom of truth and bliss.

But the peculiar character of the New Testament, of the good news brought by Christ, consists in the fact that this *visible, tangible* realization of the Old Testament dream of the transfiguration of the world, of its transformation into the kingdom of God, is transferred to the *new, second* coming of Christ, the day and hour of which "knoweth no man, no, not the angels which are in heaven, neither the Son, but the Father" (Mark 13: 32). And this new coming will be the last judgment over the world, which will signify *the end of the world* as such; or, in the words of Revelation, it will signify a "new heaven and new earth," for "the first heaven and the first earth were passed away" and a new creation will come to pass ("Behold, I make all things new").

Thus, instead of the simple, indivisible act of the *external* transformation of the world of which the Old Testament man dreamt in his idea of the kingdom of God (and of which all Old Testament people dream even today, including socialists and communists in their plans for the "salvation" of the world), the good news of Jesus Christ affirms the distinct duality of two salvational works of God. In its ontological ground, salvation is realized

82

by Christ in the form of the liberation of the soul from the domination of the world through the possibility given to the soul of returning to the Father's house, of having "perfect joy," of being at this
very moment a blissful participant in the kingdom of heaven—in
spite of the imperfection of the world, in spite of the sorrow that the
soul inevitably experiences in the world. This salvation is not only
the salvation of the soul *from* the world but also the salvation *of the
world itself*, the salvation of the ontological foundations of the world,
a victory in the invisible depths of being over the primordial source
of the world's woes—over sin, over the "prince of this world." Thus,
the closed, self-contained character of the world is overcome and
the human soul has access from the world to blessed superworldly
Divine-human being. Thus, human souls suffering in the world as
in a fortress besieged on all sides by the enemy now have free
access—despite the continuing siege—to the forces of salvation
that come to the assistance of these souls. The former hopelessness
of subordination to the enemy forces is overcome, and the genuine
effectiveness, the all-powerfulness, of these forces is broken. The
victory over evil and woe has, in principle, already been won,
though this victory is invisible, i.e., nothing has changed in the
external, visible aspect of the world, in empirical reality. Therefore,
Christ could say the comforting words: "In the world ye shall have
tribulation: but be of good cheer; I have overcome the world" (John
16: 33). The victory over the world as the incarnation of the powers
of evil is the salvation of the world as creation imprisoned by these
powers. This victory and this salvation are wholly real, though invisible. It is true, however, that people who do not have *inner experience* of this salvation will naturally not believe in it, will deny its
reality, by referring to the fact that evil and suffering reign in the
world as before. The good news of this salvation can be apprehended and used only by those who have ears to hear.

This is the *first* salvation, the first, decisive, fundamental act
(an act that has already been realized though it is invisible) in the
work of the salvation of the world, the fruit and consequence of
which all else must be—even as the clear victorious conclusion of a
war can be the already predetermined, inevitable result of one decisive battle, the immediate consequences of which are not yet visible. Indeed, it has been proclaimed to us that, along with this first
salvation, which consists in the liberation of the soul from the utter
domination of the powers of this world, there must occur (no one
knows the day or hour) a second, final and conclusive act of salva-

tion, which is the predetermined result and necessary consequence of the first salvation: there must occur the final, visible, genuinely all-encompassing salvation of the world. This final salvation will not be a simple, though radical, improvement of *the state of the world*; rather, it will signify the ascendancy of certain ideal conditions of life in this habitual world; it will signify a radical change of the basic conditions of being, which will be tantamount to the total *transfiguration* of the world. This can be expressed even more distinctly in the idea that this desired final salvation of the world will be *the end of the world as such*—the transfiguration of the world in its separateness from God, the replacement of the world by a kingdom of God in which the world will be wholly permeated and illuminated by God.

One can express this situation in the form of a paradox (and this paradox is once again "unto the Jews a stumblingblock and unto the Greeks foolishness," an improbability that belongs to the very essence of the good news): neither the first nor the second salvation is what is usually meant by the salvation of the world, i.e., neither salvation is the establishment of ideal, perfect conditions of life *within the limits of the world*. The first is not such a salvation because it occurs only in the invisible depths of being and does not change the external imperfect aspect of the world. The second is not such a salvation because it is more than even a radical improvement of life in the world—it is precisely the final, conclusive realization of the ultimate hopes of the human heart and signifies the end of all being in the world, for the world's being itself ends, replaced by blissful transfiguration, superworldly, deified being.

From its beginning and until today, Christian faith recognizes the fact of Christ's resurrection as the symbol and real guarantee of this coming salvation of the world as its transfiguration into superworldly being in God. "And if Christ be not risen, then is our preaching vain, and your faith is also vain" (1 Cor. 15: 14). It is infinitely difficult for contemporary man, having behind him centuries of education in the spirit of naturalism, to have real, living (and not only "theological") faith in this fact. But discussion of the possibility or reality of this fact would only be evidence of mental limitation. Contemporary man is like doubting Thomas: before believing, he would like to place his fingers in Christ's wounds. But precisely to such a man are directed the words: "Blessed are they that have not seen, and yet have believed" (John 20: 29). Of course, the bewildering fact of Christ's resurrection contradicts all the laws of nature and is impossible *in this sense*; but the very *meaning* of the belief in resurrection consists precisely in the fact that the triumph (invisible in all other respects) of the spirit over the world, over all the conditions of the world's being (i.e., over the "laws of nature" themselves) in which man suffers has already taken visible form at *this one point of being*, has really triumphed over the last enemy: death. The massive images in which the Gospel portrays this fact are difficult to take literally now, and not only because the various descriptions do not entirely agree with one another. We must admit that the exact content of this bewildering fact is unimaginable for us *in its essence*; and that all descriptions of this fact have only the significance of approximate, symbolic hints at the *ineffable*. For how can we imagine, represent in habitual sensory forms, describe in rational concepts, a fact the very meaning of which consists in *the overcoming of all habitual forms of the world's being*—in the concretely visible appearance of supersensory, transfigured, wholly deified being?

But the only thing that is significant for us here is to recognize this concretely unimaginable fact in its *inwardly essential religious meaning*, in its meaning as an unfathomable phenomenon and symbol of the *maximal realization* of God's power and truth on earth, as the incarnate being and visible, tangible triumph of that power and reality which usually is only invisibly accessible to the experience of our heart. In order to understand why, religiously, we not only have the right, but are compelled to recognize this unimaginable fact, we must consider what its denial would mean. Its denial would evidently mean the conviction that the blind, dark powers of nature, the powers of evil and destruction, are—in the final analysis and by their absolute powerfulness—always and with absolutely invincible necessity stronger than the Divine Spirit and are able to annihilate the Divine Spirit. In rejecting this denial, this faith in the absolute all-powerfulness of darkness, we profess the faith that the invisible spiritual power of the living truth incarnate in Christ really triumphs—in the final analysis, at an unimaginable limit—over all the blind, dark powers of the world. No truths of science, no knowledge of the "laws" of nature, can refute the self-evident religious experience that, in the invisible, deep layer of being, God is nonetheless stronger than all the "laws of nature"; and that this is clearly revealed in the rationally unfathomable fact that death was powerless to destroy the reality of the God-man, Jesus Christ.

The resurrected Christ, with us until the end of time, is the symbol and guarantee of the fact that the invisible salvation of the world continues to be an invincible, effective force, the result of which must one day be the desired transfiguration and conclusive salvation of the world. The resurrected Christ is the link that connects these two acts of salvation into a single whole.

Professing in this sense the faith in the connection of these two salvations, in the unbreakable unity of the creative Divine power that realizes them, we must nonetheless maintain a precise understanding of the essential distinction between these two acts of salvation, initial and conclusive. The essential inner salvation of the world, the salvation of life in its ontological ground, precisely as the salvation of the human soul liberated from the domination of the world and returned to its true homeland "in heaven," must be clearly distinguished as *the necessary preliminary condition* of the salvation of the world or as the first, decisive, fundamental stage of this salvation—it must be distinguished from that day and hour, known to no one, when this salvation will bear its final, visible fruits in the explicit transfiguration of the world.

Therefore, until that day, i.e., as long as the world continues to exist, as long as time continues to exist as the form of the world's being (in Revelation the angel promised that after the final transfiguration "there should be time no longer"), there will be preserved an uneliminable duality between the life-in-God of the soul that has followed the call of Christ and returned to the Father's house and the life of the soul in the world, in the midst of the untruth, sorrows, and sin that reign in the world.

3. The Duality of Christian Being. The Kingdom of God and the Kingdom of Caesar

There is a saying of Christ in which this inexorable duality (which cannot be overcome until the end of the world) of Christian existence is expressed with particular distinctness. Interpreted in many ways, the source of the greatest temptations and often of the greatest untruth in the history of Christian thought, this saying advises: "Render . . . unto Caesar the things which are Caesar's; and unto God the things that are God's" (Matthew 22: 17). But the soul that wishes to follow Christ is astounded and asks: Then not all in the world belongs to God, and there is an entity and domain of life that is independent of God? Then, contrary to Christ's clearly expressed commandment, it is not only possible but even necessary to "serve two masters" (Matthew 6: 24)?

Of course, it is possible to answer that Caesar's power is not independent of God (this is affirmed by Apostle Paul in a famous passage in the 13th chapter of the Epistle to the Romans and in Christ's words to Pilate). Thus, it is not, in any case, a question of equally and independently serving two masters, but of some other, more complex and subtle, relationship. But this clarification does not remove the paradox. Let it be the case that in rendering "unto Caesar the things which are Caesar's," we fulfill the will of God Himself and, in this sense, also serve God by this behavior, as it were. But then the question arises: Why can the service of God not be inwardly homogeneous, simple, but allows and even demands were. But then the question arises: Why is the service of God not inwardly homogeneous, simple, but allows and even demands

The paradox is especially evident if we take into consideration the historical theoretical basis of the problem that was solved in this saying of Christ. For the Messiah, the savior of Israel, sent by God to realize the kingdom of God, was (not only according to the Jewish idea of the Messiah, but also according to His own acknowledgement) a *king*. It would appear that the coming to power of the true king, the anointed and son of God, ends the kingdom of Caesar; and every human soul, bowing to the lawful king, has not only the right, but also the obligation to reject the power of the Roman Caesar. It was precisely this argument that the Pharisees attempted to exploit when they asked Christ the tempting question whether it is permissible to give tribute to Caesar. It is impossible to deny the external persuasiveness of this argument. And Christ's answer, which proposes that one clearly distinguish between "the things that are God's" and "the things which are Caesar's," and, without becoming troubled, to give tribute to Caesar, thus giving to him what belongs to him—this answer is just as paradoxical in the face of our ordinary human notions as is Christ's truth in general.

For the moment we leave aside the moral aspect of this problem, i.e., we do not consider this saying of Christ's in terms of its prescribing a certain practical behavior (we shall examine this theme in the following chapter). Here what interests us is only the *ontological duality* implied in Christ's words, the duality between the kingdom of God and the kingdom of Caesar. It is evident that this distinction between "the things that are God's" and "the things which are Caesar's" emanates directly from the understanding of the kingdom of God as a kingdom "not of this world." In this connection, Caesar's power is something much greater than simply the political power of a Roman emperor, or secular, state power in general. In the final analysis, Caesar's power should be understood as a symbol of the power of the world in general which has not yet been overcome—the de facto ascendancy of the powers of the world deriving from the very fact of the unilluminated being of the world. It is not by chance that Caesar's possession which must be given to him is *money*, the symbol and incarnation of earthly need, of the earthly conditions of human existence.

In this connection the true meaning of Christ's saying is clarified. To "render unto Caesar the things which are Caesar's" does not at all mean (contrary to the interpretation of those who especially cherish "the things which are Caesar's") to give oneself, to give one's soul, to the service of Caesar. The human soul belongs wholly to God; there is no and cannot be any duality here. God's children (and Christ's disciples and all people in their primordial inner essence are God's children) really know no power above them other than that of the heavenly Father and of the Messiah, the Christ sent by the Father. But to "render unto Caesar the things which are Caesar's" means to subordinate oneself to the will of God also in the sense that a Christian must, without being troubled and without attaching any fundamental importance to this, tolerate the kingdom of Caesar in the world—tolerate the kingdom of this world and remain externally subordinate to it.

With the sovereign irony of a being who is inseparably one with the being of God Himself, a king knowing that his kingdom is eternal and indestructible even if it is externally invisible and unincarnate—the divine teacher dissipates the doubts of timid human souls fettered by earthly ideas and feelings as well as the tempting power of the question posed by the Pharisees based on these doubts. He explains that it is possible to give to the earthly lord the symbol and incarnation of earthly goods, money; that it is possible to give to the world and its powers all that is worldly without thereby lessening one's dignity and bliss as a free son of the kingdom of God—*under the condition that God will wholly receive what belongs to Him, namely, the human soul itself.* But the condition of this possibility of combining the complete freedom of God's children with the external subordination to earthly powers is the recognition of the kingdom of God as the kingdom "not of this world." For this, it is necessary to accept as a fundamental truth the paradoxical premise (acceptable neither for the rational thought of the Greeks nor for the passionate thought of the Jews, which knows only one plane of being) that the kingdom of God is solidly grounded and possesses all the fullness of reality in another, invisible dimension of being, alongside which is preserved "before the time," i.e., before the end of the world, the unilluminated world with its inexorable power of Caesar, which power is established by God Himself within the limits of the world.

The antinomian, rationally unfathomable dualism between life-in-God and life-in-the-world is *the fundamental fact of Christian being*. This dualism first entered into the world in all its mystery and became unshakeably grounded in the world with Christian revelation. No other religion knows this dualism in such a form. A great and incomparable revolution is the fact that from the day of Christ's revelation until today wherever there is true Christian faith and genuine Christian consciousness, the kingdom of Caesar is limited by the sovereign, free life of the soul in God. All the powers of this world, all the authority of state power, boundless in all other respects, collide with an immovable wall that protects the life-in-God of the free children of God.* Henceforth, every man is a son of God, an heir to the kingdom; and Christians as a whole, in their unity, in that which is called the holy church, are "a chosen generation, a royal priesthood, an holy nation, a peculiar people; that ye should shew forth the praises of him who hath called you out of darkness into his marvellous light" (1 Peter 2: 9). In this capacity, Christians are higher than the whole world, higher than all the laws and all earthly power. However difficult, complex, and entangled the concrete relations of this free, sovereign kingdom to the world and the world's powers—the fundamental sovereignty of the kingdom, its absolute freedom from the world, is a self-evident axiom. Despite all the sins, falls, and betrayals of the historical Christian world, this its essence has been preserved until today, and until today it remains the object of misunderstanding and doubt on the part of all

---

* As far as I know, the immortal figure of Sophocles' Antigone is the only recognition in the history of human thought prior to Christ that God's truth is sovereign and independent of all the laws of Caesar and of this world. This is an example of that "Christianity before Christ" of which the ancient fathers of the church spoke.

"pagans." The prediction that "the gates of hell shall not prevail against it" (Matthew 16: 18) has been fulfilled despite all the frailty of the human bearers of the Christian consciousness, despite the fact that on the historical path of mankind there have been many situations in which the collapse of this enigmatic autonomous—or rather theonomous—sphere of being could have been expected. This is that aspect of Christian dualism which is "foolishness" for the Greeks, or rather for the Romans.

But correlative to this aspect is another aspect of this dualism, an aspect in which it is "unto the Jews a stumblingblock." This is precisely the paradox described above, according to which the life-in-God, renewed by the good news and the influx of the gracious power of God, is not directly transmitted to the world, which remains alien and hostile to this life-in-God. The life-in-God evolves in defense against and in opposition to the world. The history of Christian thought and life shows that all attempts to directly conquer the world, to include the world into the church of Christ or to transform it into the church of Christ, into the blessed and righteous church of God; that *all attempts to obliterate the boundary between the kingdom of God and the kingdom of Caesar lead only to the distortion of Christ's truth*. This distortion can be twofold. Either the consciousness of the fundamental, essential distinction between life-in-God and all life-in-the-world; the consciousness of the absolute superworldliness, the incomparable superiority of Christ's truth in relation to all possible forms of the order of earthly human life—is lost; and the church of Christ is secularized, adapts itself to the imperfection of human nature, and "the salt of the earth" loses its "saltiness." Or, notwithstanding the inevitable imperfection of the world, an attempt is made to force the world to attain the perfection of the true kingdom of God. This is the essence and error of utopianism, of which we spoke in Chapter I and to which we shall return below. Here let us only note that utopianism, the attempt to establish the kingdom of God on earth by human powers—whether this utopianism takes the form of a conscious Christian doctrine (e.g., the Taborites, Anabaptists, Christian socialists, etc.) or the form of a worldly, antireligious doctrine (e.g., Jacobinism, Communism)—is in essence a kind of Christian heresy, namely, *the Judaisizing distortion of Christian revelation*. This distortion is precisely the fruit of that "stumblingblock" which this revelation remains for the Jews, people for whom the measure of truth is its visible, tangible, incarnate fruitfulness. The access to the kingdom

90

of God opened through Christ is understood here as a *political program* of the realization of the messianic kingdom of God on earth. Christian "works" are understood precisely as the external realization on earth of an order of life that is adequate to Christ's truth. Experience has shown that this is a fatal error, whose practical fruit is the reign of *hell on earth*. We shall return to this theme below. We mention this here because it is a "proof from the contrary" of the Christian idea of the necessary duality between life-in-God and life-in-the-world, between the kingdom of God and the kingdom of Caesar; i.e., it is a practical demonstration of the dire consequences of the forgetting or denial of this duality.

Thus, Christianity introduced into the world the paradoxical dualism—which will abide in the world until the end of the world—between the holy and the profane or secular, between life as the free and blessed being in God of God's children and the life of man in his subordination to the powers of "this world," be it socio-political powers or powers of nature. The world cannot engulf or conquer the church, but neither can the church—that holy unity in which Christians jointly form the immaculate, mysterious, spiritual "body of Christ"—conquer the world, incorporate the world into itself. Rather, the church is always (or, more precisely, until the end of the world) in the position of a besieged fortress with respect to the world. It is true that from this fortress escape is always possible into the blessed, superworldly being-in-God; but, *in the direction of the world itself*, only separate attempts to indirectly influence the world, to let the world feel Christ's truth, are possible. Of course, the world can and must receive the rays of this truth, this higher, superworldly life. Insofar as this occurs, the world, like the moon, can shine only with a dim, reflected light, can in its worldly forms indirectly reflect the influence of the superworldly light. Until the end of the world, Christian being remains at the boundary between light and darkness; it remains *the light that shines in darkness*. The light cannot overcome and completely dissipate the darkness, but neither can the darkness overcome and put out the light.

4. Two Worlds: "Spirit" and "Flesh"

To explain this fundamental dualism of Christian being, i.e., to give an analysis that would make this dualism understandable, transparent, that would reveal its logical necessity—is impossible. In its essence, this dualism is *antinomian*: it belongs to that domain of higher, superrational truth which reason perceives as the unity of mutually contradictory determinations. Thus, this dualism can only be stated or affirmed as a fact; and the attempt to understand or explain it must be rejected. Nevertheless, with the aid of certain symbols and analogies it is somehow possible to describe this dualism more accurately, to penetrate into it more deeply, and to clarify that which is associated with it or emanates from it.

The first symbolic idea that comes to mind, an idea emphasized in the Gospel and Epistles of St. John, is the idea of the "two worlds." We have already used this idea several times. Our soul simultaneously belongs to two worlds, simultaneously participates in two worlds: "this world" and "that world." "This world" is the world as it lives, acts, and feels permeated with sin and under the power of the devil, the prince of this world. Therefore, "this world" is fundamentally hostile to Christ's truth and opposes His truth. To the Jews who are stubborn in their unfaith, Christ says: "Ye are from beneath; I am from above; ye are of this world; I am not of this world" (John 8: 23). Therefore, it is also written: "He that hateth his soul in this world shall keep it unto life eternal" (John 12: 25). The world ("this" world) cannot receive the Spirit of Truth (John 14: 17). The Apostles are told to remember: "If the world hate you, ye know that it hated me [Christ] before it hated you" (John 15: 18). The same Apostle says in his first Epistle that "the whole world lies in evil" (5, 19); and those who believe in Christ are called to "love not the world, neither the things that are in the world" (1 John 2: 15).

In essence, this dualism between the two worlds is the basis of the meaning of the "good news" in all the Gospels. The paradoxicality of the good news includes the affirmation that all success in this world, all service of the powers of the world, is death to the human soul, for it deprives the soul of access to "that world," which is its true homeland. On the other hand, the true way to the "other world," to the kingdom of God which coincides with the kingdom of heaven, is accessible only to powers of the soul that are despised or hated in this world. Not the brazen and powerful, not those who have joy and pleasure, not the rich, have access to bliss, but only those who suffer and are persecuted in "this world," the poor in spirit, those who cry, the meek, those who hunger and thirst for righteousness and are persecuted for righteousness' sake. The truth is hidden from the "wise and prudent," from people who know this world and how to orient themselves and be successful in this world, and is revealed to "babes," to beings who are ignorant from the point of view of "this world."

Of course, this opposition between the two worlds is not a Manicheanism or gnosticism, as it has been affirmed by certain irrationally zealous critics of the Gospel of St. John. All in the world, and hence the "world" itself, "this" world, the earthly world, given to the senses—is, in its ground, created by God through His eternal word; this is solemnly witnessed in the first words of the very same Gospel of St. John. But this unity of the primordial origin and essence of all things as the creation of God does not contradict the deep, fundamental opposition between "that" world and "this" world. We do not occupy ourselves here with fruitless argument, we do not attempt to "understand" and "explain" how God's creation could turn out to be the bearer of evil. We limit ourselves here to a statement, a distinct perception, of the facts. Following the Gospel of St. John, we must bear witness to the paradox that the world did not recognize and rejected that true light through which the world itself came into being. This dualism between the two worlds, though it is derivative in relation to the primordial origin of being, concretely remains a fundamental fact of human life.

Another symbol for this dualism, a symbol that is constantly used in the Bible, is the opposition between "spirit" and "flesh." "Spirit" and "flesh" are, of course, completely different from "soul" and "body." "Soul" and "body" are both elements of the psychic life of man. But the flesh is that element of psychic life which is connected to the animal, cosmic, "worldly" nature of man, full of evil and sin; whereas the spirit is the superworldly element of man, that side of man from which he is immediately connected to God or to higher powers in general. In the Gospel of St. John, this dualism is expressed with a simplicity that at first glance appears to border on banality, but which in reality contains the profoundest philosophy of human life: "That which is born of the flesh is flesh; and that which is born of the Spirit is spirit" (3: 6). This simple formula gives a lapidary, classic, eternally valid definition of both the rights and limits of that conception which the "wisdom of the world" proclaimed in the nineteenth century with the solemnity appropriate to a great discovery and which we have agreed to call "naturalism." According to this conception, man is a "natural being" and does not essentially differ from the other beings of nature. Darwin discovered that man, this "king of nature," is in essence the descendant of an ape-like being, the closest relative, the cousin as it were, of the ape. Having taken this path, we can easily see that man is essentially only an especially complex variant of the primordial and elementary bearers of animal life: the amoeba, protoplasm, the cell. It is true that, because of inconsistent thought, people generally do not understand the strict meaning of this conception and the conclusions to which it leads. If man is only a clump of blind forces of nature as it were, his entire being can be reduced to the turbulence of these blind animal forces. But contrary to this, the naturalistic conception (as we have seen in Chapter I, 2) is usually combined with the belief that man must and can be guided by moral considerations, that his life has some higher, special meaning. But of course it is not difficult to expose the nonsense of this idea, to show that it contains an intolerable and absurd combination of contradictory elements. Within the limits of the scientific knowledge of man, on the basis of empirical data, this nonsensical naturalistic-idealistic idea was exposed and refuted just recently, in Freud's teaching. Within the limits of naturalism itself, Freud showed with incontrovertible certainty that which could have been expected from the very beginning. If man originates from "protoplasm," if such an elemental, natural principle as the sexual act (the act of the blind merging and multiplication of cells) lies at the base of his being, then in his very essence, in the whole makeup of his corporeal-spiritual life, man in fact is the incarnation of the dark element of sex, the crystallization of that dark turbulence of the chaotic element from which he arises. To put it briefly and simply, Freud showed (first scandalizing but then delighting the enlightened European world) that "that which is born of the flesh is flesh." That which is born, as the Gospel says, "of the blood, of the desires of the flesh," "of the desires of a man," is, naturally and essentially, "the desires of the flesh," the dark, blind, natural element that dominates human life. The qualification must be made, however, that the idea of "flesh," in its essence and according to the Gospel, is broader than the concept of blind sexual dynamism. In the first Epistle of St. John (2: 16) we find the affirmation that "all that is in the world, the lust of the flesh, and the lust of the eyes, and the pride of life, is not of the Father, but is of the world"; and all this taken together constitutes the "lust of the world." Thus, in a broader and more adequate sense, the flesh as the bearer of the lust of the world is a sphere of dark, blind pleasures and the satisfaction of pride. The flesh is the element of sin, and all that is born of the flesh is subject to this enigmatic element of sin—subject

94

to that which the Apostle Paul called "the sin that dwelleth in me," which "makes me the prisoner of the law of sin" (Romans 7).

But (and this contains that fullness without which there is no truth) the statement "that which is born of the flesh is flesh" (with the fearless acceptance of all the consequences) is complemented by a correlative statement, more decisive and deeper than the first: "that which is born of the Spirit is spirit." In His mysterious, elevated nighttime talk with Nicodemus, Jesus explains to the "teacher of Israel" that besides birth from the mother's womb there is another birth: birth "from above," from the Spirit, and that that which in man is born of the Spirit is not flesh, but spirit. That which is born of the Spirit in man is equivalent to that which is born of God (John 8: 47), whereas those who are born of the flesh, though they be children of Abraham, have the devil as their true father (John 8: 44).*

If man has these two different elements, spirit and flesh or that which is born of the Spirit and that which is born of the flesh, this determines the dual order or dual direction of his life. The correlative significance of these two principles is determined by the fact that "the spirit . . . quickeneth; the flesh profiteth nothing" (John 6: 63). This means that the response to the good news, the ability to receive the gracious powers of truth and life brought into the world by Christ and in the person of Christ, is the work of the spirit in

---

* Let us note the following. It appears that in traditional theology it is insufficiently understood that—along with the recognition of the *creatureliness* of man's being—the Gospel of St. John, in the passages alluded to, openly and unambiguously recognizes in man (precisely as a principle of spirit) an element that is not merely "created" but *born of God*. Thus, we possess "the Spirit which he [God] hath given us" (1 John 3: 24). Moreover, if, following the exegesis accepted by the most authoritative specialists in the New Testament, we accept the reading according to which the end of the third verse and the beginning of the fourth verse of Chapter I of the Gospel of St. John form a separate sentence: "that which came into being was in him [in Logos] life,"† we would have the authentic word of the Gospel itself affirming the eternal (existent in the womb of God) principle of the human spirit. It seems to me that this idea gives the only direct justification of faith in immortality, the everlasting life of the soul. I discuss this in detail in my book *God-with-us*.

† In order to convey accurately the point Frank is making, I am forced to diverge from the rendering of this passage in the Authorized Version—Translator.

man: "Only he that is God heareth God's words" (John 8: 47). "Except a man be born . . . of the Spirit, he cannot enter into the kingdom of God" (John 3: 5), whereas "flesh and blood cannot inherit the kingdom of God" (1 Cor. 15: 50). Generally speaking, a Christian is called to live by or in the spirit, not in the flesh; the Apostles constantly show how dire are "the works of the flesh" and call people not to follow these works. Nevertheless, along with this general, fundamental precept or commandment, it is necessary to take into account a more complex and problematic relationship which corresponds to the dualism (discussed above) of Christian life that cannot be fully overcome. In the tragic hours of the struggle at Gethsemane, the Apostles themselves revealed by their conduct that "the spirit is willing but the flesh is weak" (Matthew 26: 41). With spiritual fearlessness and dialectical acuteness characteristic of him, the Apostle Paul discloses this dualism in the 7th Chapter of the Epistle to the Romans. Man knows the good and wants to do it, but "the good that I would, I do not: but the evil which I would not, that I do"; that is, "what I would, that I do not, but what I hate, that do I." But this means that "it is no more I that do it, but sin that dwelleth in me." "For I delight in the law of God after the inward man; but I see another law in my members, warring against the law of my mind, and bringing me into captivity to the law of sin which is in my members." "So then with the mind I myself serve the law of God; but with the flesh the law of sin."

I know of course that this famous argument is one of the proofs of the insufficiency of the law for the salvation of man and that it is necessary to fulfill the law with grace or, on the part of man, with faith. But the further fate of this problem in the history of Christian speculation shows that the dualism outlined by Paul has also a more general significance. In view of the necessity of *freedom* for the action of grace and also in view of the problematic nature of freedom in man, who is subordinate to the power of sin or the "flesh"—the struggle between the action of grace and the action of sin is inevitable for man. But the severe pessimistic conclusion drawn from this by St. Augustine—namely, the powerlessness of man enslaved by sin, the famous "*non posse non peccare*"—is (like all abstract univocal formulas) not true owing to its onesidedness. And even more erroneous in its onesidedness is Luther's conclusion that salvation consists only in the justification of the sinner through the redeeming force of Christ (*justificatio forensis*), and not in his genuine inner healing, illumination, and liberation from the power of sin. In this interpretation, the flesh is practically all-powerful and the spirit is practically powerless. However valuable in itself is the religious theme of the penitent consciousness of human weakness from which this interpretation derives, its result is that the spirit surrenders beforehand all its positions except *sola fides*, "pure faith," the powerless recognition of the truth of the spirit. In the *real* sphere, the dualism and antagonism between spirit and flesh are replaced here, in essence, by the all-powerfulness of the flesh. This contradicts not only a whole series of unquestionable precepts and promises of the Bible, but also the experience of Christian life, which in its best examples incontrovertibly bears witness to the *real power* of grace, the possibility of real inner illumination and healing, the real victory of spirit over flesh.

But refuting and pushing aside such fundamental pessimism, such spiritual defeatism, we must also reject the onesidedness of fundamental optimism. In the 8th chapter of Romans, Paul explains that our glory as the children of God will be revealed in us only in the future. Even now we have "the first fruits of the Spirit," but we groan, "waiting for the adoption, the redemption of our body." Our present, real life is such that we are saved only by hope; our hope lies in the fact that "the Spirit helpeth our infirmities." These thoughts of the Apostle, as well as the real existence of spiritual life, bear witness to the fact that the antagonism between spirit and flesh (or sin) cannot be wholly overcome in man; and that despite the possibility, and hence the necessity, of the victory of spirit over flesh, the battle between these two elements fills all of man's life; and during this life, man cannot celebrate a final victory of spirit over flesh. Even the chosen heroes of the spirit, the saints, i.e., people whose whole being is permeated by the gracious powers of the Divine Spirit, cannot forget about the power of sin and the necessity of struggling against it. Thus, in the overall economy of collective Christian being, the tireless antagonism between spirit and flesh, between the gracious powers brought into the world by Christ and the power of sin, cannot end with the absolute victory of the spirit. The supposition that Christ's grace has already conclusively and forever freed man from the danger of being enslaved by the powers of sin, that henceforth man is wholly pure and spiritual, is one of the dangerous and fatal errors that recur in the history of Christian thought. The same error, in the secularized form of faith in the innate goodness and rationality of human nature, has possessed European thought since the time of Rousseau and led it onto the fatal path of utopianism (which we discussed in Chapter I and which we shall also discuss below).

The power of sin or the flesh, even over people who are already saved in the spiritual ground or depths, is a primordial fact which is a *mystery* that cannot be solved by rational thought. But the mysterious character of this fact should, of course, not keep it from being recognized precisely as an incomprehensible but certain *reality*. Without attempting to explain this unexplainable fact, we can nonetheless attempt to illuminate or describe it from another side. The inevitable duality of human life, based on the fact that its salvation which is already realized remains empirically invisible and is combined with the visible powerlessness of man in the face of the dark powers of "this world"—this duality, forming the paradoxical peculiarity of the Christian revelation of salvation, presupposes yet another idea, which we have not adequately taken into account. This paradoxicality is based on the utterly *new understanding of the all-powerfulness of God* introduced by the revelation of Christ. Above, in our discussion of the relation between the tragic nature of life and faith (Chapter I, 4), we approached this theme, but had to defer its systematic examination. We shall now undertake this examination.

5. The Meaning of the "All-powerfulness" of God. The Mystery of the Action of the Powers of Grace in the World

The dualism between life-in-God and the world, or between spirit and flesh (a dualism that is a necessary element of Christian revelation), sets before us the task of harmonizing this dualism with faith in the all-powerfulness of God or (what is the same thing for a Christian) with faith in the genuine victoriousness of Christ's work of redemption. It is clear beforehand that no simple, rational position can satisfy us: neither the Manichean-gnostic denial of the all-powerfulness of God and the affirmation of the absolute independence with respect to God of the powers of sin, the flesh, "this world"; nor the optimistic conception that the powers of evil have already been conclusively overcome. Rather, the truth here is superrational and antinomian.

According to the Gospel, the resurrected Christ told His disciples: "All power is given unto me in heaven and in earth" (Matthew 18: 18). In their general meaning these words are an expression of that faith in the triumph of Christ's work of redemption which forms the very essence of Christian faith. But how should we understand these words more precisely? The *literal* interpretation of these words is obviously incompatible with a profoundly understood faith in them. When with these words Christ proclaimed that He was King of the world, Galilee and Judaea were not yet under the domination of Caesar, and Jerusalem had not yet lived through the fearful drama of its destruction (foretold by Christ) at the merciless hands of the Roman Caesar. More generally, the whole world— even after Christ proclaimed these words—remained and remains until now in the power of evil and untruth. Despite this proclamation by Christ of His already-established all-powerfulness, not only on heaven but also on earth, He told us to pray to our Father in heaven: "Thy kingdom come." But this prayer, this hope of the coming attainment of the kingdom of God (no one knows the day or hour) would be meaningless if Christ already had—right now— genuine all-powerfulness in the literal sense.

The words "all power is given unto me" coincide with the meaning of the words spoken by Christ at the end of His earthly activity: "I have overcome the world." But these words are in the context of a more complex proclamation, which we examined earlier: "In the world ye shall have tribulation: but be of good cheer; I have overcome the world" (John 16: 33). We have already seen that these words point to an invisible victory won by Christ in the ontological depths of being, a victory that has not yet been adequately impressed on the empirical world given to the senses, a victory after which must follow the desired final transfiguration of the world. Let us return to this theme. It is wholly evident that, understood literally, the words "I have overcome the world" contradict the words "In the world ye shall have tribulation." It would appear that one of two must be the case: Either people are fated to "have tribulation" in the world, and this means that they still find themselves under the harsh domination of the world, which has *not been overcome.* Or Christ really has "overcome the world," and the world is powerless, cannot cause "tribulation"; and the encouragement "be of good cheer" becomes meaningless.

This contradiction is removed by the distinction, already revealed to us, between two acts of salvation, two "victories" over the world. The meaning of the words we are examining, like the meaning of Christian faith as a whole, presupposes that there is an overcoming of the world, a triumph of spirit over flesh, an all-powerfulness of the saving power of God, that is wholly real, while remaining invisible, while being inadequately revealed in the empirical plane of being.

But this means that in considering *the practical action in the world* of the redeeming work of Christ or the saving power of grace, that is, their role as real effective powers in the rationally knowable empirical plane of the world's being, we do not have the right to attribute visible, tangible, empirically evidenced all-powerfulness to these powers. On the contrary, this all-powerfulness remains hidden, invisible, the object of faith as the "evidence of things not seen" (Hebrews 11: 1). But how must we conceive this invisible all-powerfulness, this (if we can be allowed a paradoxical formulation) *practically powerless or feeble all-powerfulness*, so that it be more than an empty word for us?

Of course we can answer this question by limiting ourselves to a reference to a general faith (self-evident to our "hearts") in Divine Providence, which on paths unknown to us leads the world and human souls to the conclusive triumph of absolute good and absolute truth, i.e., to a goal the attainment of which is an adequate reflection of the all-powerfulness of the all-good will of God. Faith in Divine Providence is nothing else but faith in the invisible all-powerfulness of God, secretly acting even where powers of an opposite order appear to triumph. We spoke about this before, at the end of Chapter I.

However, this general reference to the faith in Providence does not answer one excruciating question that arises in the human soul insofar as the soul is acutely conscious of the abnormality of the lordship of evil and suffering in the world. We do not understand why God, despite His all-powerfulness, is *forced*, as it were, to lead us on the path of tribulation and suffering, and to tolerate— "before the time," i.e., before the end of the world—the lordship of evil. Does not this state of affairs, as well as the faith in the coming conclusive triumph of the kingdom of God, imply that God will only *become* all-powerful at some future time? But faith in this future triumph of God would be completely arbitrary if it were not guaranteed by the consciousness of the already-realized—invisible—all-powerfulness of God. And precisely this consciousness, the consciousness that all power is given unto Him in heaven and in earth, constitutes the essence of the Christian faith, as of all religious faith in general.

The world as such, in its dark, unilluminated essence, in its essence which has not yet been empirically overcome—this world is hostile to God, the light of the Divine Logos, and opposes this light. Thus, it is completely natural that this light, insofar as it itself is part of the world as it were, penetrates into the world and acts in it in the capacity of a worldly power; the light is like the vanguard of an army that has penetrated deep into the rear of the enemy, and is surrounded for this reason by the numerically superior enemy. It is natural that the vanguard is often doomed to destruction, and its only success lies in the fact that it is able to make the enemy aware of the great army that is arrayed against it and will one day defeat it. This weakness, this condition, full of risk and danger, of the vanguard that has penetrated into the territory of the enemy is not proof of the weakness and powerlessness of the main army, outside the limits of this territory. On the contrary, this army can be great and ultimately invincible. Moreover, it could have already won somewhere else a decisive victory over the enemy despite its weakness on the enemy's territory (precisely such is the situation in which the invisible victory of Christ over the world is combined with the hostile power of the world that has not yet been overcome). If we remember that the "field of battle" of these armies is, to use Dostoevsky's words, "the human heart," we can understand how this human heart, having on the one hand the experience of the powerlessness and weakness of the light in the world, can *at the same time* have the experience of the immanent inner power, the invincibleness and all-powerfulness of the light in another plane, the experience of the already-attained yet invisible victory over the darkness in the depths of being. Once it apprehends with inner certainty the invisible being of the superworldly Light, the human heart has self-evident knowledge that this being of the Light and its revelation to the human heart are an *effective power* that illuminates and warms life. Furthermore, this Light is so dazzlingly bright, and the warmth that emanates from it so unrestrainedly penetrates into the human heart, that in some depth of being we have experience not simply of a power but of a power that in some immanent sense is *all-powerful, all-conquering*. This is rationally undemonstrable, of course, like everything else in this domain. But this requires no demonstration for spiritual experience, for it possesses all the self-evidence of a fact of experience. For spiritual being the attribute of all-powerfulness is simply a self-evident element of the super-worldly Light, coincides with the being of the Light as it were.

Understanding this fact with our mind and associating it with the empirical fact of the powerlessness or faintness of the Light within the limits of the world's being and on the paths of purely natural activity, we affirm one very significant proposition: *The power of something is scarcely always determined by the magnitude of the empirical effect produced.* Only the power of an empirical, natural force can be measured in such a way (and that with limitations associated with the distinction between potential and kinetic energy). Besides such an empirical, natural force, the whole content of which is in principle exhausted by its capacity to produce the appropriate practical effect, there is a force of another, inner order, the power of which directly coincides with its inner significance and is wholly independent of the external, practical effect produced. This is not a sophisticated play on words. A situation of this sort is disclosed not only in the religious realm. Wherever we have an impression expressed in the words "spiritual force," we also have the consciousness that the magnitude of this force is wholly independent of its practical effectiveness. How often a *genius*—a being who astonishes us with his spiritual force, and immediately reveals himself as a colossal spiritual force, far surpassing the usual medium level—is without influence on his environment! And on the contrary, how often, especially in our epoch of demagogic dictatorships, spiritual nonentity and powerlessness have, at least for a time, the deceiving likeness of all-powerful force, bewitching the whole world and bringing it to blind obedience! There is no more widespread, cruder, and more fatal error than the confusion of these two orders of things. One must be deprived of all immediate perception of inner force to judge about the force and significance of a man only on the basis of his influence. "O people—pitiful race, worthy of tears and laughter, the priests of the momentary, worshippers of success"—is what Pushkin says of this error. Heat from rotting straw can produce a terrible, destructive fire; under certain conditions, light from the sun can fail to ignite a flame or even to penetrate a closed shutter. But the straw remains a straw, and the sun remains the sun; and a burning straw does not have a millionth of the energy of the sun.

It is true that in domains that do not extend to that ultimate depth of being which is revealed to religious experience, the dis-

102

tinction between superficial, external force and inner, genuinely profound force is usually manifested in the distinction between a rapid but transient effect and a slow but prolonged effect. This is applicable both to the domain of physics and to the domain of purely human spirituality. The flame of a straw can set a fire, but this flame goes out soon after being lit. For millions of years the sun has illuminated, warmed, and given life to the earth. Celebrities of the present day who have conquered the whole world are forgotten quickly as if they never existed, but a genius gains greater and greater influence with the passage of time. Compared to this, the distinction between inner force and outer force in that ultimate depth of being which is revealed to religious experience cannot be defined so simply. The empirically inner force of the Light is revealed in the fact that, despite all its possible failures and its faintness in the world, it remains "the unfading light," and the darkness cannot overtake it and put it out. As far as its positive action in the world is concerned, the Light is not guaranteed decisive *outer* success even in the future, that is, within the limits of the empirical future of the world. Its force in the sense of its effectiveness is expressed here not in the breadth of its influnce, but in its intensity. He who genuinely possesses, and is inwardly permeated by this Light possesses a source of measureless power, invincible by any outward force; this is revealed in his unbending fortitude, his capacity for superhuman works. Such is the action of that spiritual energy which we call moral force. Kant had this force in mind when he said that the ideal force of duty is all-powerful in its nature, and therefore it is superior to all real force. From this follows the rule: "you must, therefore you can."

If this immediate consciousness of the ideal, immanent all-powerfulness of spiritual force is combined with the fundamental religious perception of the superworldly invisible reality of the higher Light, then we have the experience that this self-evident, though invisible, reality of the Light coincides in its essence with invisible but self-evident inner *all-powerfulness*. From this point of view, gnostic dualism with its sharp distinction between the distant powerless all-good Divinity and the power of the evil powers of the world turns out to be a crude rationalistic scheme, the transfer to the religious domain of concepts and laws of the external, rational, empirical layer of being. He who does not succumb to this habitual superficial scheme has, on the contrary, the immediate consciousness that the being of the higher, Divine Light coincides with its inner, immanent all-powerfulness—an all-powerfulness that is not at all diminished by its empirical weakness. *In this sense* the attribute of all-powerfulness irrevocably belongs to the very idea of God's being; and the religious consciousness (at least in principle, i.e., insofar as it really is *religious* consciousness) is not confused and tempted by the apparent, visible triumph of evil on earth. There is no need for Christ to prove His divinity by performing the external miracle of coming down from the cross, as the Jews demanded. Furthermore, such an external proof is impossible for Him, for it would contradict the very *essence* of His divinity. But even dying in agony on the cross, or rather precisely through this agony and death, He *overcomes the world.* The Gospel tells us that—even before and thus independently of the miracle of resurrection—the force of the spirit revealed in this agony possessed at that moment the soul of its witness, a centurion ("Truly this was the son of God"), i.e., revealed its triumphal nature. This constitutes the mysterious meaning of those words of God which Apostle Paul heard: "My strength is made perfect in weakness" (2 Cor. 12: 9). And this contains the profoundest essence of the idea of *kenosis: the idea of God overcoming the world precisely by His suffering in it.*

In other words, the all-powerfulness of God is not an external agency that forcibly intrudes into and overcomes the world. Rather, the all-powerfulness of God acts upon the human soul *from within,* in the form of *grace,* which penetrates into the depths of the soul that freely opens to admit this grace. All-powerfulness, the overcoming of the world, power "in heaven and in earth," are notions that should be confused neither with crude physical force nor with tyrannical power. They can be compared only to the unrestrainable force of *charm* which enchants and enslaves the human heart. Aristotle understood this when he said that God moves the world the way the object of love acts upon a lover, attracting him and conquering his heart. But if the all-powerfulness of God acts in the form of grace pouring into the human heart, the problem of the reality or the effectiveness of its action is then reduced to the unfathomable ultimate mystery of man's being: *the mystery of freedom.* It is known what role in the history of Christian speculation (and partly in the history of the theological speculation of other religions) is played by the problem of grace and freedom. We shall not present a theoretical discussion of this problem. It is sufficient to note that this problem is, in essence, an antinomian one and does not admit a rational solution. On the one hand, grace in the form of Divine charm unrestrainedly attracts and conquers the human heart; it is as if grace itself produces in the human heart the free motion toward grace, produces the free self-disclosure, which constitutes the meaning of the all-powerfulness of God. On the other hand, human freedom by definition is absolutely spontaneous, primary, not determined by anything from outside; and we know from experience that the powers of grace often knock in vain for entrance into the closed human heart, enslaved by "this world." Theological speculation, especially that of the Catholic Church, has thought up many intricate formulations, many subtle distinctions of the forms of grace, in order to mentally "get around" this antinomy. However interesting and instructive these formulations may be, they are not able to genuinely and really overcome the antinomianism of the relation. All the habitual categories under which we subsume the relations of phenomena are not adequate to that mysterious deep medium in which grace acts in the element of the free human spirit. This action is given to us in religious experience but is not completely fathomable for thought. We can only affirm that the nature of this action is indeed unfathomable and that, nonetheless, the inner, immanent all-powerfulness of grace somehow presupposes the participation of the free human will and, precisely for this reason, can be combined with the powerlessness or weakness of grace in regard to its effectiveness in the "world," in empirical life.

Given to us with utter self-evidence in inner religious experience, the mysterious immanent all-powerfulness of God, in no wise diminished by its relative weakness in the empirical world, is experienced as genuine, precisely *all-overcoming* power. This experience is therefore connected with the hope of the *conclusive, explicit triumph* of God's all-powerfulness that must occur one day. If in the world the all-powerfulness of God is invisible "before the time" (i.e., before the end of the world) and is combined with the empirical power of darkness which has not yet been overcome, if in the world "the light shineth in darkness"—the very form of being that we call the "world," standing in contradiction to the genuine all-powerfulness of God, is *inwardly unstable* and must—one day, at some limit—be overcome. We have already seen that precisely this constitutes the meaning of faith in the resurrection of Christ as the symbol and guarantee of the ultimate triumph of light over darkness. The concept of the ideal immanent all-powerfulness of God, which is compatible with the opposition to it of the dark powers of the empirical world, finds its genuine realization in the element of *eschatological faith*.

6. The Coming Transfiguration of the World. The Meaning of Eschatological Faith

The good news of the kingdom brought by Jesus Christ fundamentally differs, as we have seen, from the Old Testament idea of the kingdom of God. This difference consists in the fact that the good news establishes a clear distinction and separation between the inner, invisible overcoming of the world and the attainment of the kingdom of God through the revelation that the kingdom eternally belongs to man and is immediately accessible to him—and the outwardly visible, conclusive triumph of God, a triumph that is connected here with the second coming of Christ in power and glory, and with the end of the world as such in its present form of being.

But here, in relation to this Christian understanding, there steals into the soul the same doubt that concerns us throughout this book. Is not this transference of the *actual* coming of the kingdom of God to the end of the world, beyond the limits of the historical time of mankind in general, simply a deceptively comforting form of religious thought, which conceals a simple lack of faith in its genuine coming? It cannot be denied that in the popular consciousness of the Christian world this characteristically Christian form of promise concerning the coming conclusive triumph of the kingdom of God has really led, to a significant degree, to a lack of faith in this triumph. The expectation of the early Christians of the imminent coming of Christ and the end of the world had not been justified. And the Apostle's interpretation had for the most part lost its comforting power; this was the interpretation that for God a thousand years are like one day, or that the delay is due to God's long-suffering patience, giving us time for penitence and salvation. The delaying of something "until the second coming" became (like the ancient Roman expression "*ad calendas graecas*") a euphemism for "never" in the popular consciousness. Christian mankind has already for a long time been attempting to establish itself solidly,

securely, and forever in a "Christian manner" in the world; in particular, the western Christian world has followed this path to a
significant degree. Although it is indisputable that part of the task
of a Christian life is a dignified form of life in the world, it cannot be
denied that such a loss of eschatological hope, such a narrowing of
Christian faith by its application only to the present existence of
the world, is not only an impoverishment but a direct distortion of
Christian revelation. On the other hand, insofar as we strive to
profess consciously the faith in the real coming of the kingdom of
God through the concretely unimaginable end of the world and its
complete transfiguration, this faith is especially threatened by the
danger of degenerating into a theological pseudo-faith, of becoming a mere verbal profession of that which is no longer really certain
to the human heart. Placing hand on heart, we must confess that we
can no longer believe in the literal meaning of the eschatological
prophesies of the New Testament: we can believe neither in the
astronomical or cosmological images, such as "the sun became
black as sackcloth of hair, and the moon became as blood; and the
stars of heaven fell unto the earth . . . and the heaven departed as
a scroll when it is rolled together" (Revelation 6: 12 – 14); nor in the
image of "the son of God, coming in the clouds of heaven" (Matthew 24: 30), nor in the historical convergence of the destruction of
Jerusalem and Judaea with the end of the world. In short, we cannot
believe in that which in the New Testament eschatology bears the
distinct impression of the ideas and metaphors of that historical
epoch. But in this case what must be the true meaning of the eschatological faith in the end and transfiguration of the world?

As we have already mentioned, we cannot conceive this transfiguration of the world and the conclusive triumph of the kingdom
of God as an event in the makeup of the historical time of human
and worldly being. Rather, this transfiguration ends historical time,
ends the "world" in its current temporal form. The very meaning of
the Christian revelation of the triumph of the kingdom of God,
contrary to the Old Testament idea, consists in the fact that this
"metaphysical event" (we are forced to use the word "event" for
want of another, more adequate word) does not fit into the habitual
forms of the world's being, but destroys them, replacing them with
new forms, which at present are inaccessible and unfathomable for
us. This means that we can have a concrete idea neither of the
forms of the end of the world nor of the forms of the transfigured

being of the "new heaven and new earth." But, despite this un-fathomableness, what is the living, concrete meaning of the escha-tological faith?

This meaning can be defined only *negatively*; but in this nega-tive form it is completely definite and has decisive religious signifi-cance. The eschatological faith signifies the acute, living con-sciousness that all the current forms of human and cosmic being which we habitually consider to be everlasting, "normal" as it were, expressive of the true, primordial essence of being—that all of these forms of being are not everlasting, but are only transitory, unstable, and unnatural states; for these forms do not correspond to the true essence of God, to the genuine all-powerfulness of the gracious powers of God, and thus to the primordial plan of God for the world. In contradistinction to both the pagan and Judaic world-understandings, the Christian eschatological faith is the living feel-ing of the instability, illusoriness, and distortedness of being in that form which makes up the habitual essence of the "world." This faith is therefore the living hope that the true image of the world and man, corresponding to God's plan, will be revealed *one day*, though this "one day" lies outside of historical time and the forms of this revelation are unfathomable for us at present. In this sense, Chris-tian eschatology produces a decisive change in our entire life-feeling. This faith is an uneliminable, integral part of the Christian revelation, opening our eyes to another, better, truer being. This faith gives us the acute consciousness that *genuine reality* is differ-ent from that form of being which we call "objective reality." This faith teaches us to consider not only our personal life but also the being of the whole world in its habitual, supposedly unchangeable forms as only a kind of transitory voyage, after which begins real, conclusive life. This faith teaches us to establish ourselves in this world as if we were passengers in a train, that is, with the idea that this is only a relatively short stage, a trip leading to the real goal of our life, to the conclusive establishment of our being. Where and how we will have to leave the train, each of us at some intermediate station and all of us at the final station of the journey—this we do not know and cannot imagine. But the fact that such a final goal exists, that our life and the life of the whole world are only a path to this goal—this our believing heart knows with certainty. And this knowledge, expanding our spiritual horizons, radically changes the whole perspective of our life, our fundamental life-feeling.

Of course, this eschatological faith, like all faith, cannot be objectively grounded and does not require proof; it is given immediately, with utter self-evidence, in religious experience. It is curious to note, however, that in some epochs spiritual themes which act in completely different domains converge in one direction. Thus, in our time a series of themes psychologically sustains and fortifies the eschatological faith in its general sense described above. The general feeling of the instability, changeableness, impermanence of all the basic forms of being, which but recently seemed eternal, possesses now our entire consciousness. This consciousness is sustained by the experience of unexpected, gigantic, almost unprecedented historical world-catastrophes, wars, and revolutions as well as by contemporary physical-cosmological scientific thought, which (as we have already mentioned in another connection) has destroyed the old ideas about the conservatism of the universe, expressed in the laws of the conservation of matter and energy, and replaced them with the doctrine of the changeableness of all the elements of the world's being, of the possibility of all kinds of cosmic "explosions." And if in the pious Middle Ages the idea of the eternity of the world, borrowed from antiquity, was a temptation that could not be rationally overcome for such a pillar of orthodoxy as Thomas Aquinas—in our time the doctrine of the changeableness of all the fundamental elements of being and of "creative evolution" has revived Leibniz's brilliant idea that the supposedly eternal laws of nature are no more than "habits of nature," and has made accessible even for scientific thought the idea of the radical cosmic revolution and "transfiguration" of the world. This general intellectual tendency of our epoch makes understandable and accessible the Gospel's eschatological teaching that "for as in the days that were before the flood they were eating and drinking, marrying and giving in marriage . . . and knew not till the flood came, and took them all away; so shall also the coming of the Son of man be" (Matthew 24: 38, 39).

It is true that the same tendency of our epoch that makes habitual and understandable for us radical, revolutionary cataclysms in all domains of being including the cosmic domain, also threatens to revive the ancient, literal, Old Testament conception of the eschatological-apocalyptic hope. Minds of a sectarian, provincial spiritual character have the tendency (particularly under the influence of the spiritual atmosphere we have just described) to perceive certain signs of the coming of the end *precisely in our time*, even though the words of the Gospel make it unambiguously clear that no one knows the day and hour of the end of the world except our Father in heaven. Exaggerating the significance of all that is occurring *now* in the world, unconsciously suffering from the usual pride of contemporaries in the comparative evaluation of one's own time and the past, these sectarian minds attribute to our time the privilege of becoming free at last from the burden of the painful historical process and surviving a genuine, terrible, yet glorious "end of the world." Such conceptions are not only false in their limitation and pride, but are also fatal in practice. Either these conceptions contain an unconscious return to the Old Testament eschatology which was revoked by Christ's revelation, i.e., they factually revive the false chiliastic dream of the kingdom of God *on earth*, within the limits and in the forms of this world; and this leads to the doom of utopianism. Or, in the illusory foreseeing of the imminent end of the world, such conceptions lead in practice to something that is akin to joy at the destruction of the world, to an asceticism connected with contempt for and rejection of the world, i.e., to a spiritual tendency that is remote from the Christian commandment of love, from the Christian sense of responsibility for the fate of the world. This literal, spiritually limited understanding of eschatology, with the rectilinear practical conclusions that follow from this understanding, is, in practice, one of the deadliest of Christian heresies. Wherever the eschatological tendency directly determines action, there the responsible Christian relation to reality, necessarily based on the awareness of reality as it *really* is, is replaced by practice based on fantasy. Such a literal, rectilinear understanding of eschatology destroys the very foundations of the illuminated, reasonable spiritual hygiene of the Christian relation to life. This orientation must be clearly distinguished from the healthy general eschatological orientation, in which the eschatological religious tendency is combined with responsible Christian realism.

For this healthy eschatological orientation, which is limited by the general consciousness of the possibility of the end and the transfiguration of the world, seen as if through the very being of the world, i.e., through a perception of the instability, impermanence, abnormality of the current state of the world—the prophesy of the end of the world is like "a light that shineth in a dark place, until the day dawn, and the day star arise in your hearts" (2 Peter 1: 19). These words mean that the necessary, healthy eschatological orientation of the Christian consciousness naturally fits into the frame of that dualism of Christian being, the dualism between the kingdom of God and the world, which we have attempted to clarify. Thus, the necessary duality between faith in the coming transfiguration of the world and *our obligation to lead a Christian life in the world* is, in the final analysis, only a manifestation of the basic dualism of Christian being, expressed in the prologue to the Gospel of St. John in the words concerning the light that shines in darkness.

But now we face a new problem. The basic Christian duality between the kingdom of God and the world must have its natural expression in the distinctive character of *the moral order of Christian life.*

CHAPTER FOUR

The Duality of Life-in-God and the World, and the Moral Order of Life

1. The Universality of this Duality

*T*he foregoing discussion of the supra-sensory certainty (i.e., the inaccessibleness for sense perception and the paradoxicalness for rationality) of the kingdom of God, in which we participate even now; of the mystery of the action of grace in the depths of the human soul; of the all-powerfulness of God, manifested in the powerlessness of our empirical being—leads to one highly significant proposition: The boundary between the kingdom of God (or the gracious life-in-God) and the forces of "this world," between "redeemed" and "unredeemed" being, between life truly illuminated by the light and life in darkness and under the power of darkness—*this boundary is empirically invisible, for it passes through the depths of the human heart.* All empirically visible distinctions (whether between "sinful" and "saintly" individual souls or between corresponding "collectives," such as the distinction between the "church" and the "world" in empirical life) do not coincide with, but intersect, the *essential* distinction between life "in light" and life "in darkness." For this duality and antagonism are concealed in the spiritual depths—inaccessible to apprehension from outside—of the human soul and are therefore essentially hidden and invisible. This constitutes the eternal paradoxicality of Christ's truth, the fact that it does not coincide with any human measures, moral, dogmatic, or other. Just as, according to the Gospel parable, the stranger and false believer (a Samaritan) can turn out to be my neighbor, while my neighbor, having all the attributes of spiritual privilege (a Levite), can turn out to be a stranger to me; and even as publicans and prostitutes can enter into the kingdom of God before true believers and the virtuous—so in general the genuine boundary between the gracious life-in-God and life in the prison of this world does not have to coincide at all with the empirically visible boundary between a "righteous man" and a "sinner," between a "good" man and an "evil" man, between believers and unbelievers, between the "church" and the "world." For the true battle, as the Apostle says, is not against empirical, visible powers (in this sense, "not against flesh and blood") but "against the rulers of the darkness of this world, against spiritual wickedness in high places" (Ephesians 6: 12). In short, the battle between "light" and "darkness" is an empirically invisible battle between *spiritual* principles.

If we combine this consciousness with the conception of the kingdom of God as the heavenly homeland and eternal potential possession of every human soul, we will necessarily come to the conclusion that the duality between the life-in-God and slavery in the world is absolutely *universal,* i.e., has force in regard to *every human soul as such,* irrespective of all other distinctions between people.

This universality of the duality between the life-in-God and subordination to the powers of this world, between the principles of light and darkness in the human soul, is not at all a generally accepted, self-evident truth. On the contrary, like the entire revelation of Christ, this truth is paradoxical, at first sight seems incredible, contradicts certain deep-rooted, widespread themes of human thought. First of all, this truth contradicts the tendency to rationalism in the domain of moral valuations, owing to which the absoluteness of the distinction between good and evil, holiness and sinfulness, becomes the absolute distinction between good and evil people, the righteous and the sinful. It is not surprising that this tendency is reflected in the theological interpretation of Christ's revelation itself, and this to such a degree that the idea of the universality of the duality of human life appears to be a kind of heresy. The most extreme version of this religio-moral rationalism is the so influential (in the history of Christian thought), truly monstrous doctrine outlined by Augustine and systematized by Calvin—the doctrine of the predestination of some human souls to salvation and others to perdition. But even setting aside this extreme form of a doctrine that posits a fundamental distinction between the natures and religious fates of different human souls, this doctrine itself can find support in Gospel texts which speak of the distinction between the "sheep" and the "goats," between those who are doomed to "wailing and grinding of teeth," and those for whom salvation has been prepared. However, for those who have grasped the essence of Christ's revelation in its paradoxicality and who desire to serve the New Testament "not of the letter, but of the spirit"—there is no doubt that such texts have only a symbolic meaning and a pedagogical significance. In any case, these texts are not able to push aside the decisive religious significance of the revelation of God as a loving Father, who gives to all who ask and opens to all who knock; or to push aside the truth that Christ came "not to judge, but to save the world."

No text, no letter, of the Scripture, can suppress in us the joyful consciousness, emanating from the very essence of the good news, of the fundamental equality of human souls before God; and, moreover, of their two-fold equality: in their dignity as "children of God" and in their human weakness and imperfection. Of course, this equality does not exclude distinctions between human souls nor a hierarchy of souls; but even the greatest conceivable distinction between God-chosen saints and dark sinners does not negate the fundamental fact that they remain brothers, having an innate spiritual kinship—the fact that even the greatest saint is beset by human weaknesses and even the darkest sinner has access, in the hidden depths of his spirit, to the saving grace of God. The righteous man who forgets that he has a sinful nature is as far from the truth of Christ's revelation as the sinner who loses faith in the inexhaustible, all-embracing mercy of God. The best evidence of the genuine universality of the duality under consideration is the obligation for all people without exception (irrespective of concrete spiritual state, God-given talents, or spiritual achievements) to combine in their self-awareness the sense of their own worth as children of God and potential participants in the kingdom of God with the humble admission of their unworthiness, weakness, and

114

sinfulness. The absence of one of these two fundamental elements of the religious self-consciousness already signifies a fatal deviation from Christ's truth.

This is not the place to expound all the significance of this truth of the universality of the dual nature of man, of *the fundamental equality of all people*, both in their aristocratic worth as "children of God" and in the imperfection and sinfulness of their empirical state. This is one of those truths the genuine significance of which we understand and vividly feel only after having experienced the effect of the opposite conception. The historian knows to what extent this truth differs, for example, from the conception—developed by Aristotle and widespread in the ancient world—of the fundamental, substantial distinction between the soul of a "free" man and the soul of a slave, or between the soul of a "Greek" and the soul of a "barbarian." But in our age there is no need, unfortunately, to plunge back into antiquity to appreciate the significance of the truth we have examined. It is sufficient to compare this truth with doctrines which affirm the substantial inequality of people: doctrines which recognize, depending on race, the absolute worth of some and devalue others to the rank of helots, having no right to exist; or, in a well-known opposite variant of the same heresy, doctrines which affirm that one class of society is the bearer of pure evil, while another class is the bearer of good and salvation. In the face of such conceptions, in the face of the unbearable woes and humiliations of man, caused by man himself—in what a bright and comforting light shines for us the everlasting truth of the good news of the equal holy significance of every human person and the equal imperfection of the empirical nature of every man!

Here it is important for us to understand the genuine *ontological ground* owing to which the duality of man's being attains genuinely universal significance. This universality emanates from what can be called the *unisubstantiality* of the nature of all people. The idea of the fundamental equality of human nature must seem completely improbable for a conception according to which every individual concrete being has a self-contained self-sufficient existence and its own particular essence. On what basis must two or more separate beings, not touching one another in their existence, but self-contained, with completely different qualities and different lives—on what basis must these separate beings nonetheless be recognized as equal in their primordial essence? We tend, from this point of view, to consider it improbable that a saint and a benighted sinner, for instance, could have equal natures and could be considered brothers, having an inner spiritual kinship. This sort of individualistic idea is widespread even among believing Christians. Nevertheless, this conception is fundamentally false. It contradicts both the profound philosophical knowledge of the nature of being and genuine religious consciousness.

The world and being are not, as it appears at first glance, a simple aggregate or sum of separate, mutually independent entities, each of which has its special sphere of being and which only externally touch upon or interact with one another. Rather, the world and being are a *total-unity*: its separate parts or members are inwardly fused in such a way that they are permeated by some one, common principle. Individual persons are members or cells of one organism as it were; they are living beings whose life is based on their belonging to a common whole, on a common circulation of the blood. According to an analogy that we have already used, an analogy that derives from Plotinus and was often used in the literature of Christian mysticism, people are like the leaves of a tree, outwardly independent and perhaps not even touching one another, but inwardly nourished by a common sap, flowing to them through a common trunk and common roots.

Because all people without exception belong to the all-encompassing and all-permeating unity of mankind, all people have a common nature, however much they may differ in all other respects. But as we have seen, this common nature is essentially dual: man as a spiritual being is a "child of God"; he has something from the Spirit of God, and in this sense he is a potential participant in the kingdom of God; he has depths rooted in God. But on the other hand, man as such is characterized by the weakness and imperfection emanating from his fleshly nature, and connected with his origin from the womb of the world and with his subordination to the powers of "this world." All people without exception are co-participants in a great battle, the battle of the higher, spiritual principle against the base principle of the flesh, the battle of light against darkness. The soul of every man, from the greatest saint to the darkest, most unrepentant sinner, is the field of battle between these great, all-encompassing principles of light and darkness. And the image of the light that shines in darkness is the image which, in the infinite variety of its concrete forms, expresses the true essence of the inner being of every man.

2. Salvation of the Soul or Salvation of the World?

This ontological unity, this metaphysical mutual connectedness of people, their belonging to a certain common whole, also has an immediate consequence for the religious fate of man, i.e., for the problem of "salvation." In the New Testament and in the fundamental writings of Christian thought in general, we encounter two parallel ideas—opposed at first glance—of the meaning or object of salvation. On the one hand salvation is conceived as the combined, united *salvation of the whole world*, of all mankind or even of all creation. And on the other hand salvation is conceived as *the salvation of the individual human soul* in its separateness.* It is true that it is not difficult to see that in a certain sense these two concepts not only do not contradict each other, but even coincide. For in its profound religio-metaphysical makeup, the world is nothing else but the totality of individual souls or a kind of *kingdom of spirits*; hence, the salvation of the world is precisely the salvation of the individual souls who make up this world. This in fact constitutes, as we have seen, the spiritual revolution brought about by Christ's revelation. The old idea of salvation as the ideal ordering of the world, the making happy of the world by external means, i.e., a kind of *mechanical* or *organizational* restructuring of the world (regardless of whether this saving revolution is conceived on a political scale or even on an all-encompassing cosmic scale), is replaced here by the truth that the genuine salvation of the world consists precisely in the illumination of souls, in their entering the kingdom of God as the kingdom of "heaven." "Flesh and blood cannot inherit the kingdom of God" (1 Cor. 15: 50). And on the other hand salvation, since it is precisely the realization of the

---

* In order to avoid a misunderstanding, let us add the qualification that this distinction does not coincide with the distinction (examined above) between the invisible participation, accessible only to the depths of the spirit, in the kingdom of God and the coming ultimate, explicit triumph of the kingdom of God over the whole world. On the contrary, invisible salvation (rebirth through the attainment of the gift of God's grace, through participation in the kingdom of God as the eternal possession of man) can be conceived either in a strictly and exclusively *individual* form as the salvation of "my soul" or in a collective form as the salvation of the whole world.

kingdom of God as a *general state of the world's being*, is thus the "salvation of the world"—the combined, collective salvation of mankind and all creation as a unified whole. Meanwhile, the salvation of an individual human soul can be only its inclusion into the universal kingdom of saved, illuminated being: the soul's entering into the kingdom of God or its inheritance of the kingdom.

But this exposes the inconsistency not only of the view that the salvation of the world involves the external, mechanical re-ordering of the world, but also of the opposite view, which utterly neglects the total salvation of the whole world. We have in mind the religious individualism—so widespread in the modern Christian world—that concentrates wholly on the idea of the salvation of the individual human soul and conceives salvation as only the salvation, *one by one*, of individual souls as such. This individualism sharply contradicts the religious universalism of the Gospel consciousness. At its extreme, this individualism approaches the slogan "every man for himself," a cry of panic at a moment of general danger, which is an expression of the consciousness of the inevitable doom of the whole as such (of a ship, for instance) and therefore of the unleashing of the animal instinct of self-preservation. A careful consideration of this will leave no doubt to what extent this tendency contradicts the religious and moral consciousness of Christianity. The *religious* contradiction consists in the fact that the Christian faith in the salvation of the world is opposed here by faith in the inevitable doom of the world or at least the inevitable decomposition of the world into separate parts ("souls"), of which only some will be saved. Even a simple instinctive moral sense tells us that such a tendency contradicts the very essence of the Christian life-understanding. One who is conscious of himself as a Christian cannot think only of his own salvation and neglect the fate of his brothers. Secure in the belief that he himself is saved, he cannot calmly enjoy the bliss of salvation while indifferently viewing the torments of souls that are doomed. The very idea of salvation is distorted here by a glaring contradiction: for salvation is the attainment of refuge and peace *in God,* and *God is love.* However widespread they may be in the world that calls itself Christian, such ideas are essentially a dark anti-Christian mythology, the product of unilluminated human egotism.

But even if pure, abstract individualism, based on the religious and moral forgetting of the commonality of human life and leading to an egotistical tendency with regard to the problem of salvation, clearly contradicts the most elementary principles of the Christian consciousness; in other words, even if the idea of *the absolute independence and isolation* of the fates of individual human souls must be rejected—this does not yet remove the question: Must salvation be understood to mean *only* the total, combined salvation of the whole world, of all the beings who compose the world, or is it conceivable that individual souls nonetheless have their *separate fates?* The only answer adequate to the Christian truth is that the "either-or" alternative is replaced by the affirmation of concrete fullness that is expressed in the principle of "both-and." Two elements are simultaneously present in the fate and life of every individual human soul: an element in which the soul is connected in solidarity to the fate of mankind and the world, and in which the salvation of the soul is derivative of the general salvation of the world and creation; and an element in which every soul has a special, unique relation to the gracious powers of salvation, its own special religious fate.

The first element was clarified above. We saw that the essential metaphysical homogeneity or unisubstantiality of all people is determined by the total unity of spiritual being, by the subordination of all human souls to principles of a common order. This total unity also determines the commonality of the fate of human souls. And both the powers of evil from which man seeks salvation and the gracious powers of good, powers whose ascendancy forms the kingdom of God, are powers of a *common order*. As we have seen, all people are, whether they wish it or not, co-participants in one all-encompassing battle between light and darkness; and their common fate is determined by the issue of this battle, by the invisible victory of Christ over the world. This total unity of the kingdom of spirits, this inner mutual connectedness of human souls, creates a commonality of the fate of these souls, where each is responsible for all. Apostle Paul speaks of this when he affirms the organic total-unity of mankind and compares individual souls to the separate parts of one body, which "have been all made to drink into one Spirit" (1 Cor. 12: 13). "But now are they many members, yet but one body . . . And whether one member suffer, all the members suffer with it; or one member be honoured, all the members rejoice with it" (1 Cor. 12: 20, 26). From this point of view, it is in essence impossible to conceive of the absolute, conclusive salvation of one soul when other souls are sick or doomed, for whatever part of the body is afflicted by sickness, the affliction is a state experienced by the organism as a whole.

This commonality of the fate of human souls refers both to the achievements and to the weaknesses and sins of human nature. Inner "deification," the permeatedness of souls by the powers of grace (even if this state is attained by a hermit, who is outwardly isolated from all people), contrary to all our naturalistic ideas, also invisibly pours down on all other people, having a healing, saving effect. Solitary prayer in an isolated cell, the solitary contemplation of God, has salutary consequences for the whole world, for the powers of grace that are released here are powers of a *common* order, healing the world as a whole. This fact of the spiritual unity of the whole world, the unity of the world's fate, is the only condition that makes it possible for us to conceive—contrary to the widespread individualistic view—of the saving, redeeming power of Christ's revelation and sacrifice.

But in connection with our theme, the reverse side of this relationship is more important. As long as "this world," the world that lies in evil, exists, not one being living in the world and born of the womb of the world can attain a state of unlimited illumination and blessedness, can be "deified," can live only "in God," can completely enter into the kingdom of God. Even the lives of the greatest saints have a side in which they, through their organic and unbreakable connection with other people and with the whole world, reflect the action of the universal sinfulness of the world and are forced to bear all the consequences of this sinfulness. Because of this, the very intention of the isolated, separate, egotistical salvation of one's own soul is essentially inconsistent and impossible.

On the other hand (this is the second, correlative element) the combined participation of all people in the fate of the world's being as a whole does not exclude the direct, immediate relation of every individual human soul to God and thus to the gracious powers of salvation. Every individual soul has its unique path to God, its unique service, and its unique zeal, or its neglect of this service; in other words, every soul has its own religious fate, which is invisible and inaccessible to other souls—every soul has its own task of salvation. The common salvation of the world proclaimed and brought about by Christ consists in making the kingdom of God accessible to people, human souls. It consists in a breach of the siege of being by the dark powers of this world which causes all of mankind to suffer. The extent to which every separate, individual soul desires and is able to use this *common possibility of salvation* is the affair of precisely this soul in its immediate relation to God, to the gracious powers of salvation. Although, owing to the total unity of man's being, both the achievements and the sins of every human soul are reflected in the fate of all other souls, the immediate carrier of both healing and sickness is the separate, individual human soul—even as in a body the carrier of sickness or healing is some separate member, and the rest of the body only derivatively participates in the consequences of the state of this separate member. In this respect the carrier or object (or subject) of salvation is, in the final analysis, the separate human soul. For salvation is nothing else but spiritual rebirth, illumination, strengthening, the subject of which can be only one thing in the world: the enigmatic principle of human *personality* in all its uniqueness and mystery, which forms the very essence of my "I." Thus, the *personalistic* idea of salvation is combined with the *universalism* of spiritual being, i.e., with the overcoming of *detached individualism* in the idea of salvation.

But this means that to the ontological duality of human nature we must now add *the duality of the religious fate* of the human person, the duality of his relation to the gracious powers of salvation. On the one hand every human soul has its unique, individual, *inner* relation to God and the gracious powers of salvation, its personal spiritual life, which consists in the battle *within the person himself* between the powers of grace and the powers of sin, the powers of "this world." On the other hand every person—through his primordial connection with all other people, through his co-participation in the total unity of the world's being—is necessarily a participant in the common, cosmic work of salvation.

Owing to this duality of the religious situation and religious fate of man, the very task of salvation that man faces—the task of overcoming the powers of sin and darkness, and serving the powers of light—acquires a dual character. Together with the task of following his own path to God, of becoming spiritually strong and grounding himself in the gracious superworldly element of the Divine light, man also has the urgent task of actively participating in the common healing and salvation of the world. Besides his own sinfulness, which inwardly burdens his personal spiritual life, every man must also concern himself with the common sinfulness of the world. He must not only bear in fact the consequences of this sinfulness, but be morally responsible for it. This moral responsibility, this necessity (following Christ's example) of bearing the burden of the world's sin, is determined by the fundamental element of Christian religio-moral consciousness, by the relation of brotherly solidarity, the relation of love, the sense of responsibility for the fate of my brothers, which is the very essence of that spiritual healing and rebirth of the person which constitute his salvation, his *conditio sine qua non.* "If a man say, I love God, and hateth his brother, he is a liar: for he that loveth not his brother whom he hath seen, how can he love God whom he hath not seen?" "He that saith he is in the light, and hateth his brother, is in darkness even until now" (1 John 4: 20; 2: 9). For "God is love," and therefore the path of a person to God goes through love for one's neighbor, through the taking upon one-self of the whole burden of the world's imperfection, of the world's sinfulness. The salvation of the soul and responsibility for the salva-tion of the world form an inseparable dual-unity in the religious task that confronts every human person.

3. Moral Conclusions. The Salvation of the World and Its Protection from Evil

Contrary to the pietistic moods and tendencies to individual perfection which are rather widespread in the Christian world, it is necessary to recognize as an unshakeable axiom of the Christian conscience the following thesis: *Every man is responsible not only for evil that he causes and carries, but also for evil in the world that he does not resist.* A Christian can be indifferent neither to the suffering of his neighbors nor to the evil that they do or the evil that possesses them. He will be judged not only for his achievements in the sphere of his personal saintliness, but also for his responsiveness to the suffering of his neighbors, his activeness in the battle against the world's evil. By his very essence, a Christian must bear the burdens of his brothers, not only material burdens, but moral burdens as well.

It has not yet been sufficiently understood to what degree Christian morality differs in this sense from ordinary, "natural" morality and is superior to the latter. According to ordinary moral-ity, every man is responsible for his own actions or for that limited sphere of life that is entrusted to him and depends on his activity. The principle of personal, individual responsibility is the basic principle of law and the principle of the ordinary moral valuation of people. Only the criminal himself and his accomplices are respon-sible for a crime, no one else. The ordinary moral valuation of people assumes a clear distinction between individual persons as isolated, mutually independent centers or carriers of activity. Of course, this moral position is necessary and legitimate. But it would be a great error to think that human morality is exhausted by this position. Even in certain cases of social-legal life, individual responsibility is complemented by collective responsibility: precisely where the activity of one man influences or can influence the activity of another. The responsibility for a violation or a dereliction of law is shared both by the offender himself and his supervisors. In business corporations the material responsibility is borne not only by the persons directly involved in a transaction, but also by all the other participants in the corporation.

All this, however, is considered to be an exception to the general principle of individual moral responsibility or a derivative consequence of the latter, involving the interweaving of several individual responsibilities. The fundamental meaning of the principle of collective responsibility is revealed only when moral life is determined by *love*. Thus, parents feel themselves responsible for everything bad in their children or all the bad things their children do, for they see in these bad things the result of their own sin or error, a failure to educate, a failure of their duty of love to their children. If he is morally sensitive, every participant in a union of love or friendship should blame himself for all the lies that have crept into the union, even when the immediate responsibility is borne by another participant in the union.

This consciousness of responsibility acquires a fundamental and universal substantiation in Christian morality. Since the higher and universal duty of a Christian is the duty of love for his neighbor, love for every man and for all people; since a Christian is obliged in all respects to help his neighbor and to save him—a Christian is conscious of himself as indirectly responsible for all evil, all need in the world, for all that is imperfect and sinful in the world. For the Christian is conscious of all such evil and calamity as a result of the failure of his duty of love. In many cases of both personal and socio-political life we experience (even outside the explicit Christian consciousness) this sense of collective responsibility or, more precisely, this sense of my or our responsibility for the evil that is directly caused by others. We say to ourselves: "I should have foreseen this and prevented it; and if I have not, then my negligence, my inattention to what others do, is also responsible for the evil done by others; insufficient active love for my neighbor, insufficient concern about him, is also to blame." Such is the sense of social responsibility of all members of society for the material needs of the poor, or the sense of collective responsibility of all nations for the preservation of international peace. As we have mentioned, the Christian consciousness provides a general, fundamental, universal substantiation for the responsibility of all for the world's evil; for in the Christian consciousness the duty of love and responsibility for others is not simply a moral prescription or moral feeling, but is based on the perception of the inner, primordial, organic total-unity of universal-human life.

A highly significant conclusion follows. Even if a Christian attains maximal perfection within the limits of his own personal saintliness and maximal independence from the dark powers of this world—he remains subordinate to these powers or affected by them in the sense that he *morally* shares the fate of all other people in this imperfect world. Thus, the universal duality of Christian being, the duality between life-in-God and the subordination to the powers of this world, has (in combination with the duality between the individual, personal, inner path to God and the metaphysically and morally grounded participation of every person in the common fate of the world) its necessary reflection in the duality of morality, in the duality of the determining principles of moral life.

In his individual, personal, inner spiritual life, every man who strives to be guided by Christ's truth has the duty to follow, without compromise, the Christian commandment: "Be . . . ye perfect, even as your Father which is in heaven is perfect" (Matthew 5: 48). Insofar as he does not succeed, insofar as his spirit cannot overcome the weakness of the flesh, he will be conscious of this as sin, which he must attempt to overcome. But in his relation to his neighbor, in his activity and moral energy directed at opposing the evil of the world, *he cannot be guided by the principle of moral perfection*. Rather, he must be guided by the principle of *the maximal effectiveness and usefulness of his actions in the battle against evil*. Not being able to overcome and destroy evil completely, and conscious that he himself is responsible for evil, he must do *everything possible* to effectively counteract evil and to protect his neighbors against evil to a maximal degree. In other words, in relation to our neighbors, in relation to the world, the measure of our personal perfection can only be the maximal intensity of our consciousness of responsibility for the fate of our neighbors, of our will to help them.

A question arises here, the correct answer to which wholly

124

determines the healthy moral orientation that is adequate to the Christian moral consciousness: To what degree do these two principles—the principle of personal perfection and the principle of maximal effectiveness in the counteraction of evil—coincide in practice? To what degree can a Christian in his concern about the good of his neighbors, about their protection from evil, act according to the principle of personal perfection, i.e., to what degree can he seek to attain his goal only in the action (upon himself and upon others) of higher, gracious powers?

The correct answer to these questions demands the perception of a distinction that is often neglected or only dimly understood in discussions of ethics: the distinction between the task of *genuine, essential salvation* and the task of simple *protection from evil*, i.e., the task of the external counteraction of spiritually and materially destructive forces acting in the world, and the external facilitation of the well-being of one's neighbors and the world. As to the first task, the task of essential salvation, there emanates from the very essence of Christian revelation, Christian faith, the conviction that this salvation is the work only of higher, gracious powers, and that man in his striving for the salvation of his neighbor (or of the whole world) can and must therefore be only a conductor of these higher powers. Every intention to save man and the world by other means, by means of other—i.e., earthly—powers, is a betrayal of the fundamental meaning of Christian faith. Thus, to present one example instead of many, it is fundamentally impermissible to use force or compulsion here; the dream of destroying evil by external means and thus allowing good to triumph is, in essence, a false dream. For truly saving, gracious powers act only through the element of freedom, through the spontaneous awakening of the deep powers of man's spirit, powers which voluntarily go out to meet the powers of grace and salvation; and the only way we can help our neighbors open themselves to the action of the gracious powers of salvation is the way of *love*, i.e., the pouring down on our neighbors of these gracious powers, insofar as these powers are in our possession. Thus, although it is possible for there to be a certain competition between activity directed outward, toward the salvation of others, and the activity of personal inner perfection, both activities lie in the same plane as it were and cannot enter into fundamental conflict. For in both directions, the meaning of this spiritual activity consists in the training of the human soul, one's own or another's, to receive the gracious powers of the Divine light. The way of love, prayer, ascesis, self-renunciation, has force here both in the personal inner path of man to God and in the aid rendered to our neighbors in their striving to approach God. In this sense, one can say that at base of the Tolstoyian teaching and ethical doctrine lies a completely correct, truly Christian idea. This idea consists in the consciousness that no external, earthly sin-burdened means, no compulsion or repression, can essentially overcome evil or essentially heal the world and generate good in the world. No compulsion, including the physical destruction of the carrier of evil, can essentially, substantially destroy one atom of evil; evil is essentially destroyed only by good, by the gracious power of love, just as darkness disappears only when it is illuminated by light. The work of the essential salvation of the world is exclusively the work of the organic blossoming in the world of the higher, gracious powers of holiness, good, and love.

The greatest and truly fatal error of the Tolstoyian teaching and of all moral purism is the confusion of this task of the essential spiritual perfecting of the world with the task of the simple protection of one's neighbors and the world from the destructive powers of evil. Here, in regard to this latter task, which is also morally obligatory for man, the situation is completely different. Let us present an example that has been worn out in arguments on this theme, but which is nonetheless decisive. When a child is being tortured before our eyes, it is not enough to think of the salvation of the souls of the child and of the tormenter. The voice of the healthy conscience, and even more so the voice of the Christian conscience, says that we are first obliged to stop the violent act, to free the child from suffering. If our prayers or admonishments are so full of gracious power that they can act on the will of the tormenter and force him to repent and desist from his violent act, so much the better. But if not? How strong are the powers of grace that we can summon to aid us if even the all-powerfulness of God is, as we have seen, a certain immanent, invisible all-powerfulness that is combined with powerlessness in the practice of earthly life. Therefore, it is always possible that these powers will turn out to be insufficient in practice in a given concrete case. Furthermore, this insufficiency or weakness of the powers of grace in the capacity of empirical powers effectively acting in the world belongs to the fundamental situation of the light that shines in darkness and that cannot overcome and dissipate the darkness until the end of the world. What should we do in such a situation? Outside of all theological discussion, our conscience, our moral instinct, gives us a perfectly obvious answer: It is necessary to tear the child from the tormenter's hands; it may be necessary to bind the tormenter, to put him in jail; and in the extreme case, if there is no alternative, it may be necessary to kill him. In other words, all necessary means must be employed to stop the evil deed, including means that are completely worldly and thus more or less sinful, not excluding the terrible sin of the killing of a human being.

Thus, in the Christian work of protecting our neighbors and the whole world from evil and easing suffering, our moral responsibility for the real effectiveness of our aid to our neighbors and the world can always compel us to employ (where there is no other possibility) *worldly means of struggle*, which are inevitably burdened with sin; that is, it can always compel us to follow a path that diverges (we shall see later precisely in what sense) from the path of inner spiritual perfection. In this sphere, Christian duty compels us to take the burden of sin upon our conscience, and not to observe our personal purity in a situation where we would be responsible, by our inaction, for the triumph of evil in the world. A Christian has the obligation to sin in his external battle against evil, in the work of the protection of the world from evil, if in the judgment of his conscience the sin of inaction is greater than the sin connected with the active opposition to evil.

Thus, owing to the total unity of spiritual being, the fact of the existence of the unilluminated, unredeemed, sinful world (a fact that is a fundamental axiom of the Christian consciousness) not only inwardly burdens my soul with sin, in the form of my inner participation in the universal-human weakness and sinfulness, but also forces upon me the tragic moral obligation to participate in sin when this is necessary for the active assistance of my neighbors. For this reason, the sectarian, Tolstoyian understanding of the principle of Christian moral behavior, an understanding that is rather widespread in Christianity, is completely inconsistent. It is a great error for a Christian to take literally the Gospel commandment "resist not evil," i.e., to transform this commandment into a rule, an external law of behavior, and to extend it even to cases where it is a question of selflessly aiding one's neighbor. It is a great error to observe the untouchable purity of one's personal Christian conscience under all conditions and despite all consequences.

Precisely on this path occurs the so classical and, alas, widespread degeneration of the Christian consciousness into its opposite: pharisaism.

Let us consider another example, analogous to the first, but less hypothetical, more understandable and imposing in its actuality. Christian pacifism, the rejection of war and the refusal to carry out one's military obligation in the name of the sanctity of the life of every human being, even the sanctity of the lives of enemies attacking one's native country—this kind of pacifism can be a *great sin* for the living Christian conscience if this preservation of one's personal purity results in mass killing and brutality committed by an enemy full of the power of evil. Owing to the principle of Christian responsibility, these crimes will burden the conscience of him who, in the name of his personal purity, refused to use military force, i.e., to kill, to oppose the victory of criminal force in the world. This has nothing to do with the widespread banal error (which we shall discuss further below) according to which the truth of the Christian consciousness or even of the moral consciousness in general is inapplicable to the sphere of social life, an error that so easily perverts the moral sense and justifies sin and crime. There can be no question of a substantial limitation of the sphere of action of the Christian commandment, or even of the Old Testament commandment, "Thou shalt not kill." On the contrary, the action of this commandment remains absolutely universal in its essence. Anyone who kills is a sinner, even if this killing is committed for the most unselfish reasons, out of a sense of love for one's neighbors and responsibility for their fate, in the battle against the destructive powers of evil. Even a soldier who kills an enemy in the most just war of defense of his native country against an evil aggressor, or in the defense of freedom against a conquerer who is attempting to enslave the world—even this soldier who kills justly must be conscious that he is a sinner. And the ancient practice of the church according to which a soldier, a participant in a war, must be cleansed by penitence of all the sins of killing and violence he has committed is wholly adequate to the true Christian consciousness. So widespread in our time among "revolutionaries" of *all* political orientations, the fundamental justification and even glorification of killing and violence in the attainment of goals that are considered to be absolutely valuable—are a terrible moral perversion, which destroys human souls.

Thus, a Christian, owing to his responsibility for the fate of his neighbors in the sinful world, can be placed in the position where he cannot avoid evil. Situations are possible and, in principle, even inevitable in which the commission of a sinful act, even the killing of one's neighbor, must be judged by the truly fair and unprejudiced Christian conscience as an immeasurably smaller sin than inaction and a passive relation to the world's evil and suffering, a relation determined by the desire to preserve one's personal moral purity. Every moral purist and "conscientious objector" must be asked the question: If to kill and to participate in killing and violence is a sin, then is it not also a sin, sometimes a greater sin, to sit with hands folded and to passively observe evil acts committed before one's very eyes and to excuse oneself by saying that one is too pure to become involved in these dirty deeds? Do we then not purchase our salvation from sin at the cost of falling into the greater sin of pharisaism? The history of the last several decades of European mankind, culminating in the unprecedented unchaining of the powers of hell in the world, is a searing indictment not only of the perpetrators and carriers of the evil but also of those Christian and humanitarian moral purists who lost the stern awareness of their responsibility for the world's evil, of their obligation to effectively oppose evil. Thus, we arrive at a crucial truth, crucial precisely because it can be so easily abused. *In view of the common moral responsibility for the evil that reigns in the world, and the impossibility of wholly destroying this evil and establishing the absolute holiness of earthly life—the measure of the rightness or perfection of behavior in relation to life in the world is not the purity or sinfulness of an action, but only its necessity for the most effective protection of the world from evil.*

At first glance it might appear that this affirms the notorious immoral principle "the end justifies the means." But this is a misunderstanding. The conclusive clarification of this misunderstanding will be presented below, but even now it is possible to present an argument that removes it. The principle "the end justifies the means" is immoral not at all because under certain conditions it forgives or sanctions actions that are sinful in themselves. It is immoral because it relativizes the holiness of good and replaces the unconditional subordination to moral duty by a rational-utilitarian accounting system of moral credits and debits as it were. By analogy with free economic initiative and calculation, both the determination of the ends and the choice of means are conceived as depending on the free rational decision of man. This is completely alien to the moral situation that we are attempting to clarify. In principle this moral situation is similar to that which the science of criminal law calls the state of extreme necessity, only with the difference that the necessity of which it is a question is determined not by the need of self-preservation but by the unconditional demand (the "categorical imperative") of moral duty. In the situation described above, a man is placed against his will in the position of the *tragic necessity* of sacrificing the moral purity of one of his acts in the name of the requirement of love for his neighbor. Not at all justifying in the absolute sense his sinful act, but recognizing its sinfulness, he is guided only by the consciousness that inaction would be an even greater sin. The subsuming of this situation under the categorial relation of "means" and "ends" is not adequate to the essence of the matter. The determination of an "end" does not depend here on human decision but is imperiously prescribed as a moral duty. And the "means" here are not coldly calculated only according to their effectiveness, but are evaluated in the totality of their consequences, intended and unintended. They are evaluated in their entire concrete moral nature; they are imposed on our consciousness as the only morally obligatory (despite their sinfulness) path of our activity.

Thus it is a question not of a rational, utilitarian calculation of means for the attainment of a certain end, but of a certain *integral solution of moral tact*, which is guided by the striving to find, in the given concrete conditions, a way out that is *least burdened* by sin, or that most satisfies the demands of moral duty, in the face of the tragic impossibility (owing to the imperfection of the world and of the person who is performing the moral act) of absolutely sinless behavior. In our moral actions in relation to the world, we are obliged to be guided not by the striving to observe our personal moral purity, isolated from the fate of our neighbors, but by the striving to attain the *relatively maximal perfection* of our behavior with regard to the real realization of effective, responsible love for our neighbors. The genuinely right moral solution is determined not by the observance of the letter of the moral law, not by soulless obedience to abstract general rules without attention to the concrete needs of real life—but only by *love*, the demands of which are always concrete. In other words, the genuinely right solution consists in the relatively best realization of the moral truth, of that which Aristotle called by the untranslatable word ἐπιεικές: the suitable, the appropriate, the concretely right. About the right moral solution we can say only one thing: it is such that, taking into account the whole fullness of the concrete situation, the whole concrete significance and all the consequences of our actions, we must act *precisely in this way and not otherwise* in order for our action, despite its imperfection and sinfulness, to correspond to a maximal degree to our duty to ourselves and our neighbors, to our feeling of responsibility in the service of God and people.

Moral purists, adherents of personal purity and the individual salvation of the soul, recoil in fear from the risk of moral solutions that even remotely hint at the immoral principle "the end justifies the means." But these purists are blind to the opposite moral danger that an action which is good in the subjective motive or intent of the person who performs it can turn out to be deadly and therefore immoral *in its objective content* in the given concrete conditions in which it is performed, i.e., that it can have deadly objective consequences and therefore make the person performing it responsible for a great sin. The fact is that it is insufficient to have good intentions to perform a morally right act, that is, "the road to hell is paved with good intentions." More precisely, *the truly good will* must contain moral tact, moral courage, a sensitive moral attentiveness to the genuine needs of people, and wisdom and breadth in the evaluation of the genuine significance of our actions in the given concrete situation of the world. But owing to the above-examined fundamental truth of the Christian consciousness, namely, the uneliminable imperfection of the world that will exist until the final transformation of the world, it is always necessary to take account of the fundamental truth that *a certain minimum of imperfection and evil is inevitable in the world*, that we are forced to bear this evil and even to participate in it, and that therefore we must beware that the aspiration to the immaculate purity of behavior does not increase the quantity of evil in the world. In order to choose genuinely moral behavior, it is insufficient to be as meek as a dove; it is also necessary to be as wise as a serpent.*

---

* This idea can be illustrated by a multitude of contemporary examples. Let us present instead one highly instructive example from the history of the papacy. At the end of the thirteenth century, when the papacy was particularly powerful, when it was most involved in politics, and when it was therefore especially burdened with sinfulness, an attempt was made to save the Church by elevating a saintly monk to the pope's throne: the hermit Peter, who took the name Celestine V. Peter was full of active faith in evangelical poverty and evangelical detachment from the world. The

It goes without saying that this truth can become a source of abuses in the case of an insufficiently strict and objective moral consciousness, and even more so in the case of conscious evil intent. Every sin, even an involuntary one, *even a morally obligatory one*, burdens the soul, and—becoming a habit, in the case of an insufficiently sensitive conscience—can pervert the soul. Furthermore, owing to the infectiousness of sin, even a morally obligatory sinful act always has unintended harmful consequences, which must be sensitively taken into account; the habituation to such acts tends to suppress this sensitivity. In general, there is no moral truth that cannot be abused; and we have seen that, for sinful human will, precisely the Christian truth is an especially convenient pretext for abuses, as a result of the fundamental impossibility of having any precisely definable external measures of this truth. Therefore, the possibility of abuse is not a substantial argument against the thesis we have developed.

Of course, the basic condition of the right application of the principle of the concrete effectiveness of our moral activity is the clear distinction between the task of protecting the world from evil and the task of the essential overcoming of evil. The confusion of these two tasks always has deadly consequences. Either it makes us plunge into the deadly temptation of the impossible task of generating good and dissipating evil by sinful means of compulsion, which makes us forget that this task is accessible only to the free action and perception of love. Or it clouds the consciousness of our responsibility for the suffering of our neighbors, our obligation to be active in the protection of the world from evil. A clear distinction between these two completely different tasks has a determining significance for the entire moral-social practice of life in the domains of pedagogy, criminal law, state policy, and social activity.

---

short rule of this holy man consisted of a series of shameful failures. Owing to his naivete, ignorance, inability to suppress evil, his will was dominated by the worst intriguers; anarchy and calamity only immeasurably multiplied in the Church and in Italy under his rule. After only half-a-year he had to admit that he was not fit to rule and abdicated. Dante puts his soul—despite his personal saintliness—in the first, outer circle of hell, to which are doomed characterless, morally weak-willed people. Two saintly women of the end of the fourteenth century stand in instructive contrast to Celestine V: Str. Bridget of Sweden and St. Catherine of Siena, who were wise advisors of popes.

The foregoing discussion clarifies the inevitable dualism that emanates from the dualism, examined above, of the makeup of Christian being. We can and must trace this dualism still deeper.

4. Grace and the Law. The Inner Order of Moral Being and Moral Activity in the World

Since the first reception of the Christian revelation and its first effect on moral life, human thought has faced a difficulty, first clearly understood in St. Paul's Epistles: the harmonization of the gracious life-in-God with the ordinary order of moral life, determined by the subordination of life to the moral law. Paradoxical in its general essence and therefore in all its applications, the Christian truth is also paradoxical as a factor that determines moral life. Since time immemorial, people have become habituated to the perception that the moral life is determined by *the law*, by commandments of a general character, expressed in the formula "thou shalt" (or "thou shalt not"). Such a commandment or prohibition compulsorily directs, or limits, the naturally unrestrained, anarchic will of man. In the Old Testament consciousness this moral law was understood as the commandment, or prohibition, of God Himself (historically this law was inextricably connected with the liturgical and ritual law); in the ancient world it was usually understood as a sort of holy norm of "natural law": as Apostle Paul says, "the work of the law [is] written in their [the Gentiles'] hearts." And about eighteen centuries after the Christian revelation, Kant rediscovered the essence of moral life in the "categorical imperative": the command equally obligatory for all people, understood as an unconditional command, which we voluntarily obey. It is completely natural that even Christ's first and closest disciples tended to understand Christ's testament as a "law"; and only the religious genius Paul succeeded in clearly grasping the uniqueness of Christ's revelation as a factor of moral life, i.e., in understanding that this revelation determines human life not in the form of a law of behavior but in the form of redeeming and saving grace, given to the human soul through an act of faith and therefore realized in freedom. Insofar as the soul is open to and full of grace, the soul is already not subordinate to the law—not because the action of the law has been destroyed (Christ came not to "destroy" the law but to "fulfill" it), but because moral action (an action that is much greater and more effective than that of the law) is realized for the Christian soul in a new, higher form of free influence and the use of the gifts of grace. From this follows the general rule of Christian life: "Where the Spirit of the Lord is, there is liberty" (2 Cor. 3: 17); from this follows the Apostle's commandment: "Stand fast therefore in the liberty wherewith Christ hath made us free, and be not entangled again with the yoke of bondage" (Galatians 5: 1). The force of God that *really saves* man frees him from the obligation of concerning himself with subordination to the will of God in the form of the fulfillment of "the law." The difference between the moral determination of the will through the law and the purifying power of grace is like the difference between the rules that caution bathers about swimming in dangerous waters and the actual rescue of a drowning man.

Thus, the real gracious power that immanently permeates the soul and the transcendent law as an external commandment differ essentially with respect to *the form of the influence* they have on the moral life; and this distinction is also reflected in the distinction with respect to the object of this influence. The law—moral as well as juridical—normalizes, determines, or limits human behavior, human actions. Every "thou shalt" (or "thou shalt not") implies: "do this, not that," "act this way, not another way." Such is the content of the classic example of "the law," the Ten Commandments: "thou shalt not kill," "thou shalt not commit adultery," and so on. Even when it appears that the law normalizes not action but psychic state, it is directed at the determination of the will immediately manifested and realized in actions; such is the meaning of the commandments "honor thy mother and thy father," and "thou shalt not covet thy neighbor's house," "thou shalt not covet thy neighbor's wife," etc.

However, the commandments of Christ, fulfilled with the aid of gracious power, have a wholly different meaning, that is, a wholly different object. These commandments determine not the action, but *the inner spiritual order* from which actions issue, always remaining inadequate to the inner order. Such are the basic Christian commandments of love for God and love for one's neighbor. Such is the meaning of the sharp opposition between the New Testament and the Old Testament in the Sermon on the Mount. To the prohibition against killing is opposed the prohibition against being angry with one's brother. To the prohibition against adultery is opposed the statement that "whosoever looketh on a woman to lust after her hath committed adultery with her already in his heart." The righteousness of actions, "the righteousness of scribes and pharisees" who fulfill the law, is insufficient to allow one to enter into the kingdom of God. On the other hand, sinners, "publicans and prostitutes," will be the first to enter into the kingdom of God— if only they are full of inner penitence. Christ's commandments are not rules of behavior, but principles determining the right *inner being* of man. The grace that is given to the Christian aids him not to act in one way or another, but to be as he should be in order to pass through the "gate which leadeth unto life." Precisely because Christ came into the world not to judge but to save, His commandment is not a law of behavior, but the revelation of true inner being, and the purpose of His grace is not to make man righteous in the sense of obedience to the law, but to heal inwardly his infirm, morally sick being. Expressed in its most general form, this is the commandment to "be . . . perfect, even as your Father which is in heaven is perfect" (Matthew 5: 48). This commandment speaks not of actions but of *being*. Thus, life-in-God, the way to which is revealed to us by Christ and which he helps us to achieve, is not life as it is determined and limited by the law, not life as the slavish subordination to the commands and prohibitions of a lord and master, but a new free, inwardly illuminated being. The goal of Christian life as the gracious life-in-God does not consist in the realization of certain actions through which we obediently and slavishly fulfill the will of God. Rather, this goal consists exclusively in becoming as we must be in order to "enter into the kingdom of God," in order to genuinely realize life as being-in-God. Therefore, Christian life as such does not at all consist in outer actions. On the one hand, it consists in *inner* activity, invisible to the world, which is directed at the attainment, conservation, and maximal fullness of being-in-God. And on the other hand, all the actions of the Christian soul, inner or outer, are only an expression and index, always inadequate, of the soul's being as being-in-God, permeated by the powers of grace. In themselves, our actions cannot be *Christian* in the strict and immediate sense of this word. They are Christian only insofar as they express and disclose true Christian being. This is not contradicted by the words, "Ye shall know them by their fruits." If on the one hand these words emphasize that true inner being is always active and fruitful, on the other hand they indicate the organic dependence of the outer realization on the inner being. One must be or become a good tree, and then the fruits of this being will

135

grow from it as naturally, spontaneously, and organically as fruits grow from a tree. Of course, the gifts of grace owing to which we attain this basic Christian goal presuppose on our part the moral effort of the self-revelation of the soul for the acquisition of these gifts. And there exists a whole complex art or, if you will, a whole science, developed on the basis of the experience of many generations of masters of Christian life, an art and a science of the means and forms through which we can best and most easily realize this inner spiritual activity, necessary for the acquisition of the gifts of grace. Although one must not forget that the Christian truth is fundamentally paradoxical, that this truth can remain hidden from "the wise and prudent" and be revealed to "babes," this does not free us from the obligation of the intense and wise inner moral activity of self-perfection, an activity whose general name is *asceticism*. But the source, the goal, of this activity is not "works," but *life, being*. All our actions, inner or outer, do not have intrinsic, immanent value in this connection. They are either means to the attainment of higher, illuminated being or the spontaneous fruits of this being.

But this gracious being-in-God is realized under conditions of man's existence in the world, i.e., in the unilluminated, *graceless* sphere of being. Thus, Christian being, from which love for one's neighbor necessarily issues, must in its very essence be moral activity in the world, directed toward the struggle against evil, toward the protection of the world against evil, the protection of the powers of good in the world. But the energy of moral will in a sphere unilluminated by grace necessarily takes the form of the subordination of the sinful worldly element to the action of the law, to rules that determine or limit the will. The meaning of the law consists in the fact that in it is realized the element of *discipline*, that element of guidance and limitation of human will without which life would perish in the chaos of anarchy. In the law, the dark individual self-willfullness of man is subordinate to a general formative principle, through which a power of a higher order acts, the power of reason and good.

It follows that in man's life the law is overcome only insofar as it is replaced by the free action of grace. Where this does not occur (by definition, this does not occur in the "world," be it the world that is external to my soul or the worldly powers that dominate my soul), the obligatory power of the law asserts its rights. Juridical or state law, as well as the law in the form of customs, rules of decency and proper conduct, etc., is only a secondary, inadequate reflection of the moral law which is burdened by all the imperfection of human subjectivity. It is only a reflection of "natural law," that order which under the given concrete conditions is necessary to protect life from evil and to insure the most favorable conditions of life. On the one hand, this law, as the totality of rules of behavior, has the character of strict, unshakeable rules, the violation of which is impermissible and is a sin or evil; and on the other hand, these general rules, precisely as a consequence of their abstract commonality, are insufficient to achieve in every concrete case their goal: namely, living truth; and they can even conflict with one other. Thus, moral activity in the world is determined in the final analysis by a certain *moral tact*, the living sense of precisely what law, and in what form and to what degree, must be applied in the given concrete case in order to genuinely achieve the common goal of the law—the struggle against the evil of the world; or more precisely, what moral act, what concrete moral solution and action, corresponds under the concrete conditions to this common goal of the law. In view of the fact that the world's evil cannot be completely overcome, it is precisely this healthy moral tact which compels man to tolerate the lesser evil, and sometimes even to commit the lesser evil, in order to overcome the greater sin.

The foregoing conclusively clarifies why this position—which in a certain sense can be called the position of *moral compromise* and which is unavoidable in practice in our responsible moral activity in the world—does not coincide with the immoral principle "the end justifies the means." For only insofar as moral demands and moral valuations touch directly upon actions can man find it necessary to commit sinful actions, actions that go counter to the holy and universally obligatory common norms of the moral law. But since, as we have just seen, the essential Christian morality does not in general touch upon actions but determines the order of man's spiritual being, it is not possible to conceive of any concrete situations that would force man to violate these essential commandments of truth and that would justify their violation. On the contrary, these commandments must and can remain absolutely inviolable even if it is necessary to violate the norm of "natural law," the norm of actions. Let us return to a previous example. The commandment "thou shalt not kill" is one of the holiest, most fundamental norms of morality, both as natural law and as a law of behavior. Nevertheless, we have seen that there are cases when a Christian is compelled to take the sin of killing upon his conscience for moral reasons. But the commandment "love thy neighbor as thyself" is absolutely inviolable for all situations of life, for all requirements that issue from the task of moral activity in the world—for this commandment concerns *the content or order of Christian being.* Its violation cannot be justified by any practical necessity and is always an expression of the sinfulness or moral infirmity of man.

Let this seem a paradox, and a seductive paradox, but we must have the spiritual perspicacity and the spiritual courage to clearly and unambiguously take account of the situation: under certain conditions man can be forced to act with a severity approaching cruelty; in extreme cases he can be forced to kill his neighbor, to take upon his soul this terrible sin. But never and under no circumstances does he have the right to hate a man. This proposition is not at all the fruit of some subtle play of theological thought. On the contrary, it has an essential, determining significance for all of human life, including pedagogy, criminal law, and politics, among other domains. Everyone agrees that, when necessary, a father or pedagogue can take severe measures in regard to children, but he must meanwhile be guided by love for them. The same thing is applicable to all other aspects of social life. In the interests of the social good and social security, the state must punish crime; and extraordinary conditions are possible under which the state is forced to adopt severe, terrifying measures. But under no circumstances does the state have the right to be guided by motives of hate or revenge; beyond the limits of the objective goal of punishment, the state organs must in practice manifest a humane relation to the criminal, respect for his person. A state can find itself compelled to fight a war; and in this case a Christian soldier is morally compelled, in the fulfillment of his duty, to kill his enemy. But neither the state as a whole nor an individual soldier has the right to hate his enemy. Nothing in the world, no holy love for one's homeland, no duty to defend the good, should compel hatred for the enemy. The Christian soldier who is compelled to kill his enemy is obliged under all circumstances to maintain pity and love in his soul for the enemy as for his brother. He must pray and summon the powers of grace to preserve untouched in his soul this brotherly relation, this love, this life-giving foundation of human relations. In general, compromise in the fulfillment of the holy norms of the moral law; the necessity, in concrete moral activity in the sinful world, to have recourse to actions that are sinful from the point of view of the moral law, does not in the slightest lessen the purity of moral being, does not deflect the Christian from following the true path in the domain of the essential moral-spiritual life. However *psychologically* difficult such a combination might be, it is possible and obligatory in principle. The stubbornness of the moral will, based on the understanding of this relationship and directed toward its unwavering observance, is a necessary condition of morally healthy human (personal and social) life. The realization of this condition is possible for the simple reason that it is a question here of wholly different objects: moral activity in the world determines actions, whereas the essential commandments of Christian faith refer to the formation of the inner order of spiritual being.

Do not think, however, that this view dooms the Christian moral commandment of love to practical fruitlessness, limiting the sphere of its action only to the inner states of the spirit. The whole practical significance of moral perfection will become clear for us later. Here it is sufficient to note only one essential and incontrovertible fact: no external actions, however much evil they may contain, are as destructive as the spirit of hate. Let us consider one example instead of many: mankind would have recovered long ago and relatively easily from the destruction caused by the war of 1914-1918 if the spirit of hate, embitterment, and thirst for revenge accumulated during the war had not poisoned the whole economic and political life of the following decades. The fruit of this spirit of hate was the Second World War, an immeasurably more terrible war, which has sown infinitely greater dragon seeds of hate and thirst for revenge.

Despite all the holiness of certain fundamental norms of the moral law or natural law, the concepts of good and evil, in their primordial meaning, are applicable only to the spiritual order of inner being, to the moral state of man. If we substitute these concepts of the order of inner being or moral state for the ambiguous word "will," we must then agree with Kant's judgment (coinciding in this connection with the meaning of the Christian truth): "There is nothing in the world that can be called good or evil in the primordial and precise sense except the human will."

We repeat: we understand very well that this view conceals the risk of abuse and can easily become a temptation to do evil. We will of course be reminded of the "holy fathers" of the Inquisition, who, subjecting their victims to torture and burning them at the stake, affirmed (and perhaps even sincerely believed in some sense) that they continued to love and pity them. But it is again necessary to point out that an indication of the risk of abuse is not a substantial refutation; and that the invisibility or hiddenness of Christ's truth makes it maximally prone to blasphemous distortion. To this general qualification we must add that, however great the moral evil of the Inquisition, it is relatively superior to the practice of certain contemporary doctrines, which preach the destruction of people out of hatred or contempt for them. The conscious or hypocritical distortion of the truth evokes moral indignation in the face of the sinfulness of man's nature, but conscious brazen denial of the truth is already a sign that man is possessed by the satanical principle.

In order to counteract any possible distortions of the duality of the spiritual and moral life of man, its degeneration into the moral bifurcation of the person, into the service of two mutually contradictory goals or values, it is necessary to understand that this duality is an *organically integral dual-unity*, i.e., it is necessary to understand the *inner unity* that permeates this duality and determines the entire moral order of human life, an inner unity that thereby moderates and limits the duality under consideration. But before turning to a clarification of this formative unity, we must consider several misunderstandings emanating from a false interpretation of this duality.

5. False Interpretations of the Duality of Moral Life

At the beginning of this chapter we touched in passing upon the basic source of false interpretations of the fundamental duality between life-in-God and subordination to the powers of the unilluminated world. This source is the tendency to "rationalize" this distinction and thereby to identify this invisible boundary (passing through the secret depths of the human heart) between two spheres of Christian life with some visible, externally graspable distinction—with a distinction that, as such, essentially belongs to the makeup of the "world" and precisely for this reason cannot coincide with the fundamental duality between participation in superworldly being and submergence in the element of the world. There is a constant tendency to falsify, to distort this invisible duality, to identify it with some externally graspable distinction: be it a distinction in behavior, a distinction in social order, or a differentiation of the kinds or domains of human life and activity. We would like to give special consideration to these false interpretations.

The crudest, but in a certain sense the most natural, distortion is the division of people according to their externally determinable moral behavior into saints, true disciples of Christ, the saved, etc., and into sinners, who are unworthy of participation in the kingdom of God and who therefore are subject to exclusion from the church as the "communion of saints." Being a natural moral reaction to the hypocritical external profession of the faith of Christ, this distinction nevertheless fundamentally contradicts the very essence of this faith as the religion not of the external moral law but of the invisible saving grace. It contradicts the words of Christ, who said that He came not to judge but to save the world, and that not the healthy but the sick need healing. Confusing the invisible life of the human heart with moral behavior, grace with the fulfillment of the moral law, this tendency represents pharisaism within the limits of Christianity. The tendency, natural in itself, to see moral purity and holiness as a sign of genuine illumination is combined here with moral valuation not on the basis of a perception of the genuine inner state of the soul (which state is essentially invisible, open only to God) but on the basis of a universally obligatory measure of external behavior. Furthermore, it is combined with the false recognition of an absolute distinction between saint and sinner, the pure and the impure, the converted and the unconverted. All moralizing sectarianism, from the Montanists and Donatists in the ancient church to modern-day Baptism and Pietism, is this kind of unconscious replacement of the radiant, saving truth of Christ by legalism and, hence, pharisaism.

There is also a natural, almost involuntary tendency to identify the invisible distinction between the two spheres of being in which every man participates with the distinction between two spheres of human life, namely, the religious sphere and the secular sphere, understood as externally distinguishable domains of human life and activity: on the one hand, the domain of prayer, contemplation, participation in the liturgy; on the other hand, the domains of economic, social, and state activity, and scientific, artistic, and cultural creativity. This distinction is identified in turn with the distinction between the "church," or the life of man as a member of the church, and the rest of his life, i.e., the "worldly" part. And insofar as church teaching recognizes a special rank of priesthood, this duality in the final analysis easily takes the form of a fundamental distinction between the moral life and obligations of the priesthood and the moral life and obligations of the laity.

All this is the result of a rather natural, but inconsistent misunderstanding, which distorts the essence of the matter. Let us begin with the most elementary thing. Without entering into the dogmatic problem of the legitimacy and necessity of the special rank of priesthood in the Christian church, let us only note one thing: if the service to which a priest is called naturally imposes on him certain special obligations of which the layman is free, this distinction is not a distinction in regard to the moral life of the priest and layman. The reason for this is simple and rooted in the very ground of the Christian faith: a Christian cannot be a "layman" in the strict and precise sense, for he belongs not to the world, but to Christ and God. The whole foundation of his spiritual and moral being is the kingdom of God, the being-in-God, which in its essence is "not of this world." In this sense, the dogma of universal priesthood simply coincides with the very essence of the Christian faith. Let us repeat the words of the Apostle Peter: "Ye are a chosen generation, a royal priesthood, an holy nation, a peculiar people; that ye should shew forth the praises of him who hath called you out of darkness into his marvellous light" (1 Peter 2: 9). If called to stand before the altar, to perform the sacraments, and to guide in faith the other members of the church, a priest must naturally observe his moral purity *even more strictly* than other Christians, this distinction cannot be an essential, qualitative distinction in regard to moral life. In essence, even this purely quantitative distinction is only an inevitable concession to the moral decline of Christianity, owing to which it is necessary to tolerate the fact that most "Christians" have neither the strength to sanctify their lives nor the taste for such sanctification. On the other hand the priest is just as imperfect and sinful as the layman. The priest too lives in the world, is connected with the world, and is forced to take account of the power of the world over himself. The erroneous identification of the distinction between the essential life-in-God and the life of the Christian in the world with the distinction between the priesthood and the laity threatens to lead to one of the most fatal errors of Christianity: clericalism.

It is somewhat more justifiable to base the distinction between monasticism and the rest of Christianity (including the nonmonastic clergy) on the duality in the structure of Christian moral life. The fact that since the time of the widespread propagation of the Christian faith among the masses (which was naturally accompanied by the intrusion into the church of elements that were only superficially christianized, elements of a worldly nature), many Christians have felt the natural urge to protect the intensity and purity of their Christian life by external separation from the sphere of worldly life, by departing into solitude or the lonely life of a small community of believers—this fact really is an external, visible manifestation of the fundamental duality that permeates Christian moral life. Contrary to the prejudices of Protestantism, Christian monasticism is basically an eternal reminder to the world of the fundamental Christian truth that "my kingdom is not of this world." The fundamental duality of Christian moral life really does correspond, to a certain degree, to the duality of Christian duties or forms of life: the life of prayer and contemplation, detached from the world; and life in the world, full of moral activity. "Useless" in its external aspect, monastic life is (insofar as it is in true harmony with its calling) a certain organization for the accumulation and protection of spiritual goods, without which the practical supplying of the world with these goods would be just as impossible as the distribution of material goods if these latter were not produced and stored in warehouses.

Of course, one must not forget that the fundamental boundary between the two spheres of Christian life is always inner and invisible, essentially passes only through the depths of the human spirit, and that no visible, social differentiation can be adequate to it. Therefore, the duality between the essential life-in-God and the subordination to the world also exists behind the walls of the monastery. Monastic life is connected with the world by the very conditions of human existence: by its economic and juridical basis, etc. The moral life, both in the good and in the bad senses, is determined by this connection. It is well known how monasteries have influenced nearly all the domains of the worldly life of the people among whom they have existed. A number of monastic orders have directly set as their practical task the religious and moral action on the world. On the other hand, it is also sufficiently well known, alas, how often monks have brought in their souls the powers of the world even into the monastery and how often they have been imprisoned by these powers in the monastery. And contrarily, Christians who live in the world and are open to all the temptations of the world are compelled—*insofar as they are at all Christians*—to observe in the depths of their soul the life-in-God detached from

143

the world, i.e., to perform invisibly the function of monks. And if the Christian faith presupposes a universal priesthood, then in this sense it also presupposes a kind of invisible universal monkhood, realized in the depths of souls. Every Christian must in a certain sense be a "monk" in the eternally pagan world.

Just as inconsistent is the widespread identification of the duality under consideration with the distinction between the "religious" life of man and his "worldly" or secular life; or, in the collective plane, the distinction between the church (understood as a union or organization of believers) and the worldly powers of the state, politics, secular culture, and so on. From this point of view, a Christian is a Christian only insofar as he gives his powers and time to "religious" life, insofar as he prays, fasts, attends church, and so on. Beyond these limits, a man is not a "Christian" but the performer of some secular function, a soldier, bureaucrat, merchant, or scholar; and the Christian church is but one of the entities and powers of the world, like the family, the state, professional associations, trade, industry, science, art, etc.

In reality, however, the "religious" life of a Christian is not some particular sphere of his life and activity, but *his very being*. Of course this being has its center and its periphery; but the spiritual energy radiated from its center is universal and permeates the *whole* life of the Christian, in the entire variety of its domains and manifestations. No matter what a Christian does, and no matter to what he dedicates his activity, he must remain a Christian everywhere and in everything. He must do everything "religiously," in accordance with the demands of Christian truth. Therefore, in the collective plane the church is not just one of the many entities or powers of social life; it appears to be such only from outside, i.e., when it is perceived by a consciousness that is directed at the objective world and is not inwardly rooted in the reality of the church. In its inner essence, the church is the potency in this world of the kingdom of God, in which God is "all in all." Being the unity of believing and saved mankind, the "body of Christ," the church is essentially universal and extends its spiritual energy to the whole fullness of collective human life. It is true that the church must not dominate the world by that external domination which the state pretends to, but this is not because the church is only a part of the reality of human being, but because the element of domination in the sense of external power contradicts the very essence of the Christian church. The church must pour its gracious powers on all

144

the fullness and manifold variety of human being, and illuminate with the light of Christian faith and fill with the energy of Christian being the family, the state, economic life, science, and art.

Thus it is a question not of the externally real, visible distinction between the church and the other domains of the world (as if the church itself is a part of the world), but of an invisible distinction within the limits of the universal, all-embracing Christian life or the universal, mystical reality of the church—the distinction between essential being-in-God (the core of Christian being, already redeemed, full of grace) and the emanation of the Christian light into the world, into the sphere of darkness. Since it is immanently religious or metaphysical in character, this latter distinction cannot coincide with the external distinction between different functions and domains of earthly human life.

A distinctive variant of the doctrine of the limitedness of the existence and action of the Christian church and of the presence of a sphere of life that remains outside the religious life of a Christian is the view widespread in the Christian world (especially characteristic of Lutheranism) according to which only the so-called private life of man is subject to Christian illumination or moral forming. According to this view, in regard to the members of his family, his servants, all his friends and acquaintances, all people that he encounters in his private life—a believing Christian must realize in all their purity the principles of the Christian life prescribed in the moral commandments of the Gospel. But the public domain, the domain of social and state life, is viewed here as a sphere that has no relation to the Christian as such (in any case, as long as it does not infringe on his religious life). Public life has its goals, rules, and laws, which have nothing in common with Christianity; and Christian duty is exhausted by St. Paul's counsel: "Let every soul be subject unto the higher powers" (Romans 13: 1). Therefore, in this domain, the behavior of a Christian does not differ in any way from the behavior of a decent, law-abiding pagan or unbeliever. It is possible to combine without any pangs of conscience the obedient execution of even the cruelest, most inhuman, and unjustifiable commands of the powers-that-be with a sincere Christian consciousness.

This idea is one of the most bizarre errors of Christian thought; it is based on inner timidity, slavish self-consciousness, spiritual self-abasement in the face of the powers of this world. Formally, this idea is based on the consciousness of the duality

145

between the kingdom of God and the kingdom of Caesar, of which we spoke above in another connection. But rationalizing this duality, this idea completely removes the kingdom of Caesar from the sphere of religious-moral life, makes the service of Caesar autonomous, and thus coordinates it as it were with the service of God. A profounder philosophical-political meditation on this point is not necessary. It is sufficient to note that for an inwardly free consciousness (such must be the Christian consciousness) society and the state are, in the final analysis, a kind of great human family and, in principle, are not different from a family in the literal sense. The moral relations of the Christian to his fellow citizens, to the order of communal life with them, and thus to the power of the state, which in the final analysis is only the instrument and expression of the organized unity of this communal life—these moral relations are realized in the same plane of being as his duties toward the members of his family, and his friends and acquaintances. Whatever the meaning of the distinction between public life and private life, this distinction is not essential in regard to the moral consciousness. The obligations of the Christian remain the same for his *whole* life in the world. His concerns and responsibilities extend equally to both of these aspects of one and the same sphere of his life, namely, that sphere which is constituted by his belonging to collective human being, his moral relation to his neighbors. In this entire sphere, the Christian must radiate outward the gracious powers of his own inner being, while, on the other hand, he is compelled to take into account the imperfection that characterizes all worldly, unilluminated being, with all the practical consequences that this entails. Family relationships, the education of children, relationships with friends, etc. often demand the same discipline, the same severe measures of protection from evil, as social life. And on the other hand, social life must be as substantially illuminated by the powers of Christian being as so-called personal life.

How could such an inconsistent view arise? What could be its objective cause? Answers to these questions will substantially help us to clarify the theme that concerns us.

The error of this view is that it elevates a purely quantitative distinction to the level of a qualitative, substantial distinction. This qualitative distinction consists in the following. The smaller the circle of people with whom we are in contact, the easier it is for the relation to them to have the character of a living relation to the given concrete person in his uniqueness. It is precisely this type of

146

relation that is presupposed by the Christian commandment of love for one's neighbor; only in the form of such a relation can the gracious power of the Christian life-in-God stream outward. And on the other hand, the larger the circle of people with whom we deal, the more we must take into account certain collective and, in this sense, impersonal elements and factors of the life of these people; hence, the more our love for them, our concern about them, will be expressed, on the one hand, in the observance of certain general norms (the "law") in regard to them, and, on the other hand, in actions aimed at protecting them from evil in a general way, which (as we know) usually requires "worldly" means, burdened by sin. In a "collective," the element of the unilluminated, sinful world is stronger than in the sphere of relations of person to person. Thus the direct radiation of gracious powers is more difficult to achieve in a collective than in a small group of people, each of whom we can meet as a person, and can thus hope to directly "infect" with the gracious power of Christ's light.

This distinction is quantitative, not substantial. And therefore the distinction between private life and public life is perhaps *even less* adequate to the immanent duality in the structure of Christian moral life than other apparent distinctions we have examined. But the cause (which we have just indicated) of this substantially inconsistent distinction contains a notion that is useful in another connection. This particular notion helps us to understand the essence of that element which serves as the connecting thread between the two spheres of life that we have just examined.

6. The Principle of the Unity of Moral Life

We noted above that the affirmation of the duality in the spiritual and moral life of man conceals the potential danger of a real moral bifurcation of the person. The duality of Christian life, the duality between being-in-God and moral activity under the conditions of the imperfection of the world, risks creating the impression that the Christian soul is split into two mutually unconnected and completely heterogeneous parts, the impression of a drastic rupture that completely destroys the wholeness of the soul. But in fact this split, this rupture, is a very common phenomenon in the world that calls itself "Christian." Like the notorious double-bookkeeping in theoretical thought, the irreconcilable combination in the human mind of "faith" professed on Sunday in church and the unfaith (based on the everyday and scientific interpretation of the world) which is the conviction of the weekday—the sphere of moral life contains a widespread unreconciled and irreconcilable combination of faith in the Christian moral teachings with the complete rejection of these teachings when it is a question of their practical application to earthly life.

But of course it is utterly evident that such a split of the moral (as well as theoretical) consciousness is a phenomenon of spiritual disease, a kind of sinful distortion, however widespread this phenomenon might be. It is clear from the very outset that the fundamental duality that necessarily emanates from the very essence of the Christian consciousness cannot coincide with such a distortion. Insofar as the gracious, redeemed life-in-God of the Christian is a genuine reality, this life must somehow be substantially reflected in the character of his activity in the world. The duality must be not an irreconcilable rupture, but a duality grounded in some unity; it must be an organic, inwardly harmonious dual-unity. A man whose activity in the world is *wholly* determined by elements and motives of a worldly order and differs not at all from the activity of a pagan—thereby reveals that he actually belongs to the "children of this world"; and the gracious inner life which he thinks to preserve turns out to be imaginary. The gracious life-in-God, owing to which Christians are the "salt of the earth," must be effectively expressed in the "salting of the earth." Otherwise this salt is worthless and will be "cast out." The light of Christ's truth must not be put "under a bushel." It must be placed high so that it shines for the world.

The image of the "light," the image which is the general foundation of the present work, will aid us in clarifying the true nature of the relation we seek. If we have spoken of the inner moral *being* of a Christian and distinguished it from his moral activity in the world, we must not forget that the very essence of this being, its substance as it were, consists (in complete analogy with the nature of light) in the *energy* that cannot but be radiated outward. The true name of this energy is *love*. "God is love" and therefore being-in-God is permeated and saturated with the gracious power of God's love. And if this being is a kind of inner state of the soul, it is also (because love in its essence is active energy) the radiation outward of

148

the gracious power of love. The soul, inwardly full of love, loves as naturally and inevitably as the light shines. All cases in which the soul, supposedly submerged in God and full of love, does not love, does not spontaneously radiate love, compassion, sympathy, goodness on the surrounding world and, first and foremost, on living human souls—all such cases (rather frequent in the pietistic literature of all the Christian faiths) bear witness to the illusoriness, inauthenticity, perversion of the inner religious life. In its primordial source or immediate essence, the commandment to love one's neighbor is for the Christian not a kind of external command, normalizing his behavior or the direction of his will. Rather, this commandment is *the clarification of the very essence of his Christian being* in regard to its utterly spontaneous consequence. In other words, love is that determination of Christian being in which is extinguished or overcome the very distinction between inner being directed toward God or existent in God and moral activity outward; for, like the light, love is an inner state, the very essence of which consists in radiation outward. Thus, love is the element that determines the *unity* of Christian life.

It is essential to understand here that from the point of view of Christian faith this unity is an absolutely all-embracing, universal unity that knows no boundaries in the life of the Christian. There is no situation, no life-problem, no state of the world, which could fundamentally prevent the possibility of love or demand from us a relation opposite to love in regard to our neighbors and the world. We already saw this above, when we noted that the necessity of actions burdened by sin does not free the Christian from the duty to love. From this point of view, the duality between Christian being and Christian moral life is not a duality between the relation of love or the action of love in the world and some other relation or action outside the limits of love, for the Christian can have no relation to the world and people except love. Rather, this duality is a duality that is rooted in *unity*, in the universal, all-embracing principle of love. This duality is a dual-unity of two different forms of disclosure or effective action of one principle: love. The distinction, discussed above, between inner being and outer activity, or between the inner order of the soul and moral behavior in relation to the world, is clarified now as the distinction between the direct radiation of the gracious power of love and the system of intentional actions guided by love, a system that we can call *the politics of love*. At every moment of our moral life and, strictly speaking, in

149

relation to every situation in which we deal with the as yet unilluminated element of this world (are we ever in any other kind of situation?) two things are simultaneously demanded of us: our essential, gracious being-in-God must—outside of all discussions and considerations concerning consequences—pour down as a spontaneous stream of love on our neighbors, on all life that surrounds us, and thus illuminate, warm, strengthen, and unify this life; and, in our responsibility for the fate of our neighbors and the world, we are obliged to realize our love on such paths and in such actions that make it maximally useful and fruitful (as we have seen, in this form of the activity of love, we are even sometimes obliged to participate in a lesser sin if this is necessary to protect the world from a greater sin). Thus, even though the Christian moral life is divided into the duality of *the essential radiation of love* and *the politics of love*, illuminated, intelligent, taking into account all the conditions of the sinful being of the world—the Christian moral life does not stop being the *unity* of that principle which forms the universal essence of Christian life, namely, the principle of love.

The politics of love! At first glance this concept may seem to be an expression of some hideously hypocritical, pharisaical pietism, something essentially unnatural, suitable only for old maids and pastors of saccharine piety—a concept that crumbles to dust in the face of the genuinely healthy, severely sober, responsible moral consciousness. According to a very widespread conception, such a combination of words seems a contradiction in terms: love, as they say, appears to be one thing while politics, a complex or system of measures and actions determined by sober utilitarian calculation and necessarily free in the choice of means, appears to be another thing, wholly incompatible with love. However, the spiritually more deeply penetrating gaze discloses that the politics of love, both as politics and as love, is precisely that which the Christian conscience demands of us in our active relation to the world. For, as we learned above, this relation must be determined by the consciousness of responsibility for the concrete, fruitful realization of good or the opposition to evil. But precisely this consciousness of responsibility is the expression of the genuinely intense, active love for one's neighbor. In the face of this responsibility, irresponsible sentimental love, unarmed for battle against evil and unprepared for the fruitful assistance of one's neighbor, and politics guided by goals other than love for people, are both inconsistent. Truly responsible, active love inspires us to "politics," the system of intelligent actions that takes into account the concrete conditions of human life; and true, right politics is inspired by love, by the aspiration to the good of one's neighbors. In a world that suffers from the politics of hate and from dreamy, irresponsible love, we must affirm the courageous Christian idea of the politics of love. The politics of love, a system of actions guided by a responsible understanding of both politics and love, has a decisive significance for the genuinely Christian solution of problems in all domains of social and state life.

Thus is clarified for us the organically integral dual-unity of Christian moral life: alongside the fundamental situation of the direct radiation into the world of the gracious power of love, which is independent of the concrete state of the world, for the grace of love is needed everywhere and always, we have—in the consciousness of our responsibility for the fate of our neighbors—the obligation to carry out the politics of love, the obligation to form our actions by calculating their maximal concrete fruitfulness, by taking into account the best practical realization of the commandment of love in the given concrete situation of the world. Thus, despite the duality of the forms of its manifestation, the order of Christian life remains inwardly one, for it is wholly determined by the one principle of love.

It is true that this unity does not prevent these two forms of the manifestation or realization of love from being profoundly unlike each other. In the direct radiation of love, it is the gracious power of love which acts, and man is only a "medium" of the Divine powers that heal and save the world. On the other hand, in the deliberate, planned system of actions which is the politics of love, love is only the primordial source of the motive force which determines the ultimate goal of activity, while the actions and efforts directed at the world belong by their nature to the purely human sphere. And this kind of Christian activity can resemble—in its outward aspect, in the means it uses—the "wisdom of this world" or at least the activity determined by the purely human, natural love for people and the worldly concern about the satisfaction of their needs.

Nevertheless, the universal principle of love not only outwardly unites these two heterogeneous forms of activity and constitutes their hidden single root as it were, but also inwardly permeates them, impressing its formative stamp on the system of deliberate actions realized by worldly means. In practice, in living concreteness, this moderates the sharpness and substantiality of

151

the distinction as it appears in its abstract, logical determination. For the direct radiation of the gracious powers of love, being universal in its essence, can and must accompany purely human moral activity, injecting a stream of gracious warmth into the cold soberness of the latter, owing to which even this purely human, worldly form of activity can shine with *the reflected light of Christ's truth*. If this activity must be severely courageous in its very essence; if in the consciousness of its responsibility for the fate of one's neighbors and the world, it must rather take upon itself the sin of the immediate causation of suffering than be weakened by dreamy, sentimental, irresponsible kindness—the power of love operating in this activity is nonetheless immediately expressed in the fact that this activity will avoid all unnecessary severity and be animated by *humaneness*, by respect and love for the sanctity of the human person. Outside the sin-burdened worldly means made compulsory by extreme necessity (clarified above), the activity of the Christian, based on faith in the holiness and ultimate triumph of love, will be directly guided by love. Even in its outward manifestation, this activity will remain that which forms its inner motive force: *responsible love, the active fruitful respect for the sanctity of man.*

All that man does bears, in the final analysis, the living impression of his *concrete personality*, i.e., the state of *his inner being*. Thus, the concrete aspect of the whole life and activity of a Christian, of a man the profoundest roots of whose being touch God, are grounded in God, and who participates in the kingdom of God, this concrete aspect necessarily differs or must differ from the life of a "pagan," a man unilluminated by the light of Christ's truth and wholly enslaved by the forces of "this world."

CHAPTER FIVE

The Kingdom of God and the Religious Value of Creation

The foregoing considerations have not yet completely clarified the problems of moral life with which we are dealing. These considerations have not touched upon the deep, primordial reason why the fundamental ontological duality between the pure Divine light and the darkness of the unilluminated world must be reflected in the duality of the principles of moral life. We still have to resolve one more doubt, arising spontaneously here. It would appear to be a natural supposition that the ontological duality between light and darkness, i.e., the de facto imperfection of the world's being, should determine the intensity and persistence of our moral activity, but should not have as its consequence the duality of the directions or forms of this activity. For the content of our moral duty cannot, in essence, depend on the de facto state of being. And even less can it depend on the imperfection of this being, for we are summoned precisely to *overcome* this imperfection, to dissipate the darkness by the power of the light in which we participate. That good and evil have their own, immanent criteria, independent of the de facto empirical state of the world, is simply the fundamental axiom of the moral consciousness, outside of which the independence, i.e., the adequate action, of this consciousness is inconceivable. No powers of the world, and no weaknesses and imperfections of the world, are able to change that which is truth and that which is untruth. To the very essence of moral life belongs its ascendancy over, its independence of, empirical conditions, and, consequently, its moral stubbornness, its moral rigorism. According to Kant's profound formulation, which we have already mentioned, *the obligatory* is possible always and under all conditions, for the very absoluteness of moral duty is a power that overcomes all empirical motives, all obstacles to the realization of good. In this *general* sense, the principle expressed in the French saying "*fais ce que dois, advienne ce que pourra*" is undeniably valid. The voice of conscience, the command of the supreme, ideally all-powerful will of God, demands complete obedience and is therefore independent of all empirical conditions.

How can this absolute ascendancy of the morally obligatory be harmonized with the realization, clarified above, that the moral life, reflecting in itself the ontological duality between the Divine light and the darkness of the world, is itself inwardly divided, and divided in such a way that in that aspect in which it is activity in the world it must take into account the sinfulness of the world and assume the character of a certain compromise, be burdened by sinfulness? We have already seen that the necessity of participation in the sinfulness of the world, of taking the burden of this sinfulness upon oneself, must be not an expression of the weakness, the flabbiness and pliability of the moral will, but rather the result of the pitilessly severe, strict observance of moral responsibility, i.e., the fulfillment of a moral duty. Moral rigorism, the uncompromising obedience to the voice of conscience, the command of God, demands of us an active, effective battle against the world's evil, a battle whose conditions can compel us to sacrifice the principle of our personal, individual perfection. Without an understanding of this dialectical action of moral duty, which obliges us under certain conditions to sacrifice our personal purity and to take sin upon our souls; without this consciousness that moral duty is, in the final analysis, not the duty of purity but the duty of *love*— moral stubbornness, moral rigorism, degenerates into its opposite, into pharisaical self-satisfaction, indifference, and egotism.

In other words, according to its own inner motives and criteria or according to the values that guide it, moral life as such has— in the face of the duality between God and the world—a certain immanent dual structure. If such a dual structure did not exist, it would be impossible to conceive of a situation in which the commission of a sinful act, the violation of personal purity and saintliness, would turn out to be the fulfillment of a moral obligation.

1. A New Aspect of the Duality of Christian Life: Two Goals of Moral Activity

The assumption that there is an immanent duality in the goals or values of moral life was in essence already contained in the distinction between the task of essential salvation and the task of external assistance to the world, its external protection from evil. We saw, after all, that precisely this distinction is the source of the inevitable dialectical duality and, hence, sometimes the tragic collision between two directions of moral will. We must now attempt to examine this relationship more profoundly, to ask how this duality of tasks is possible and how it is combined with the necessary inner spiritual unity of the Christian ideal.

Christian life in its ultimate, absolute essence and meaning has only one goal, knows only one good: the kingdom of God, life that is wholly permeated by the light of Divine truth and is therefore saved and blessed. This is so unambiguously evident in the Gospels and follows so clearly from the whole spirit of the Gospels that it cannot cause the slightest doubt. Having opened people's eyes to the kingdom of God, having shown them the way to this kingdom, having revealed Himself as this way, Christ (it would appear) decisively commanded people to have only one goal in life: the aspiration to, the search for, the kingdom of God. "And seek not ye what ye shall eat, or what ye shall drink, neither be ye of doubtful mind. For all these things do the nations of the world seek after: and your Father knoweth that ye have need of these things" (Luke 12: 29-32; see also Matthew 6: 31-33). In reply to Martha, Jesus says: "Thou art careful and troubled about many things: but one thing is needful" (Luke 10: 41-42). It is in this sense that one must understand the stricture that it is impossible to serve "two masters" at the same time. And this essentially coincides with the only commandment that contains all the fullness of the Christian ideal, the goal of Christian life: "Be ye . . . perfect as your Father which is in heaven is perfect."

We repeat: in this general sense it is completely undeniable that the Christian life has only one goal. But this one higher goal not only can be attained in different ways, but can have different variants or sides, can be concretely embodied in different aspects.

Here as everywhere, to be "ministers of the New Testament" is to be ministers "not of the letter, but of the spirit: for the letter killeth, but the spirit giveth life" (2 Cor. 3: 6). The same Sermon on the Mount that commands us to seek before all the "kingdom of God and His truth" and not to concern ourselves about anything else, also commands us to give alms to the poor, i.e., to concern ourselves about the satisfaction of the worldly, material needs of our neighbor, without any thought for the significance of this aid for the salvation of our neighbor's soul. And the Gospels underscore with great insistence the absolute religious significance of this task of active love for one's neighbor, expressed in giving food to the hungry, drink to the thirsty, refuge to the stranger, and clothing to the naked, and in visiting the sick: the coming last judgment over the human soul, the inheritance of "the kingdom prepared from the foundation of the world," depends directly on the fulfillment of this task.

Thus, one thing is clear outside of all theoretical considerations. Even though *for myself* I must before all seek the kingdom of God and not concern myself about my earthly needs; even though I must help my neighbor become strong in this direction of will—nevertheless, the satisfaction of the earthly needs of *my neighbor* is for me the only genuine measure of my love for him, which, being the fruit and expression of love for God, is thus the necessary proof of the authenticity of my search for the "kingdom of God and His truth." Meister Eckhart, one of the greatest of Christian sages, who lived wholly by the goods of the kingdom of God, speaks of this justly and simply: "If you are taken to seventh heaven and contemplate God, and your neighbor asks you for something to eat, it would be better for you to descend to earth and make him a bowl of soup than to keep on contemplating God." Wherever and whenever the search for the kingdom of God, for oneself and for others; or, more generally, wherever religious interests make us indifferent to the earthly, material needs of our neighbors, the Christian faith is distorted into religiously inconsistent and morally intolerable pharisaism. It is utterly incorrect that the "church" is the union or organization whose only task is concern about the spiritual, "religious" education of people, about the satisfaction of their "spiritual" needs. This sort of "church" is not the true church of Christ, not the mystical "body of Christ" in which all are one. It is rather a collection of pharisees or unrepentant sinners, a collection of people who have forgotten the fundamental commandment of love for one's neighbor, and precisely for this reason (according to St. John) abide in death or darkness. The true church of Christ is that primordial Christian church in which "the multitude of them that believed were of one heart and of one soul," so that "neither was there any among them that lacked," for "distribution was made unto every man according as he had need" (Acts 4: 32, 34–35).

But how should one understand this task of the Christian moral life? What, precisely, is its genuine *Christian* meaning, its religious ground? The fact that Christian love for one's neighbor, which includes concern about the satisfaction of his material needs, has a *self-evident, purely immanent value*, which excludes, as it were, the very question about its ground—this fact is not an objection against our need to understand it; that is, to understand how it is compatible with the commandment to seek only the kingdom of God. For it is evident that love for one's neighbor obliges us to do *good* for him, to give him goods that are of genuine value, but not at all to help him attain that which has no value or even is evil. To help a drunkard obtain drink, to help a debaucher in his debauchery, to help a robber or usurer get rich at the expense of other people, these things, evidently, are not part of the task of Christian love for one's neighbor. From this it follows self-evidently that the Christian commandment to feed the hungry, to give drink to the thirsty, to clothe the naked, to visit the sick, and so on, presupposes that the satisfaction of such needs of my neighbor has a *positive religious value*, despite the commandment not to seek that which you should eat and drink, but to seek only the kingdom of God. But how can one harmonize the two? It would appear that the fundamental commandment to seek the kingdom of God and not to concern ourselves about anything else has force not only as a commandment of our personal inner spiritual life, but also as a commandment that determines the direction of the activity of our love for our neighbor. And of course this is the way it is. The commandment to seek the kingdom of God includes the commandment to help our neighbors in this search. This determines the obligatoriness of activity directed at the spiritual assistance of one's neighbor, an activity that is inseparable from Christian being, inseparable from the being of persons who are conscious of themselves as inwardly rooted in God. The presence in us of spiritual depths illuminated by the Divine light, this presence which is our faith in and love of God, opens our eyes to the true, principal need of each of our neighbors, of every man as such, compels us to see that this principal need is a *spiritual* need, what the Gospel calls the search for

157

salvation or the kingdom of God. For how does it profit our neighbor if we help him acquire the whole world but he loses his soul? The spiritual assistance to man, the assistance to our neighbor in the principal, fundamental, primordially unique goal of human life, namely, the search for "salvation"—this assistance is, of course, the fundamental and necessary form of love for our neighbor. And contrary to the view widespread in the world that calls itself "Christian," this assistance is not at all only the duty of the "pastors of souls," but also the obvious duty of every Christian, of every man who himself uses the goods of the Divine light.

But along with this duty to assist one's neighbor in his fundamental and principal need, there is also the duty, commanded to us unambiguously and imposingly, to actively assist one's neighbor in his material, earthly need. Evidently, this cannot be explained except by the recognition that this material assistance is the realization of a kind of positive value, affirmed by the Christian consciousness. And precisely for this reason, material assistance is the necessary form of the fulfillment of the universal commandment of love for one's neighbor.

2. The Essence of Christian Love for One's Neighbor. The Holiness of Man in His Creaturely Nature

Insofar as love for one's neighbor as expressed in active assistance directed at the satisfaction of all his concrete (including material, earthly) needs not only has a positive value from the point of view of the Christian consciousness, but is even the direct measure of the authenticity of our Christian faith, we stand before a peculiar paradox. Our own rootedness in superworldly, Divine being, our illuminatedness by the light of Christ's truth, the intensity of our search for the "kingdom of God and His truth," must find expression in a love for our neighbor that includes an active concern about his earthly needs. And on the other hand, absence of interest, indifference to the earthly suffering and needs of one's neighbor, shows that we are not yet "in the light," that we are yet "in darkness," that we are not "the children of God" but the children of Satan, "the prince of this world." This is stated by the same Apostle who tells us: "Love not the world, neither the things that are in the world" (1 John 2: 15). How can we understand this contradiction?

Love for one's neighbor in the Christian sense is evidently something wholly other than a purely elemental feeling or sympathy rooted in the *empirical* nature of man. As is well known, the Greek language has a special word, *agape*, to express this concept, by which it is distinguished from all purely fleshly or psychic attraction to or sympathy for a person, *philia* (the French use the marvelous word "*charité*" to express this concept). This does not mean, of course, that Christian love for one's neighbor must unfailingly be conscious of its religious ground, so that its unconscious manifestation is worthless. On the contrary, here as everywhere, the measure of the true spiritual illuminatedness of a person and his nearness to God is not the content of his conscious thoughts, convictions, and beliefs, but the real state of his soul: his "heart." The parable of the Good Samaritan expresses this sufficiently clearly, as does the parable of the two sons, one of whom expresses his readiness to carry out his father's will, but does not do so, while the other expresses disobedience, but in fact carries out his father's will. All human kindness, all caring about the fate of one's neighbor, the ability to be inwardly touched by his need, all this bears witness to the fact that the human heart has depths that transcend man's purely fleshly nature. All this is the sign of a spiritual fire, of the action of God in our soul, even if we are not conscious of this action. Love for one's neighbor, commanded by the Christian revelation and emanating from the ontological makeup of Christian life as rootedness in God, who Himself is love—this love can be unconscious of its religious ground. But this does not prevent it from having this ground. We must and can love our neighbor in the Christian sense of this concept (*agape*) whether or not we "like" or "love" him in the sense of purely human, subjective-emotional attraction (*philia*).

In this Christian sense, love—most proximally—is good will; selfless interest in the good of one's neighbor. And if we ask where does this love come from, what in this love makes possible our selfless interest in the good of another person, the answer to this consists in the fact that love in the Christian sense is the openness of the soul to the perception of the holiness, the absolute value, of one's neighbor, of every human soul as such. Thus, this love has not only a religious ground (for this openness of the soul is an index of the action in us of grace), but also a religious meaning. It is connected with the basic content of Christian revelation, the revelation of the Divine-human ground of man's essence and being. This revelation for the first time opens man's eyes (see Chapter II, 4) to the

159

true dignity of every human being as a principle emanating from God and sanctified by the presence of God within it. A new thought is now added to this universal religious ground of love for one's neighbor. If above, in harmony with the basic theme of Christian faith, we underscored the *dualistic* character of being, disclosed by Christian revelation (see Chapter II, particularly II, 4), the opposition between the birth of man "from the light," "from God," and his creatural being, or the opposition between "spirit" and "flesh" in human beings—now, paying attention to the fact that the truth of revelation is always the fullness and combined action of opposite determinations, we must consider the reverse relation. Possessing the high dignity of "the children of God," being the son of the heavenly Father and the heir to His kingdom, man is also a *creatural* being, rooted in the world and an inseparable part of the world. It is true that this is what constitutes the duality of human nature, but this duality is a kind of *dual-unity*; and as a dual-unity it is also a unity. Although these two natures of man do not merge and must be distinguished, they are inseparable. Man cannot simply be divided into these two parts; he is concretely conceivable only as their unity. Thus, the holiness of man as a spiritual being is thereby the holiness of his *concrete person*, i.e., the holiness of the *creatural* bearer of God's image. Hence, the higher origin and dignity of man makes holy his very *being*, his life in all its concreteness, including its creatural nature. The spirit born of God is incarnate in the *living soul* of man. The Old Testament faith considers that the living soul of man was formed when God breathed His "spirit" into the nostrils of a being made of "the dust of the ground." How much more so then must the New Testament religious understanding of man be permeated with the consciousness that God has given us His Spirit (1 John 3: 24); and that therefore not only our soul, but also that in which it is incarnate, our body, "is the temple of the Holy Spirit." In Christian dogmatics, this consciousness is an explicit and necessary consequence of the fundamental belief that the Word of God, the eternally existent Son of God, was incarnated in the creatural being of man, in Jesus of Nazareth, the son of Mary.

From this derivative holiness of man as a creature follows the obligation to treat with reverence the concrete living soul of one's neighbor in all its wholeness, to consider holy the very being of man, concretely existent in its earthly aspect. But man as he exists in his fallen, imperfect nature and in the imperfect world necessarily has earthly needs. He is condemned to eat bread in the sweat of his face: his concrete, earthly being depends on a whole series of earthly, material conditions, on the satisfaction of material needs necessary for his existence. And if in regard to *himself* man must not concern himself about what he is going to eat and drink, but must place his hopes on his heavenly Father, must seek, before all, the kingdom of God—then in regard to our neighbor we must act in such a way that this concern of the Father is manifested precisely *through us*, through the activity of our love for the holiness of man even in his creatural being and creatural needs. Although God in Himself, in His essence, is a Spirit, and thus man too, insofar as he is connected with God and God is present in him, is also a spirit and in this sense (as the good news has revealed) is free from all earthly needs and possesses boundless riches—nevertheless the holiness of the human spirit born of God, as it is concretely incarnate in the living, creatural nature of man, sanctifies this creatural nature as well. Precisely for this reason, one who feeds the hungry, clothes the naked, visits the sick, thereby realizes his love for God Himself; or, as the Gospel expresses it, he does all this for the Lord Jesus Christ Himself. For Christ, appearing on earth in the "slavish form" of a man, is present invisibly and mystically in every human being and even in the earthly, creatural, fleshly nature of every human being.

Precisely for this reason, the one goal and value of Christian life, i.e., the "kingdom of God and His truth," is naturally divided into *two fundamental tasks* of our life: the search for the salvation, redemption, deification of the world, its transfiguration into the kingdom of God; and the protection of the very *being of man* and, hence, the *being of the world*, of which man is a part. This second task means that we must concern ourselves with the concrete subject of being, for whom the kingdom of God is prepared. Precisely in the realization of the duality of these tasks, we (to the extent we are able) become perfect like our heavenly Father, who not only saves the world He has created, but also protects it, sustains its being, making "his sun to rise on the evil and on the good" and sending "rain on the just and on the unjust" (Matthew 5: 45).

3. The Positive Value of the World. The Holy Primordial-Ground of the World

Until now the concept of the "world," in harmony with the predominant use of the word in the New Testament and particularly in the Gospel of St. John, has had in our work the significance of a kind of negative principle. "The whole world lies in evil." About the world, we are commanded: "Love not the world, neither the things that are in the world" (1 John 2: 15). The "world" is the kingdom of Satan, "the prince of this world." The world cannot receive the spirit of truth (John 14: 17). And most importantly, the kingdom of God is "not of this world," just as Christ Himself is "not of this world" (John 17: 14). In the Prologue of the Gospel of St. John, the idea of the light that shines in darkness coincides with the judgment that the true light was in the world, and the world, which came into being through Him, did not know Him and did not receive Him. The world is a principle opposed to and antagonistic to the kingdom of God, the light of the Divine Logos.

Nevertheless, this understanding of the world as a negative principle does not at all coincide with the gnostic rejection of the world, or with some fundamental, Manichean dualism between Good and Evil, God and the devil. For this world, the negative elements of which are so distinctly remarked and severely condemned, nonetheless came into being through the Divine word, without which nothing could have come into being. The paradox that the world did not know the Light and rejected the Light that came into the world consists precisely in the fact that the world itself came into being through the Light. The Light "came unto his own, and his own received him not." And if it is said "love not the world," the same Evangelist John says that "God so loved the world that He gave his only begotten Son" (John 3: 16). If the world were only an expression of a negative principle of being, then the very concept of the salvation of the world would have neither meaning nor justification. However, the same Gospel of St. John that so severely condemns the world contains the great words: "I came not to judge the world, but to save the world" (John 12: 47). These are words of Divine love, which through all the imperfection of the world perceives and knows the higher, absolute value of the world and is therefore concerned about its salvation—like a loving mother, who even in the most vicious and criminal son sees and loves the living soul, holy to her, of her child. The evil of the world—that negative principle which, according to the Old Testament consciousness, possessed the world as a result of the Fall—could only distort and weaken but not destroy or fundamentally hurt the holy primordial-ground of the world, determined by God Himself and therefore positive.

This positive value and holiness for us of the ontological primordial-ground of the world are determined not only by the fact that the world is God's creation, about which God said that "it was good." The positive value of the world is determined still more by the organic belonging of man to the world, by the commonality of the creatural nature of man and the world. In man, all of creation is sanctified, the whole world is sanctified.

In the nineteenth century, evolutionism of the Darwinian type made the discovery that man is not an exceptional being, not a being of a special order, fundamentally different from the rest of the animal world or the rest of the organic world in general, but a being who is inwardly akin to the rest of the world, for he issues from the womb of the world. This discovery of the kinship of man with the rest of the world was understood and preached as the exposure of the falsity of man's claim to have a higher origin and as proof that man "in essence" is not a reality of a higher order than an "ape," or even a "protoplasm" or "amoeba." But recognizing the kinship between man and the rest of the world, we can and must draw the opposite conclusion. Darwinian evolutionism encounters the invincible, purely logical obstacle that, starting with the higher, it is possible to understand the lower as a reality partially and imperfectly identical with the higher; but that, starting with the lower, it is not possible to explain the higher. For the greater obviously contains the lesser, but the greater can never be derived from the lesser as such. Just as we judge the ability and significance of a man (e.g., an artist or thinker) not by his initial, imperfect trials, but only by his higher, more mature achievements, so we must judge the evolutionary development of the general nature of the being called man. At the present time even the purely natural-scientific, biological point of view no longer has any doubt that the "evolution" of higher forms from lower ones has the character of "creative" evolution, i.e., that the reality of a higher order is derived not at all from the lower reality as such but from the potency of its own being, a potency that is already concealed in the lower being and reveals itself only in a higher stage. To put it more briefly and simply, from the fact that a certain kinship between man and "ape" has been demonstrated, it does not at all follow that man "in essence" is not more than an "ape." Rather it follows that, despite its fundamental distinction from man, the ape is something like man's "younger brother."

Generalizing this latter idea and connecting it with our basic theme, we must say that the belonging of man's soul to the world, the fact that the world has a reality that we call man and whose higher dignity we are immediately conscious of, demonstrates that the reality of the world, owing to its kinship with man, also has a certain higher value and dignity. If in one sense the world as "flesh" is a principle that is hostile, opposed, antagonistic to the spirit, in another sense the world, also like the "flesh" or "body," is that in which the human spirit is "incarnate" and acquires a visible, tangible sphere for its action. And if the human body is not only "flesh" in the pejorative sense, but also the temple of the Holy Spirit in us, which we have from God (1 Cor. 6: 19), the world as a whole is also a kind of common body, the "temple" of the spirit that lives in it. If the world is a creature in the pejorative sense in which the creature is opposed to the Creator, as the "earthen pitcher" is opposed to the "potter," nevertheless, the fact that the world came out of the Creator's hands signifies that it bears the stamp of the Creator. Furthermore, arising through Logos, without which nothing comes into being, and being also the space and material in which this Logos, becoming a person, thereby became incarnate—the world, like man who is a part of it, in a certain sense resembles this Logos, is indirectly, like man (though in a different way), "the image and likeness of God." As the Apostle says, "the invisible things of him [God] from the creation of the world are clearly seen, being understood by the things that are made, even His eternal power and Godhead" (Romans 1: 20). The salvation of man is not only conceived as the salvation of the whole world in the sense clarified above, but, in view of the kinship and solidarity of all creation, the salvation of man is connected with the salvation of all creation: "the creature itself also shall be delivered from the bondage of corruption into the glorious liberty of the children of God" (Romans 8: 21). In the spirit of this love for the holiness of creation, Jesus teaches us that God feeds the birds of the air and clothes the lilies of the fields as Solomon in all his glory was not clothed. And one of the most perfect Christians who ever lived, St. Francis of Assisi, saw in all the creatures of the world his brothers and sisters, and loved them all with that illuminated Christian love which is grounded in the living feeling of the holy dignity of creation, of the presence in creation of the traces of God's glory.

Thus, despite all the imperfection, all the sinfulnes of the world or creation, the world has a kind of primordial ontological ground in which it is a positive religious value, something holy. That which the world *truly is* coincides with that which the world *should be*, with God's plan for the world. This primordial, genuine, profound being of the world, this holy principle is, of course, essentially different from what the world *has become*, from the imperfect empirical state of the world, distorted by sin. But, differing from this empirical state, the true, positive essence of the world has not perished (as affirmed sometimes by the onesided radicalism of the Christian consciousness which is shaken by the fact of sinfulness) but continues to be present, shining through the sinful empirical shell of the world—just as the living soul of man, the image and likeness of God, cannot perish even in the most vicious, criminal, sinful man, but is only crushed by the weight of sin, hidden beneath the darkness of sin. Furthermore, this positive, holy primordial-ground of the world is that real power or agency by the action of which the world continues to exist in general, protects itself against destruction. For evil and sin are powers of destruction; and if they were to totally rule the world, the world would crumble, would cease to exist.

The positive, holy primordial-ground of the world's being is present and acts concretely in the world in the form of a kind of harmony of separate parts and functions of this being, in the form of *order*, in the form of that which the thought of antiquity designated by the untranslatable word "cosmos." Constituting the holy, Divine primordial-ground of the world, this action of ideal forces on the imperfect empirical state of the world forms that complex of normalizing principles which human thought (both ancient Greek thought, starting with Heraclitus, and Old Testament thought) apprehends as "natural law" or as the law of the world's life, established by God Himself.

Thus, although according to Christ's revelation the fullness of the kingdom of God, the fullness of Divine truth, is attainable only through the end of the world, through its transfiguration into a new, higher, perfect form of being—nevertheless (and this is the second, just as essential, part of the relationship), prior to this conclusive transfiguration of creation, i.e., precisely within the limits of the imperfect being of creation, there are certain holy principles that protect the world from the destructive powers of evil. From this follows our moral obligation to observe these positive principles, to be their servants as it were, in their function of the protection of the world from destruction by evil powers, i.e., the obligation to obey, in our moral life, the natural law, the law of God, to recognize His authority as the normalizing principle of worldly and human life.

165

Until the moment comes (as we have seen, not a moment of time but a mysterious, unfathomable moment, which overcomes and revokes time itself) when the gracious powers of salvation dissolve the world of the present aeon and transform it into the kingdom of God, in which God is "all in all," and the kingdom of the law is replaced by the kingdom of all-triumphant, all-permeating, all-embracing grace—until that moment the world must be subordinate (as we have seen in another connection in Chapter IV, 3) to the law that protects it from the powers of evil. This law is—in conditions of the imperfection of the world—the disclosure and action of God's plan for creation and, thus, an expression of the holy, positive primordial-ground of the world. Thus, the task of the protection of the very being of the world, holy by its primordial ground, coincides with the task of obedience to the law, respect for its holiness. Below we shall see precisely what constitutes the basic content or the general character of this law. Here we shall limit ourselves to the indication that precisely this relationship contains the ontological ground of that duality of tasks of the Christian moral life about which we spoke above, namely, the combination in this moral life of the task of salvation with the task of the protection of the world.

4. The Heresy of Utopianism

Several times in the course of this book, we have already had to mention the error of utopianism and to expose it as a kind of heresy, i.e., a harmful, fatal distortion of the genuine truth. We have seen that the error of utopianism is based on the confusion of two utterly heterogeneous tasks or ideals: the hope for the conclusive transfiguration or salvation of the world, which in its essence surpasses all human powers and even lies outside the limits of the world's being in that categorial form in which it is accessible in general to us; and the task of the establishment of the absolute fullness of the truth by the external organization of life, by the efforts of man, and precisely within the limits of the habitual, familiar world ("this world"). Now we have the opportunity to give a fundamental evaluation of this heresy and to disclose the general reason why it has fatal consequences.

History provides irrefutable empirical evidence of the fatal consequences of utopianism, of the fact that the striving to establish the kingdom of God on earth by external, human organizational measures not only turns out to be unattainable in practice, but inevitably leads to a diametrically opposite result, to the unchaining and triumph of the powers of evil, to the kingdom of hell on earth. Starting with the Taborites, Thomas Munzer, the Anabaptists, and proceeding to the Jacobins and Communism, all concrete attempts to use human, state, and legal means to attain complete equality, bliss, and absolute justice, i.e., the kingdom of absolute truth on earth, have led fatally to a tyranny (to a degree unknown in other, habitual forms of the world's being) of evil, repression, and humiliation of man. Originally inspired by elevated, noble feelings of pity for the woes of people and the desire to establish a just order, the kingdom of good and truth — all human "saviors of the world" have, by a fatal dialectical process, been transformed into bloodthirsty tyrants, oppressors, and executioners. Thus understood, the task of the salvation of the world has always led in practice to the meaningless and merciless shedding of torrents of human blood, to universal enslavement and brutalization, to the kingdom of poverty and the tyrannical humiliation of man. But what is the general inner cause of this enigmatic fatal transformation?

First of all, the nature of the error lies, most proximally, in the intention to "save the world" by means of the *law*, i.e., by the establishment of some ideal, compulsorily realized *order*. It is curious that all the Christian utopians, the Taborites, the Anabaptists, the militant Puritans, in practice replaced the New Testament, Christian understanding of the truth by the Old Testament religions of the law, the Old Testament theocratic ideal. Therefore, all these utopians have called for a merciless war against the "Amalekites" and "Philistines," for the destruction of the godless. All have felt compelled to declare compassion for the enemy to be impermissible disobedience to the severe will of God (the Taborites even ended by openly rejecting Christianity and converting to the Old Testament religion). All utopians transfer the function of salvation to the law, to measures of state compulsion or, at best, moral compulsion—a function that, in essence, only the free powers of God's grace are capable of performing. Thus, the fatal consequences of the error of utopianism can be explained, most proximally, by the fact that upon the law (the principle that in its essence has the task of the protection of the world from evil) is imposed the impossible task of the essential salvation of the world, a task that contradicts the true essence and function of the law. Since the law in its essence is incapable of performing this task, it is necessary, in a vain attempt to perform this task, to immeasurably intensify the force of the law, to have recourse to tyrannically harsh and despotic forms of the law, normalizing all aspects of human life. But, though correct, this explanation does not yet sufficiently clarify the problem in all its concrete fullness.

This problem can be most easily clarified by a concrete, typical example. In nineteenth-century Russia, Belinsky was a classic example and prototype of the coming Russian revolutionary (who in turn is a typical example of a utopian). Belinsky's point of departure is the affirmation (in opposition to Hegel's pantheism, which sacrifices the destiny of the person in the name of the general development of the world) of *the absolute value of every human person* and the demand directed to the world's being that conditions be established which guarantee a dignified, meaningful, happy existence for every person. Like Ivan Karamazov's celebrated speech in Dostoevsky's novel, this demand takes the form of a *revolt against the world*, the exposure of the untruth that reigns in the world, the affirmation that the good of an individual human person is of greater value than the fate of the world's development. Like Ivan Karamazov, who may have been modeled after Belinsky, Belinsky is prepared to affirm that all of the world's progress is not worth a single tear of a tortured innocent child. This formulation of the problem clearly discloses the Christian theme that a living human soul is of greater value than the whole world. But from this point there begins a fatal slipping into a deadly error. Having come to the conviction that the only order that guarantees the good of every person is socialism (or "sociality" as he calls it), Belinsky cries out with the fierce fanaticism of a Jacobin: "If the triumph of sociality calls for a thousand heads, I demand a thousand heads." Thus, a man concerned about the fate of *every* human person, a man who blames the world's order for the fact that progress is achieved at the expense of concrete human lives, is compelled by the logic of his thinking to accept the necessity of the killing of people—and of subjectively innocent people—for the triumph of a just and rational order.

The same paradoxical train of thought was repeated three quarters of a century later, in the form of collective action and on a grandiose scale, by Russian socialism as embodied in the Bolshevist, Communist revolution. But here it was revealed that the practical attainment—in the form of communism—of absolute truth requires not thousands, but many millions of "heads." Starting from the same argument as Belinsky, the communists sacrificed these millions of human lives with no pangs of conscience. But, in practice, this experiment showed that these hecatombs of human sacrifice too were without purpose, that they did not lead to the attainment of the radiant goal which was used to justify them. The bloody torture of living people, the crippling and repression of concrete life in the name of the attainment of absolute truth on earth, continues without end and without leading to the desired goal. But then, in the long process of this crippling of life, one more unexpected transformation occurs that is not part of the original plan of its initiators: the final goal itself, the kingdom of absolute good, begins to disappear from the consciousness, blocked by emotions that are necessary for this arduous path to its attainment. Power gradually passes into the hands of people whose character is adequate to the cruel, bloody work of the crippling of life, into the hands of villains and executioners, who naturally think of nothing but the protection—by all means of repression and falsehood—of their power. The radiant dream of salvation and the happiness of all people is transformed into the somber glorification of hate, cruelty, inhumanity as normal motive forces of human life. And we are possessed by a tormenting question: how is the search for truth fatally transformed into the triumph of pure evil?

The source of this paradox lies revealed in Belinsky's train of thought. The attempt to construct a new, ideal world encounters an obstacle in the imperfect world that really exists. Before constructing a new world, it is necessary to clear a place for it, to destroy the old world. But this so-called old world actually coincides, at least to a significant degree, with the general conditions of the imperfect being of the world in general. To destroy the "old world" is to destroy the world that really exists, to recognize this latter world as an evil that must be destroyed. In utopianism, the task of perfecting the world (we shall return to the problematic of this task below) is reduced in practice to the destruction of the world as it is in its general constant conditions of being, and to the attempt, using human powers, to re-create as if "from nothing" a wholly other, *ideally perfect* world. But this really existing imperfect world, created not by human will but (in spite of its imperfection) by higher, superhuman powers; this world which is the creation of God though it is burdened with sin—this world is naturally stubborn in its being, resists attempts to destroy it, and, in this resistance, turns out to be naturally stronger than its destroyers and dooms to fruitlessness the most energetic and intense efforts to destroy it. And if the "saviors of the world," the adepts and builders of a new unprecedented world, suppose that they are destroying not the very being of the world, but only the evil that reigns in it, experience shows that evil or imperfection in the makeup of this world so organically permeates its being that it cannot be destroyed without destroying this being. This determines the inevitable embitterment of the builders of the new world, the inevitability that they must gradually become habituated to a more and more universal and therefore a more and more merciless, bloody—and *fruitless*— destruction. Hence, the task of the positive construction of a new ideal world turns out to be impossible in practice; this task is put off to an indefinite future, and is replaced in practice by the task of destruction, a task that is endless because it is impossible. Instead of the promised and desired kingdom of good and truth, the king-dom of God on earth, the fanaticism of the utopians creates a collective based on unlimited, unbearable despotism. For a time, this collective can appear to be externally powerful in the way that the forces of evil in general are powerful on earth. But this powerfulness is eroded from within by forces of internecine hatred and is ex-posed sooner or later as weakness and instability. The subordina-tion of the world to forces directed at its destruction is tantamount to the unchaining of the forces of evil in the world, to the lordship of hell on earth. Thus, the attempt to realize the kingdom of God or heaven on earth within the limits of this, inevitably imperfect, world degenerates with fatal inevitability into the de facto ascen-dancy of the powers of hell in the world.

But this train of thought, this fatal destiny of utopianism, which, attempting to eliminate the imperfection of the world by the construction of a wholly new world conceived by man, leads only to the chaos of destruction, to the unchaining of the forces of evil— discloses a peculiar, particularly delicate ontological connection. If the world's being is determined by the presence and action in it of its holy primordial-ground, a presence and action that has the con-crete form of certain normalizing principles of superhuman origin and authority, the form of a "natural law"—these principles, eman-ating from God's plan for creation or, what is the same thing, from the ontological depths of being, these principles not only do not insure the absolute perfection of the world when they act within the fallen, sinful world, but are themselves full of imperfection and bur-dened with sinfulness. The true, ultimate plan of God is realized in these principles only in a lessened, imperfect form, in which these principles themselves reflect to a certain degree that very evil which they are supposed to counteract (much in the same way that in human society the protection of human life from violence is impossible except in the form of organized violence, i.e., the police or army). Precisely this constitutes the inevitable imperfection of *the law and of life that is subordinate to the law*, an imperfection from which the very task of the salvation of the world emanates. And this latter task is realizable not through the law, but through grace which fulfills the law and transforms the world's being.* And as we have just seen, the error of utopianism consists precisely in the fact that it attempts to institute something impossible: a *perfect law*, i.e., the attainment of the perfection of the world through the law, through compulsory organization.

5. The General Character and Fundamental Content of "Natural Law." The Meaning of Christian Realism

Our present subject will become clearer if we examine the general character and basic content of those ontologically rooted normalizing principles of the world's being which are subsumed under the name "natural law" or the Divine law that rules the world. In essence, this natural law is *unchangeable* and *unshakeable*. People can deviate from this law, violate it, but no human entity has the right or the actual power to revoke or change it. We have just seen how inconsistent are all such attempts to revoke or change this law, and how such attempts are fatally doomed to immanent punishment. Of course, we must remember that natural law does not at all coincide with some set of concrete norms, as it was often affirmed in the past, particularly in the seventeenth and eighteenth centur-

---

* Well-known is that subtle and profound religious dialectic which the Apostle Paul discloses in the concept of the law: Being a means of defense against sin, the law itself is derived from sin and in this sense reflects the imperfection and powerlessness of being that is burdened by sin. Paul has in mind the insufficiency of the law for the realization of the task of *personal* salvation. But as we have attempted to show, an analogous dialectic is revealed in regard to the law insofar as it is given the significance of a means to the conclusive healing or salvation of the world as a whole.

ies. Absolutely unchangeable or unshakeable concrete norms exist neither in the positive law nor in the domain of customs and mores, nor even, to a certain extent, in the domain of morality (that is, when morality is taken as a set of concrete rules of behavior that normalize the order of life in a community). There is no precisely determined, unshakeable concrete order of human life, which is obligatory in all ages and under all conditions. On the contrary, this order is not only factually changeable, but must change depending on the given state of human nature and on the concrete conditions of human life in different epochs and for different nations. There is no "natural," unchanging form of rule (e.g., monarchy, republic, etc.); there is no unchanging form of organization of the economy or unchanging concrete form of property; there is even no unchanging, uniquely right concrete form of conjugal and familial life. That which is called "natural law" is only a complex of certain *general, ideal guiding principles*, necessarily having, depending on the empirical conditions of place and time, a very diverse concrete incarnation in real positive law, in institutions, customs, and ways of life. In the order of human life, it is possible to perceive only a few general institutions and forms that precisely in their *general* essence are irrevocable and immanently present in human life despite all the changeableness of their concrete content.

The general meaning of natural law consists in the fact that it affirms a certain maximally (under the given concrete conditions) *rational* and *just* order, corresponding to the essence of man as the image of God in the creatural world, and to the guiding principle of love. The measure of the *rationality* of an order is that it guarantees that a collective, social system functions with a minimum of friction, i.e., that a social system functions in a way that is most beneficial, under the given concrete conditions, for the conservation and development of human life. In other words, the rationality of an order is determined by the fact that it facilitates to a maximal degree the realization of the higher, ideal principles of human being under conditions emanating from the imperfect state of the world (we will discuss this in greater detail in the following chapter).

The *justice* of an order consists in the principle of *suum cuique*, i.e., in the fact that the order insures the "natural rights" of every human individual, i.e., those needs and claims of the individual which emanate from his nature as the creatural bearer of God's image. This means that the rights of every given human individual must be defined in such a way that they do not reduce the rights of

172

other people, and that they do not violate the basic condition of human being: harmonious communal existence in the social unity. In other words, these rights must be defined in such a way that the maximal equilibrium and harmony of the free subjective powers of all people are established. The principle of justice is an ethical expression of the equilibrium and harmony of the world's being as a system of free, and freely connected, individual beings, as a kingdom of spirits realized under conditions of imperfect earthly being. The essence or fundamental meaning of natural law consists in the best possible harmonization of the principles of *freedom* and *solidarity*, in the affirmation of an order in which individual freedom does not take away from necessary solidarity (the general condition of communal life), and solidarity or general order is not realized at the expense of the suppression of individual freedom. Both the observance of human freedom and the harmony or solidarity of communal existence are determined by the aspiration to so normalize life that, in the plane of the external conditions of life determined by the law, both respect for the sanctity of the human person and love for one's neighbor find their active expression to a maximal degree. The order of law, insuring the freedom of the human individual and imposing certain conditions on all necessary measures that are opposed to the freedom of the individual, is an order that emanates from respect for the individual person as the image of God, from respect for a being whose activity is determined, as a general rule, by his inner, spontaneous, creative powers, by his urges and valuations as they are born in the unique individuality of his person. If man were not burdened by sinfulness and his being fully accorded with God's plan for him, his free urges would be a spontaneous expression of *love* as the essence of God, and there would be no need to limit these urges. But since these urges are always subjective and thus burdened with sinfulness and egotism, the order of law must limit this freedom in the interests of the harmony of communal life. Thus, in essence, natural law is a kind of compromise between two antagonistic principles and values, a compromise emanating from the duality of human nature, from the combination in man of the holy element of God's image and the sinfulness and imperfection of his concrete creatural-fleshly nature. It is clear from the character of the compromise inherent in natural law, that this law can in no wise be the absolutely ideal order of human life. Moreover, the very notion of an *absolutely ideal or perfect order or "law"* is a contradiction in terms.

173

On the contrary, natural law is a set of normalizing principles, inevitably reflecting in its content both the holiness of man in his ontological primordial-ground and his sinfulness and imperfection in his empirical makeup.

Against the idea of natural law in the Christian world-view is directed, from certain radical movements of Protestant thought, the substantial objection that this idea is essentially of ancient, "pagan" origin (the Stoic teaching of natural law that later entered Roman law!). This objection states that natural law can, at best, be understood as the idea of divine law and can thus be conceived as a part of the Old Testament religion; but that Christian faith, which is the religion not of nature and not of the law but of grace, is essentially incompatible with the recognition of natural law. This rather widespread objection is incorrect in two respects. On the one hand, there does exist a natural law that is based precisely on Christian faith, a natural law that *in its very content* differs from the natural law of paganism and even, in part, from the natural law of the Old Testament. Absolute respect for the holiness of the human person, the resulting principle of the fundamental freedom and equality of all people, and the principle of solidarity in the sense of the moral responsibility of people for the fate of their neighbors—all this determines the distinctive content of the natural law of the Christian world and was unknown in a distinct and consistent form prior to the Christian revelation. This gives rise to a number of essential moral-juridical norms of precisely *Christian* natural law: e.g., the fundamental impermissibility of slavery or bigamy, the impermissibility of the unlimited power of the father over the lives of the rest of the family, and the obligation of society to provide for its needy members. (The fact that the Christian world in its sinfulness sometimes sank below even the moral-juridical level of paganism and the Old Testament world does not, of course, refute the validity of the fundamental principles of Christian natural law.)

The foregoing objection is in error in an even more fundamental respect: namely, insofar as it is motivated by the idea that the Christian religion is in essence a religion not of "the law" but of "grace," or a religion that denies the religious value of all "natural" principles and overcomes "nature" by superworldly, supernatural grace. To this we must answer the following. It goes without saying (and we discussed this above) that the Christian ideal of perfection, the Christian idea of life illuminated by grace, in its essence transcends all law or order, and that therefore the concept of Chris-

174

tian moral law in the sense of an order adequate to the Christian ideal of perfection is a contradiction in terms. But our foregoing discussion (see Chapter IV, 3) concerning the relation between grace and the moral law showed that law is necessary insofar as the world's being is as yet unilluminated. Although it rejects the possibility of an ideally perfect order, although it affirms that perfection necessarily transcends all law, that it "fulfills" the law, the Christian consciousness nonetheless affirms a "law" that is necessary and obligatory *precisely in this its imperfection* as an expression of the natural order (i.e., the order that is in harmony with the will of God) precisely because it is adequate to the imperfect state of the world and human nature, and is a *necessary and uneliminable corrective to this imperfection.* In its general essence this law has everlasting force till the conclusive transformation of the world, i.e., till the advent of a new, higher aeon of conclusively saved being. And it is necessary to recognize as a profound and fatal error that direction of religious radicalism which, shaken by the sinfulness of the world and by the untruth reigning in the world, comes to the conviction that there can, in general, be no distinction between truth and untruth in this world, for all being is utterly poisoned by sinfulness. Contrary to its fundamental aspiration, this kind of religious radicalism inevitably leads in practice to the justification, the sanctioning of all kinds of evil in the world, to the atrophy of the moral valuation of human behavior and the human orders of life.

Thus, the idea of natural law as the order that is in harmony with God's will concerning the imperfect, unredeemed being of the world, is a legitimate and absolutely necessary idea. This is not the place to develop fully the systematic content of this natural law. But in the general framework of our discussion, it is essential to note at least several of the principles of this natural law as well as a small number of the generally known orders and institutions emanating from it: namely those orders and institutions that primarily express its designation determined by the ontological duality of human nature, discussed above. This is necessary because the prevailing intellectual orientation has, in part, the tendency to onesidedly affirm individual abstract principles of natural law, without understanding that they must be harmonized with other, correlative principles; and, in part, the tendency to deny radically the necessity of certain orders and institutions that emanate from natural law. Thus, liberalism and especially anarchism tend to affirm individual freedom as the absolute center and unique natural foundation of human communality. There is almost no need to mention, in contradistinction to this, that which is already demonstrated by life: for instance, that unlimited individual freedom in economic life leads to the unchaining of egotism and the unbearable suppression of the weak by the strong; and that, also in the political domain, freedom cannot be unlimited but is necessarily limited by the principle of the observance of order and solidarity. But the last several decades have been dominated by ideologies that affirm the absolute significance of the principle of solidarity or harmony in human communality, owing to which a person is denied all rights and is viewed as a blind tool, as a soulless particle of the social whole, incarnate in the all-powerful machine of the state. If, in the political domain, the world (at least the Western world) has apparently become convinced that such an ideal is unnatural and fatal, nevertheless, this ideal continues to wield power over minds in the socioeconomic sphere in the powerful movement of socialism.

In precisely the same way, the principle of equality, legitimate in itself when it is understood as the equal right of all men to an existence that is dignified and guaranteed against want, the equal right of all men to develop their inherent capabilities, and, above all, when it is understood as the universal right to participate in the construction of society—this principle becomes destructive if it is not balanced by the just as natural and unshakeable principle of *hierarchy* as free inequality, as the freely accepted order of the division of society into higher and lower entities, in accordance with the natural inequality of human capabilities. Based on the principle of equality, democracy has as its genuine foundation the commonality of the *aristocratic* nature of all people as the children and free collaborators of God; but precisely this aristocratic principle of democracy must be balanced by the aristocratic principle of inequality and hierarchy, i.e., by the natural distribution of people in an ascending and descending order, depending on the degree of their intellectual, moral, and spiritual perfection. In the contrary case, the principle of equality becomes a source of the forced, *unnatural* (i.e., opposed to natural law) abasement of the higher, the suppression of the higher by the lower.

But it is necessary in particular to note the natural-law nature and, consequently, the permanence and normative necessity of certain institutions which for the past 100–150 years have been simply rejected as antiquated and harmful prejudices. These institutions have been so criticized, condemned, and mocked by revolutionary and utopian tendencies that so-called progressive people

176

almost cannot hear the names of these institutions without a mocking smile, and that, by affirming their necessity, their value, their irrevocable rootedness in the very foundations of reality, one risks being taken for a dark and limited reactionary. Taking upon ourselves this risk, we affirm that, despite all the variety of their concrete forms, institutions such as the family, private property, and the state are not historically determined phenomena of human life which can be easily destroyed, revoked, and replaced by completely new, unprecedented orders. Rather, in their *general* essence these institutions are eternal principles of human being in which is expressed the necessity (determined by the creatural nature of man) of protecting the world, of protecting the holy primordial-ground of creatural being from chaotic, destructive powers. The New Testament, this fundamental document of the Christian moral consciousness, contains clear indications of precisely this meaning of the institutions considered. For instance, in the well-known words of the Epistle to the Romans (13: 1–5), it is affirmed that state power (and precisely state power as such, i.e., all state power that performs the function of protecting human life from evil, the function of executing "wrath upon him that doeth evil") is "ordained of God," so that "whosoever resisteth the power resisteth the ordinance of God," and therefore we must be "subject, not only for wrath, but also for conscience sake." This teaching retains its force despite the fact that the very notion of power is affirmed by Christ as incompatible with the perfect, authentically Christian relation between people (Luke 22: 25).

In precisely the same manner, although love of the flesh is an expression of the imperfection of the creatural nature of man, and "after resurrection," i.e., in the kingdom of God, according to Christ, "they neither marry, nor are given in marriage, but are as the angels of God in heaven" (Matthew 22: 30)—nevertheless, precisely in the imperfect being of the world, marriage is an inviolable holiness, for God Himself joined together male and female, making them one flesh (Matthew 19: 4–6); and therefore, according to the Apostle, conjugal love is the earthly symbol of the mysterious connection between Christ and the church (Ephesians 5: 25–32), the incarnation on earth (in conditions of the imperfect, distorted, sinful being of the world) of the *greatest holiness*, the unity of being sanctified by the saving presence of God Himself. Thus is sanctified the principle of the family, though, on the other hand, the ideal of Christian perfection demands the overcoming of familial relations as an order that constrains the spiritual freedom of man in his striving to God ("And a man's foes shall be they of his own house-hold"; "if any man come to me, and hate not his father, and mother, and wife, and children, and brethren, and sisters . . . he cannot be my disciple"—Matthew 10: 36; Luke 14: 26).

Although the New Testament does not openly express the sanctity of private property, but rather underscores the spiritual danger of riches, and affirms that the rejection of all property is the condition of total perfection—nevertheless the Old Testament commandment of respect for the property of another is understood to be implicitly valid, and the right to the free disposition of one's property (see Acts 5: 4, the story of Ananias and Sapphira) is considered to be the natural and necessary condition of the voluntary rejection of property, of the possibility of voluntary sacrifice in the name of Christian love. This indirectly represents a general directive: the principle of private property is (in view of man's earthly needs, insofar as man remains unilluminated) the condition of the real possibility of the free development of personal capacities and the realization of moral will, and therefore it is an institution that is based on the creatural nature of man and is necessary by virtue of this nature. Precisely for this reason the task of attaining a just and rational order consists not in the revocation of private property— which can lead only to the enslavement of man—but (along with the necessary limits to the possibility of the abuse of property) in its distribution to all people, in the overcoming of conditions under which there are people who are deprived of property. Thus, all these institutions or orders of natural law are characterized by the fact that, although they do not attain Christian perfection (which overcomes and transcends all of them), they are an expression of principles that are holy in their moral necessity for human existence under the conditions of the fallen, imperfect world.* In other

---

* Several contemporary German theologians distinguish between "orders of creation" (Schöpfungsordnung), i.e., orders that are part of the very plan of God's creation, and "orders of protection" (Erhaltungsordnung), i.e., orders that have become necessary after the Fall. An example of the first is the family; an example of the second is the state. This distinction seems utterly artificial to me; there is ground for it neither in the text of the New Testament nor in the general spirit of the Christian life-understanding, nor, finally, in some fundamental ontological distinction between the "orders" themselves. On the contrary, all such orders must be understood as an expression of God's will and God's truth precisely in the conditions of the fallen world; they are all conditions of the protection of the world from evil.

words, these orders or institutions express a kind of moral discipline of human existence, conditioned by the general, permanent imperfection of the creatural nature of man.

As such, these institutions have a dual nature. On the one hand they are a necessary *corrective* to the imperfection of the creatural nature of man and an expression of the higher, holy primordial-ground of creatural being itself. On the other hand they themselves are *consequences* of the inevitable rootedness of man in creatural, worldly being and therefore reflect the *imperfection* of the latter. The necessity of taking into account in human moral life (within the limits of man's being in this world) this duality, this combination of the holiness and obligatoriness of the moral principles of real human life with their imperfection—this necessity determines the meaning of what can be called *Christian realism*. And precisely this relationship conclusively clarifies for us the essence of the error of utopianism.

Pascal, with his characteristic terseness of genius, expresses this relationship in the following way: "Man is neither an angel nor a beast. The trouble is that all attempts to make him into an angel make him into a beast." Such goals of utopianism as the forced destruction of *private property*, this natural expression of individual freedom in the sphere of the imperfect, creatural, nature-dependent essence of man; the destruction of the *family*, this primary collective determined by cosmic forces, this womb which alone can nourish and nurture human being; or the elimination of the *state*, this collective self-protection of man against the chaotic, destructive powers inherent in his creatural nature—all such goals are unnatural attempts to tear man's being from the soil of the world in which it is rooted. These attempts inevitably lead to man's losing the fulcrum of his being, the solid soil on which he can find support in this world, while the chaotic, anarchic, destructive powers of his creatural being gain room for unlimited action. Precisely for this reason, man becomes a beast in practice when attempts are made to make him into an angel.

This provides a deeper clarification of what we discussed above. Genuine Christian wisdom necessarily includes *the consciousness of the inevitability in the world of a certain minimum of imperfection and evil*, i.e., the impossibility of the attainment—in the plane of "the law," in the plane of the external organizational order of the world—of the ideal perfection of human being, for *the law itself* must take into account and reflect the imperfection of man. And this consciousness leads to the conviction that the unnatural attempt to totally annihilate imperfection and evil in the plane of the world's being is inevitably connected with the danger of immeasurably multiplying the evil and woe of the world by shaking the foundations of the world's being.

Vladimir Solovyov says that the task of the state can never be to establish heaven on earth; it has another task, not less essential: *to prevent the appearance of hell on earth.* The same thing can be said about the sphere of "the law" in general in human life, about all the necessary compulsory norms and institutions that emanate from natural law.

As we have already noted, the principle of Christian realism retains its force and value despite the fact that for unscrupulous thought it can easily become a source of abuse, an occasion for justifying egotism and indifference to the suffering of our neighbors, to the lordship of untruth on earth. The fundamental distinction between Christian realism and purely earthly, ordinary realism, which is shameless indifference and adaptation to the evil that reigns in the world, consists in the fact that the recognition of the inevitability of evil in the world is combined in the Christian consciousness with *the active striving*—in another plane of being—*to attain absolute perfection*, with the search for the kingdom of God and His truth. Do not think that this fundamental distinction remains only an abstract, mental distinction and is not reflected in the practice of moral life. Christian realism is the consciousness of the danger and falsity of the utopian striving to a perfect order of human and worldly being, to perfection in the plane of the law; but in the Christian consciousness this realism is combined with *the absolute, unlimited striving to attain the free perfection of life and relations between people, to attain the free action of the powers of love.* Furthermore, it is combined with the conviction that there are no predetermined limits to the practical efficacy and fruitfulness of such striving through inner moral illumination and, hence, through the radiation of gracious powers into the world—to help our neighbor, to perfect life in the plane of its free illumination and ennoblement. This perfecting consists in the maximal development and intensity of the fundamental Christian energy: *love.* If there are immanent limits to the perfecting of earthly orders and institutions and, thus, to the success of the *compulsory* improvement of these orders and institutions, there are no predetermined limits to the active, healing, saving power of love. It is possible to doubt the attainability of such a compulsory social order, in which the very possibility of any kind of material need would be overcome automatically and once and for all. But this awareness not only does not weaken, but should even intensify our striving to realize the free, active loving assistance to the needy and troubled, our responsibility for the material fate of our neighbors. The current widespread lack of faith in the successfulness and fruitfulness of the effective power of love, in free —individual and collective—efforts to aid our neighbors, this lack of faith in "working miracles" on this path, is only a sign of our sinful weakness, our religious unfaith. And historical examples of the success of love's holy, heroic work (e.g., the work of monasteries, holy orders, etc., when they were in flower) and numerous examples of the success of individual activists of love in our own day expose the inconsistency of this unfaith.

It is precisely this dual consciousness, which corresponds to the fundamental duality (described above) of Christian life, i.e., the duality between grace and the law, or between gracious being and natural being—it is precisely this dual consciousness that constitutes the peculiar character of Christian realism and its distinction from habitual, ordinary, everyday—i.e., ungodly—"realism." Christian realism is not worship of and enslavement by the world; rather, it expresses rootedness in gracious, superworldly being, from which emanates the consciousness of the imperfection of the world and of the relative value of all human, i.e., purely worldly, reforms of the world. Precisely the *absolute radicalism* of the fundamentally superworldly position is the basis here of sober realism in the evaluation of all reforms within the limits of the world itself and by means taken from the world itself.

Christian realism is sorrow in regard to the imperfection of the world, the consciousness that this imperfection cannot be eliminated by the means of the world itself, and hence the clear and stubborn consciousness of all the responsibility of man for the creative penetration into the world of superworldly gracious powers. (The following chapter will present a more detailed examination of the relation between personal moral activity and social forms of being, a relation whose clarification has a decisive significance for the determination of the Christian position in the social question.)

6. The World as a Phenomenon of "Light in Darkness"

The considerations clarified in the present chapter add a certain new nuance of meaning to our basic theme, the problem of the light that shines in darkness. Heretofore, we have examined the relation between light and darkness in its primordial, fundamental ontological meaning. In this primordial meaning, the light is the light of the Divine Logos, the superworldly light, which in its essence transcends the world and says of itself: "I am not of the world." And in this connection the "world" means the element that opposes the light; the world is the kingdom of darkness, antagonistic to the light and receiving it not. In this sense, the world is the domain of "the power of darkness," the domain of being ruled by the "prince of this world." About the world in this sense it is said that "it lies in evil," and we are commanded: "Love not the world, neither the things that are in the world" (1 John 2: 15).

But a new concept of the world has been revealed to us which does not shake this fundamental dualism, but only fulfills it with a new idea: namely, the concept of the world as the creation of God, as the ontological ground of the being of man, this image of God and the bearer of the Spirit of God, and thus as the incarnation of the power and glory of God. It is utterly evident that the Gospels and the New Testament attach two different, seemingly opposite meanings to the world. As we have already pointed out, the commandment "love not the world" is just as valid as the affirmation that God "so loved the world that he gave his only begotten Son" for it, and the words of Christ that He came to "save the world." In the first case, the world is identified either with the darkness itself or with being insofar as it is submerged in darkness, is distorted by evil and sin. In the second case, the world is the creation of God, the kingdom of creatural and human being, but a kingdom that is tormented by the prince of this world, suffers from the darkness that has enveloped it, and thirsts for salvation. In this latter case, the world is not opposite to the kingdom of God, but is that living bearer of being which is designated to be transformed into the kingdom of God and for which this kingdom is "prepared from its foundation." On the one hand, Christ speaks of the world as an enemy that He has overcome ("Be of good cheer; I have overcome the world"), while on the other hand His work consists precisely in the salvation of the world. Paradoxically sharpening this dual, ambiguous concept of the world, we can say, in complete agreement with the authentic meaning of the Gospel as the good news: *the salvation of the world consists precisely in its liberation from the power of the world*; that is, in the salvation of creation and the image of God from the state of darkness or submergence in darkness.

This ambiguity of the concept of the world would be of no interest, would be utterly insignificant, if it could be considered a mere defect or contradiction in the terminology of the Gospels and New Testament. But, in fact, this ambiguity is grounded in *the duality of the ontological nature of the world*. Earlier we discussed the meaning of the salvation of the world, which in its essence is inconceivable within the limits of the world itself, i.e., inconceivable in a state where the world retains its usual nature or categorial form, but which rather signifies a transfiguration of the world that is connected with the *end* of the latter in its usual sense, that is, the transition to a *new creation*. From this discussion it is clear that the world as we know it is an imperfect, distorted creation; and in this sense, the New Testament views the world as an imperfect *state* of creation, distorted by sin. But the world also has an aspect in which it is the primary substance or the living bearer of creation. In this sense, the world, having a kinship to its Creator, is something valuable, holy, beautiful. And the world in this aspect is an object of God's love, an object of salvation, or (what is the same thing) the subject for which is promised and prepared transfigured being in the kingdom of God.

Understanding the world in this sense as the concrete reality of creation and using the key symbol of light and darkness, we must say that darkness is only the outer shell of the world: the world "lies in evil," in darkness. The world is submerged in darkness, but the world itself, in its primordial inner makeup, *is not darkness*. Being the creation of the Divine light, originating from Logos, bearing the stamp of this origin, the world conceals in its depths the principle of light, which, as a kind of "natural light," forms the original essence of the world. This natural light, belonging to creation itself, is the reflection of the Divine light, a reflected light, like the light of the moon.

But, owing to this, the problem of the world's being expressed in the words "the light shineth in darkness" is not exhausted by the fact that the Divine primordial-source of the light encounters the opposing darkness of the world. Together with this primary relation, another relation, derivative of and complementing the primary one, has force: "the light shineth in darkness" also in the sense that, lighting "every man that cometh into the world" (John 1: 9) or (what is the same thing) *permeating the substantial foundation of the world* and, in this its secondary form, making up the profoundest essence, the invisible heart of creation—the light abides only in these invisible depths of the world's being, while remaining outwardly surrounded and constrained by the dark shell of the world, which resists the light and which the light cannot completely dissipate and illuminate.

Among the confessional disagreements concerning the interpretation of Christian revelation, one of the most significant, precisely in its vital, practical consequences, is the disagreement concerning the problem of the relation between "nature" and "grace" (to use traditional theological terms). According to the Catholic (and Orthodox) interpretation, the world in its ontological primordial-ground, as the creation of God, *already contains* potentially and imperfectly those same positive elements which in a perfect form constitute the essence of the powers of grace, so that, as Thomas Aquinas' celebrated formula proclaims, "grace does not eliminate nature but perfects it" ("*gratia naturam non toillit, sed perficit*"). This interpretation is sharply opposed by the Reformation's conviction that there is a fundamental opposition between the sinful nature of the fallen world and the superworldly powers of grace, the conviction that there is an abyss between the two, that the passage from one domain to the other can be accomplished only by a kind of leap. The protest of the religious consciousness of the Reformation was wholly legitimate, was a valuable reminder of the essential foundation of Christian revelation, insofar as this protest was directed against the practical secularization of Christianity as a result of the forgetting or the insufficiently intense awareness of the fundamental distinction between nature and grace, between the world and the kingdom of God, between the sinful imperfection of man (including the human representatives of the church of Christ) and the ideal perfection of the powers of grace that emanate through Christ from God Himself. In our clarification of the fundamental Christian life-understanding in the symbol of the light that shines in darkness, we underscored the fundamental significance of this fundamental dualism between the kingdom of God and the world.

But here, as everywhere in the religious consciousness, the adequate truth is not contained in some abstract theological thesis, but is knowable only as an all-embracing fullness, i.e., as a unity of opposite determinations. Faith in the higher, incomparable, superworldly essence of the kingdom of God and His grace, in the fundamental and absolute opposition of grace to the "darkness of this world"—this faith, if not complemented by anything, easily leads in its onesidedness to fanatical hatred and contempt for the world and is capable of leading one away from the path of benefi-cent, meek, forgiving love, this fundamental commandment of Christian revelation. But, as we have seen, the basic goal of Chris-tian life—the search for the kingdom of God and His truth or (what is the same thing) the striving to be perfect like our heavenly Father—is necessarily attained simultaneously in two forms: in the form of the immediate directedness of the will at the kingdom of God; and in the form of reverent love for the image of God on earth, for the holiness of man in the concreteness of his creatural essence and, hence, for the holy primordial-ground of all creation as such. Theoretically, this dual directedness of the will corresponds to the recognition that—despite the opposition between the kingdom of God and the world, the opposition between light and darkness—the same superworldly light of the Divine Truth that is the unique goal and value of our life is also reflected and embodied in every human person as such and, hence, in the univervsal primordial foundation of the world. Even the concept of the church as the collective human protector and bearer of Christ's Truth on earth would be impossible if not for the recognition that the Divine light is really present in the makeup of the creatural world. Thus, pre-cisely from the fundamental *superworldly* religious position of our consciousness, we draw not contempt and hatred for the world, but tender, gracious, reverent love for the world, love for the holiness of the Divine primordial-ground of the world. This love is a *sorrowful* one, of course, full of the consciousness of the imperfection of its object, something like the love for a (physically and morally) sick child, whose weakness we are conscious of together with the pow-ers of good, potentially hidden at the foundation of his person. We shall not fall into the error of profane, antireligious humanism and "cosmism"; we shall not believe in the illusion that man and the world are good and can easily and naturally attain perfection. But neither shall we fall into the reverse error of religious acosmism and antihumanism; we shall not consider the world and man to be the "children of hell," directly opposed to God and grace. Rather, the fundamental meaning of the dualism between light and darkness, and between God and the prince of this world, must be comple-mented by the view (derivative of this fundamental meaning) that the light that shines in darkness also shines, by way of reflection, in the primordial depths of every human soul and of all creation in general. In the evaluation of the world, the Christian consciousness coincides neither with pessimism as such (how could the *good news*

185

be identical to pessimism?) nor with naive, illusory optimism based on the forgetting of the fundamental fact of the sinfulness of the world. The Christian consciousness rises above both of these positions and contains both as subordinate elements of its own fullness.

This constitutes the fundamental distinction between the Christian consciousness and all abstract dualism of Manichean or gnostic type. Although, as we have attempted to show in detail, the Christian consciousness contains as an essential element the recognition of the dualism between light and darkness, a whole spiritual abyss separates the Christian consciousness from that somber world-view which despises and hates the world as a pure incarnation of darkness. If it is said that God "so loved the world that he gave his only begotten Son" for it, and if the highest commandment of our life is the striving to the perfection of our heavenly Father, it is also clear that in this regard we must follow His example and *love* the world (of course, in a wholly different sense from the one in which we are commanded to "love not the world"). The rejection of the world as the sphere of darkness must be combined with love for the holy primordial essence of the world, in which the world reflects the light of the Logos that created it. Although we reject the world in its empirical nature as the sphere of action of the powers of darkness, we must love everything in the world that expresses its primordial ontological essence, every incarnation of a concrete "living soul" in the world. The recognition of its essence as the reflection and image of that Divine light which created it, is the ontological premise of the Christian commandment of love for our neighbor, of the reverent relation to the dignity of man as the image of God and even as the "child of God."

All this is more than abstract theological considerations. The history of mankind in general and the history of Christianity in particular bear witness to the fact that the recognition of only the transcendental holiness of superworldly Divinity, accompanied by the rejection of the world and man as a sinful, impure element opposed to Divinity, is a spiritual position that is an obstacle to the creative perfecting of the world and man, and in its fanaticism this position leads to the lordship of destructive hate and inhumanity. Indeed, such a position is directly opposed to the fundamental meaning of Christian faith as news of *Godmanhood*, the primordial kinship between God and man, and thus, indirectly, the kinship in general between the Creator and creation, despite the whole depth of difference between them. History has borne witness to the fact that only the contrary spiritual position is genuinely fruitful and beneficent, the spiritual position according to which the Holiness of Divinity is worshipped not only in its detached superworldly essence, but also in its immanent presence and reflection in the makeup of creation itself. One of the most fatal misunderstandings in the history of Christianity is the fact that the idea of the holiness and dignity of man, active love for man, as well as the reverent attention to and interest in the nature of the world (an attention and interest that produced the modern scientific investigation of the world), arose and developed to a significant degree *in opposition to the world-view of the Christian faith*. Humanism and (if we may use a new term) "cosmism," all cultural creativity based on love for man and the world, took the form of an anti-Christian and even antireligious spiritual tendency, though in fact these things are natural consequences of Christian faith, the good news, and would be inconceivable without the latter. In the history of Christian faith and thought, there have been exceptional achievements, in which a reverently loving attitude to creation, to man and the world, has emanated precisely from the depths of the detached, illuminated, superworldly consciousness. Such are the miraculous appearance of St. Francis of Assisi, the free mysticism of Meister Eckhart, the grandiose intellectual synthesis of Christian philosophy of Cardinal Nicholas of Cusa. Such also are certain types of Russian Christian thought. But beginning with the Renaissance and Reformation, and later in the age of Rationalism and the Enlightenment, religious thought in its dominant current lost its illuminated harmonious unity and took the form of an unnatural antagonism between Christianity and humanism, as well as between Christianity and reverent attention to God's world. After the difficult and edifying experience of the Middle Ages, there is no more insistent task for the Christian consciousness than to regain the true, primordial meaning of the Christian faith, namely, the unbreakable bond of this faith with true humanness and with the religiously grounded love of creation.

Love of creation and of its peak and highest expression: man; respect for man as the creatural bearer of the Divine light—this is the basis of one of the fundamental commandments of the Christian consciousness: namely, respect for *freedom*, the cult of freedom as the only medium through which light can struggle and overcome darkness. If freedom as self-willfullness is a phenomenon of man's falling away from God, owing to which man is inevitably enslaved by the devil (Dostoevsky described this situation with extraordinary power and persuasiveness), then freedom as the general spontaneity of inner life and motivation is the super-earthly element in man, in which his likeness to God is revealed: "Where the Spirit of the Lord is, there is liberty" (2 Cor. 3: 17), for the Spirit acts only in and through freedom. Despite all the imperfection of man and, hence, of his freedom, despite all the inevitability that freedom is also the freedom of wandering and error, nothing on earth can replace freedom, and all attempts to save or help man outside of and contrary to freedom are blasphemous and fatal errors. The "law" can and must limit freedom to the extent that freedom, as the freedom of evil, is directed at the destruction of the world. But all positive moral creativity is the work of grace, which acts only in and through freedom. The forgetting of this truth is a very great sin, which for many centuries afflicted Christianity—a sin which is the source of Christianity's weakness and of all opposition to Christianity. For respect for the free inner essence of man is the necessary expression of the true love for man, this central Christian commandment.

The theoretical, dogmatic foundation of this moral position consists in the thesis, developed above, that, in its primordial ground, creation—man and the world—as such is not the kingdom of darkness, but the light, the reflected light, that (like its Divine primordial-source) shines in darkness, and is compelled, in the empirical plane of being, to experience the opposition of the darkness which forms the shell of the world's being. Christianity as the religion of *Godmanhood* not only is not Manicheanism or gnosticism, but is even not abstract theism, which knows only the transcendent, superworldly God and posits an impassable abyss between the Creator and creation. Rather, Christianity, the religion of God's incarnation, is essentially *panentheism*, i.e., the recognition of *the rootedness of man and the world* (in their primordial deep essence) *in God*, the immanent presence of Divine powers, of the energy of the Divine essence, in creation itself. The recognition of the transcendence of God in relation to the world and the dualism between the Divine light and the darkness of this world is combined with the affirmation (according to the bold but apt and precise formulation of Nicholas of Cusa), of "the unity of the Creator in the Creator and creation." Only this position gives a solid foundation to the combination of religious radicalism (faith in the ascendancy of the absolute truth of God over all the powers of this world) and religious realism (the loving, tolerant relation to the holiness of human and worldly being, even though this being is darkened and distorted by the forces of sin). This position is contrary both to the banal, cold indifference to evil, the readiness to submit to the powers of this world, and to frenzied fanaticism, in which the dream of the salvation of the world degenerates into hate and contempt for the concrete nature of man and the world, into the unnatural thirst to subjugate and annihilate man and the world for their salvation.

CHAPTER SIX

Moral Activity in the World and the Task of Perfecting the World

1. Introductory Considerations

*T*he task of perfecting is the basic task and, one can say, the very essence of Christian life. For it is said, "Be perfect as your Father which is in heaven is perfect." This commandment is a summation of all the commandments of Christ's revelation. The striving for perfection, the tireless inner work of perfecting, is the necessary, determining feature of spiritual life as such. When this striving does not exist, when the creative effort of the spirit ceases, when man is completely satisfied with what he has attained and does not strive to attain what is better—then it is not the case that spiritual life is halted at a certain level, but that it is distorted in its very essence and frozen. For in its essence spiritual life is precisely tireless creativity, continuous self-overcoming through striving to attain what is better.

Most proximally, the perfecting we have in view refers to the inner spiritual being of man, which belongs to a wholly other domain of being than the world and the external medium that surrounds us. God's fundamental commandment calls us to perfect not other people, and not the world as a whole, but *ourselves*. And, as we have seen, this commandment prescribes for us not some definite action, but a definite, precisely maximally perfect state of the soul; a kind of inner spiritual being, which directly for each of us is precisely the order of our own being. But since the content of this inner perfecting is *love*, the commandment of perfecting coincides with the commandment of the development in oneself of the gracious powers of love. Being in its essence a kind of radiation outward, the power of love is expressed in *moral activity*, in loving activity for the good of one's neighbor, in the outpouring of good into the world. Thus, moral activity in the world, this general imperative of the commandment of love, coincides with the task of *the perfecting of the world* in the broadest and most general sense of this concept.

But in order to orient ourselves in the problem of the perfecting of the world as a task of Christian activity, we must clearly distinguish between different meanings of the concept of the perfecting of the world. The first and most significant distinction that we must clearly perceive in order to avoid misunderstandings is the distinction between the task of the perfecting of the world and life as the continuous overcoming of the insufficiencies of the world, as the battle with sin, the satisfaction of human needs, the amelioration of suffering, completely independent of the idea of the absolute improvement of the state of the world and the elevation of the level of the world's being—and this task of the *absolute perfecting* of the world, in the sense of the augmentation of the absolute quantity of good in the world as a consciously set goal of our activity. And here one must say that the fundamental, general, and constant task of Christian moral activity in the world is unquestionably the task of the perfecting of the world in the first of these two senses. The Christian moral position sets for itself only one conscious goal: to do good, to pour the power of good into the world, and to struggle tirelessly against the sin, evil, and disorder of the world, against the powers of destruction active in the world. Concretely, the Christian consciousness is concerned very little with whether tomorrow will in fact be better than today or whether the next era will in fact be better than the present one. The Christian consciousness leaves this task to Divine Providence.

Furthermore, Christian love in its essence is directed not at "mankind" or at the world as a whole, or therefore at a future state of mankind or the world, but at the amelioration of life, the satisfaction of need, the moral healing of the *concrete man*, our neighbor in his present concrete state. The Gospels and the Epistles never even mention the task of the perfecting of the general state of the world,

191

but they insistently and constantly call believers to active love for one's neighbor, to a constant daily concern about him, which should go hand-in-hand with the task of inner spiritual perfecting. And this is completely understandable. Whatever its moral justification and necessity might consist in, the perfecting of the general state of the world cannot at all be the task of *every* Christian soul, an obligation that can be placed alongside the two fundamental tasks of Christian life: inner perfecting and active, loving assistance to our neighbor. This follows (as we shall see in greater detail later) already from the fact that the task of the perfecting of the general state of the world demands for its realization not only good will, but special knowledge and skills, a special calling and gift of God, which are hardly given to all. If every Christian as such is called to *evaluate* the given state of life, to apprehend the harmony or disharmony of this state with Christ's truth; and if (see Chapter IV, 2) every Christian bears moral responsibility for the fate of all of his neighbors, i.e., for the general state of the world, and *in this sense* must strive to improve the world—nevertheless, not everyone can bear the burden of positive creativity in this domain. Furthermore, even the Christian church as a whole can in certain epochs be in such a relation to the world, to the powers dominant in the world, that this task of the general perfecting of the world lies outside the church's moral horizon or at least finds itself in the background. Such, for example, was the position of the early Christian church. Usually considered to be a model of the maximal fullness and intensity of Christian truth, this church did not at all set for itself the task of the perfecting of the world as a whole, of the general conditions of human life, but taught that it is necessary to combine spiritual perfecting and active love for one's neighbor with humble acceptance of the existing general state of the world. Below we shall see why and in what sense this task of the general perfecting of the world is nonetheless a part of Christian duty.

Directly below we shall attempt to clarify in greater detail the meaning and ground of the distinction between these two concepts of the perfecting of life. Here we must point out that this distinction intersects yet another distinction within the limits of the concept of the perfecting of the world. This is the distinction between paths or means of perfecting, determined by the distinction between those layers or sides of life at which the perfecting is directed. Perfecting can be the *essential-moral* introduction of good into human souls, i.e., moral education and the spiritual correction and enrichment of life. Or, perfecting can be directed at the *order* of life, at the norms effective in this order, at the relations and forms of life; and then it is socio-political perfecting. As we shall see below, these two aspects together make up the task of Christian politics in the broad sense of this concept.

The main object of our discussion is the perfecting of life or the world as a task of the *moral activity* of man. But to clarify this, it is necessary to connect this theme with the problem of the perfecting of the world as a purely ontological problem. We must understand what is the significance in the structure of the world's being of the possible perfecting of the latter, and to what extent this perfecting is possible in general. Furthermore, the fundamental task of perfecting as the solidification and development of *moral good in the world* must be posed (on the basis of what was said in the preceding chapter about the general value of creation) in connection with the perfecting of the world in other respects.

2. The Perfecting and Preservation of the World

In a certain sense the idea of the perfecting of the world, the desire to make the world happier, more rational, kinder, more beautiful, to eliminate or lessen the evil, suffering, ugliness, disorder, unreason reigning in the world—this idea and this desire are a constant, primordial, uneliminable, everlasting dream of the human heart. Schiller says:

Es sprechen und träumen die Menschen viel
Von künftigen, besseren Tagen;
Nach einem glücklichen, goldene Ziel
Sieht man sie rennen und jagen.
Die Welt wird alt und wird wieder jung
Doch der Mensch hofft immer Verbesserung.*

This dream is wholly natural and legitimate, of course. In its most general sense, this dream simply expresses the innate striving of man, as of every living being in general, for better conditions of life, for the greatest fullness of the satisfaction of his needs. In a

---

* "People speak and dream of future, better days; they all run and chase after the happy, golden time; the world ages and is renewed, but man always hopes for improvement."

more specific sense, this dream is an expression of our moral life, our moral relation to reality. Since the moral ideal, just as the ideal in general, is independent of empirical reality, but is rather the sovereign judge of empirical reality—moral activity, like all creative activity, is the attempt to embody the ideal in life or to approximate the actual order of being to that which appears to us as the ideal state of being. One can say that at every moment of our practical, active life, we are occupied with the *correction* (large or small, general or particular) of being, with the adaptation of being to our needs, requirements, desires, and ideals. The doctor who treats the sick, the policeman who arrests a criminal or restores a disrupted order, the pedagogue who teaches and shapes children, the politician who by making laws and treaties adjusts the order of life within a nation or relations between nations, even the mother who bathes her child or cleans her apartment, and the cook who prepares dinner are all occupied—each in his own way and his own domain—with the elimination of the unsufficiencies of life, the satisfaction of life's needs, i.e., the achievement of a greater agreement between human needs and the actual state of the world.

However, it is evident from these examples that this broad general concept of the correction of being is *broader* than the specific concept of its perfecting. We distinguish this everyday, banal, continuous work of the satisfaction of man's needs, the correction of the continuous spoilage of being, the restoration of that in being which perishes and is annihilated—we distinguish this from the task of the correction of being in the sense of its enrichment and improvement, the task of the *reform* of being. In reflecting on this distinction, we affirm that there is an activity directed at the correction of that which is spoiled or at the replacement of that which is destroyed and dead by something that is of equal value, or at the maintenance of the habitual level of being; and that there is another kind of activity, an activity directed at raising the level of being, the enrichment of being by *new* goods, an activity directed at the perfecting of life in the narrower sense. We distinguish between the activity of the mechanic who repairs a broken machine from the activity of an inventor of new, improved machines. We distinguish the activity of a doctor who treats a sick man from the activity of the medical geniuses who discover new, better ways of curing diseases. We distinguish the ongoing activity of a pedagogue from the reform of an educational system or the ongoing work of an administrator from state and social reforms, and so on. These examples and

194

the idea that they illustrate are so banal that their mere mention would appear to be pedantic. But it often happens that that which is most habitual and banal is the most difficult thing to notice, and it is useful to mention it. In particular, the banal idea just mentioned eliminates a misunderstanding which has taken deep root during the last few centuries in the interpretation of the nature of social and moral life.

This misunderstanding consists in the prejudice that a once-established order or level of being is unchangeably stable. That which is attained appears to be established for ever, indestructible. This leads to the idea that all correction, all activity directed at the adaptation of reality to our needs and desires, is an improvement, a perfecting of being, its enrichment, the elevation of its qualitative level, its value-level. This is the basis of the utterly arbitrary idea that progress is predetermined, an idea which we refuted at the beginning of this book and which only recently has begun to lose its popularity. According to this idea, even as it is possible to advance only forward, so that a man who has traveled a part of his path is always closer to the destination than at the beginning of the path—so a once-attained state of being cannot be lost, cannot disappear, and that therefore we always advance in all respects without having to worry about that which has been attained, about that which we already possess. Until but recently the biological theory of evolution considered it self-evident that evolution in the general sense of development (i.e., in the historical sequence of the appearance of types or forms of organisms) is *progressive* evolution, the appearance of more and more perfect, complex, life-adapted organisms or species. And the substantiated fact of the existence, together with progressive evolution, of regressive evolution, a retreat back on the path of the perfecting of living beings, was either ignored or seemed a rare exception, something that marred the general comforting picture of evolution. This superficial and essentially false biological doctrine was transferred to the social sciences; or, perhaps, the already formed idea of cultural and social progress facilitated the crystallization of this biological doctrine even before this idea received seeming support from this doctrine.

The ultimate scientific foundation of this view was an idea that took hold in the physics and chemistry of the nineteenth century in the form of the laws of the conservation of matter and energy, namely, the idea that destruction does not exist in the world, that the world is essentially stable, that (to use the nineteenth-century German philosopher Riehl's formulation) the world is a "conservative system." It is true that this conception assumes not only that nothing perishes in the world but also that nothing originates, nothing is created, in the world; that in the world there is neither destruction nor creation; that the world in its ground is eternally immobile, is such as it is, and that, in essence, there is nothing left to do in the world, there remains no room for the meaningful creative activity of man. This was a revival of the ancient teaching of the Eleatics that all change is only "apparent." But with an inconsistency characteristic of human thought governed by subjective sympathies and desires, this nineteenth-century socio-moral conception assimilated herefrom only the idea of the impossibility of destruction, in order to glorify the ease and power of *positive* change, namely, the creation of the new and better.

In our own time the conceptual fog on which this tendency of thought is based has already been dissipated to a significant degree. As we have already pointed out in our Introduction, the horrible cataclysms experienced by us—the unexpected revival of savage barbarism in cultured Europe, the use of the highest achievements of scientific progress for the destruction of life and culture—have dissipated faith in the ease, continuity, and predeterminedness of progress. Historical knowledge has shown the alternation of flowering and dying cultures, the alternation of ages of culture and barbarism. The further development of the life sciences has shaken the simplistic harmonious conception of Darwinism concerning the development of organisms through their continuous, progressively more efficient adaptation to the environment; the life sciences have discovered that such processes as progressive and regressive evolution are, to a significant degree, spontaneous. Finally, the most recent development of the physical and chemical sciences has shown that even the fundamental, elementary composition of being is not at all so unchangeably stable as presupposed by the laws of the conservation of matter and energy; and that, for example, in some cases matter disintegrates and disappears; and if energy in its essence is indestructible, nevertheless the overwhelming majority of physicists believe that the quantity of activity produced by energy fatefully decreases due to the principle of entropy, so that the world is approaching a state of the uniform dissipation of energy, tantamount to the calm of death. And if other physicists believe in the existence of creative powers, which can

196

make up for this continuous loss of the useful work of the world, these creative processes are only conceived as compensation for the destructive processes.

But there is no need to study in detail the abstract achievements of contemporary science to distinctly recognize that the greater part of human activity is directed at the simple maintenance of life on a once-attained level. A gigantic amount of the economic energy of mankind is spent on the constant restoration of exhausted, i.e., annihilated, goods necessary for life, on the simple maintenance of life. People work in order to live tomorrow not worse than today or simply in order not to die of hunger tomorrow. As a general rule, the social organism functions not otherwise than an individual organism, which maintains its life through nourishment and respiration, replacing the consumed, burnt-out particles of the body with new ones. Likewise, in the life of the species the birth of new organisms compensates for the death of old ones. These and similar elementary facts bear witness to the fact that an enormous, intense energy is necessary to maintain life in the steady state, i.e., at the previous level. The same thing applies, of course, to all domains of human culture: persistent efforts are needed in order to maintain in the succession of generations the accumulated store of knowledge and moral skills, in order to prevent the lowering of the general level of life. But the political experience of our time teaches that an intense effort is necessary to protect the once-attained store and level of culture from powerful forces directed at the destruction of this store and level. All further enrichment, all "progress," is only an additional attainment, which can and (according to our dreams, our desires) must accumulate on top of the conservation of that which is already possessed but which is not at all assured; and this enrichment cannot be the only goal of our activity. However frequently conservatism degenerates into the egotistical striving of the ruling classes to protect their privileges, their exclusive exploitation of the higher level of life, from the striving of other classes to participate in these privileges—conservatism, as the task of maintaining and defending the material and spiritual achievements accumulated in the past, saving them from the doom that constantly threatens them, is one of the uneliminable tasks of the human spirit, a task that, at the very least, is just as essential and necessary as the striving for "progress," the further perfecting of life. These tasks often (and even usually) collide and compete, are in a relation of mutual conflict, but this occurs only when they are formulated incorrectly, when their fundamental intent is distorted. For, in essence, all progress not only is accumulated on top of the conservation of that which has already been attained (one cannot add a new floor to a house by destroying its foundation), but is also created by powers accumulated in the past. Even as, according to Disraeli's wise thought, freedom is guaranteed only by tradition, so, in general, all successful and stable creation of the new is wholly determined by the stability of the healthy powers of the social organism, firmly rooted in the old, habitual, native soil. Furthermore, these two tasks are not only connected to each other and in harmony, but they have at their base an identical nature. For the protection of old, already-attained goods is not a passive watch over their security (a police watch, as it were); rather it is an active creation to compensate for the old which constantly dies and disappears. The birth of new cells of an organism during its growth and maturation, and the birth of new cells to replace those which have burnt out and died—generation and regeneration, as the biologists call it—are one and the same creative process. And even the simple battle with foreign microorganisms that have invaded the organism and cause disease is waged by the same creative energy of the organism.

These general considerations of elementary life-wisdom acquire an especially clear and distinct meaning when they are examined in relation to the basic religious theme of our book. We confront a rationally unexplainable but uneliminable general fact of human being: the mysterious power of evil and sin in the world. The enemy we must battle is not an external, temporary, accidental enemy, but a permanent inner one, concealed in the depths of our heart. This enemy is sin. The power of destruction and death is, in the final analysis, everywhere (in organic life not less than in the sphere of morality and culture) the power of sin, "darkness." Precisely for this reason, the task of the simple protection of life acquires such primary importance. If in the battle against the primordial inner enemy, the "prince of this world," we succeed in turning him back, forcing him to retreat, weakening his power, we must consider this an especial success, but even simple tireless resistance, simple courageous defense against him, is a success, and, in any case, our permanent duty. And we must never forget that a final victory is impossible here, that, even after the greatest victories, we must remain vigilant, for the enemy will collect his powers for a new offensive and the indestructible force of evil will be revealed in the most unexpected new forms.

3. Constancy and Change of the World. The Perfecting of the World as the Affirmation of Its Unshakeable Foundations. The Perfecting and Salvation of the World.

The other side of the foregoing relationship is the relation between the changeableness and constancy of the world. Perfecting is a form of change of the world. Faith in the possibility of perfecting presupposes clear answers to the questions: To what degree can be world be changed? What changes are possible? What is the true meaning of these changes? These questions coincide with the question: What are the limits of history?

Only in the nineteenth century, scarcely more than 100 years ago, was history born as a science and did mankind acquire the possibility of taking account of its past, the general character of its development—not in the form of legend, but in the form of more or less reliable, critically verifiable knowledge. This past encompasses those five or six thousand years which probably coincide with the total duration of what merits the name "history"—a process of relatively rapid and ever-accelerating events and changes of the make-up and conditions of human life. This revelation of the picture of the world's history made it possible to recognize for the first time that mankind as a whole, like an individual man, has a consistent life-history; for the first time, mankind learned the history of its childhood and youth, the dramatic process of its maturation. The static picture of the general unchanging makeup of man's being was enriched by an elucidation of its dynamic element, by the awareness that mankind finds itself in a constant process of movement, that it continuously moves somewhere, moves "forward" as people usually say, though this "forward" does not signify anything precise or definite. This birth of historical self-awareness coincided with the emergence and solidification of that deceptive idea of continuous, predetermined "progress" whose inconsistency we have already sufficiently clarified. During the entire nineteenth century, historical development—just as biological evolution in the life sciences—was simply identified with progressive development, with the growth of "civilization." It was pointed out above that this naive idea can now be considered overcome, deposited in the archive of errors. But another, more general, one-sidedness that the birth of historical self-awareness introduced into human ideas about the world has not yet been overcome. The nineteenth and twentieth centuries are considered to be the "centuries of history," an epoch in which the theme of history dominates human thought. The old idea of the immobility, the unchangeableness, of life is replaced by the idea of universal changeableness, of life as a turbulent process of motion, constant change. According to the general idea of life that is dominant now, life has nothing constant, stable, permanent; everything in life changes, grows old, and is replaced by the new.

It is clear from our previous discussions that we do not agree with this prevailing "historicism." It is a onesided conception, a historical phenomenon that is destined to pass. The idea that nothing is constant in being *except the all-embracing process of change itself* contains an internal contradiction, for if universal changeableness is a constant, unchanging feature of all human life, there is no ground to deny the possibility of other unchangeable properties and laws of life. Historicism is a subtype of relativism and is therefore characterized by the philosophically generally known internal contradiction of relativism: in affirming as an absolute, unshakeable truth the relativeness of everything, relativism denies its own content in the very form of its affirmation. The concepts of the relative and the absolute (unconditional) are correlative and lose all rational meaning outside of this correlation; the same thing holds for the concepts of change and unchangeableness. Where change is, there is something changing; and this latter concept is equivalent to the concept of the constant.

Beyond all philosophical theories, common sense knows that in the world and human life much changes, but much remains unchanged. All forms of being change, but the essence of being does not change. As the French saying goes: *"plus ça change, plus c'est la même chose."* A man could not remember his childhood and youth, if he did not know that they are precisely his childhood and youth, if his essence were not fundamentally self-identical. Likewise, we could have no historical knowledge, we could not understand the past, we could not finds words to express it, if we had nothing in common with the past, if the past were more than a variation of the permanent, common theme of human life, familiar to us from our own experience. Homer's war, with its chariots, the face-to-face combat of heroes, bronze swords, is utterly unlike to-day's wars, with tanks and airplanes; but Homer's war was also a *war*. Its cruelties, death and destruction, the unchaining of hate and vengeance, as well as the sorrow filling the human heart from the horrors of war, are all familiar to us from the experience of yester-day and today. And in Homer's epic, in the picture of the distant past that is foreign to us, we find what is close and familiar—a specimen of the eternal, unchangeable fate of man. Hector's scene of farewell with Andromache, the fire and destruction of Troy, Hecuba's wailing, are these not pictures of the yesterday and today of our lives? Or how could we read and acquire edification from the Bible if our life today—despite airplanes and the wireless, despite socialism and universal education—were not the same human life about which the Bible speaks? As before, good struggles against evil; as before, the dreams of the human heart founder on the cruelty and indifference of the powers reigning in this world; as before, the wise men of this world mock the faith in good and truth; as before, man, despite everything, lives by hope. The old truth of Ecclesiastes is true today: "The thing that hath been, it is that which shall be; and that which is done is that which shall be done; and there is no new thing under the sun. Is there any thing whereof it may be said, See this is new? it hath been already of old time, which was before us" (Eccl. 1: 9–10). And if the Apostle says, "the form of this world passeth away" (1 Cor. 7: 31), he has in mind the longed-for end of the world. This very concept of the "form of this world" signifies that the "world" has a certain unchangeable form, remains, despite all possible changes, what it was, is, and will be until its end.

In this its New Testament sense, "the form of this world" has, most proximally, a negative meaning: it is the form of the world determined by the presence in the world of the universal fact of sin. But as we have seen, "the form of this world" has another aspect in which it has a positive meaning: an aspect in which it is the crea-tion of God and derivatively (by the fact that man belongs to it) the image and likeness of God. In this latter sense, "the form of this world" is the totality of the everlasting, divinely established founda-tions of being. On the one hand, these foundations express God's plan for creation; and on the other hand, they are the divinely established unchangeable corrective for the fact of the Fall, the totality of principles and forms protecting the world's being from the destructive powers of sin.

Thus, the unchangeableness of the general essence of the world's being is something greater and more significant than merely a factual feature of this being, affirmed by observation or thought. This unchangeableness has a normative significance: it is an expression of the unshakeableness of the divinely established order of being, the unshakeableness of that "natural law" which cannot be eliminated or violated with impunity. Whatever the nature of the historical process of the change of forms and makeup of universal-human life, this process cannot consist in the mere departure from the unshakeable foundations of being, in their replacement by wholly new foundations. The nature of this process consists, rather, in the manifold varying of the concrete incarnation of these ideal foundations, in a more or less perfect expression of these foundations. The ideal goal of the aspiration to the perfection of the world consists in the attainment of the maximal adequacy of the concrete forms of human life to these unshakeable, eternal normative conditions or foundations of the world's being. As Rilke says wisely:

Wandelt sich rasch auch die Welt,
Wie Wolkengestalten,
Alles Vollendete fällt
Heim zum Uralten.*

If above, in accordance with habitual, popular ideas, we distinguished between reform (i.e., the creation of what is better) and correction (i.e., the restoration of what is ruined or destroyed), we see now that from a profounder point of view or in a broader philosophical perspective these two things coincide in the final analysis. For all reform, all improvement, all perfecting of being is, in the final analysis, only the correction of the spoilage that has crept into being, the attempt to restore the healthy state that corresponds to the unchangeable essence of being. When our activity is directed at the correction of what is spoiled, at the restoration of what was destroyed yesterday or in the recent past, we speak of the simple *protection* of the world in its old, habitual state. When our activity is directed at the correction of the spoilage that crept into the world

---

* "Even if the world changes rapidly, like the contours of clouds, all that is perfect returns to the primeval."

long ago, at the new acquisition of what was lost long ago, we speak of the *perfecting* of the world. In the final analysis, all perfecting of the world is the battle against destruction and calamity introduced into life by sin. The reform of life is justified and beneficial not when it is the fruit of the simple human intent to make life "better," to discover and to introduce in the world an order that we think is better, more ideal. The reform of life is justified and beneficial only when it responds to some essential, acutely felt *need*—when it corrects some glaring injustice, sets aright some intolerable disorder, re-establishes the social harmony, saves people from some tormenting calamity. "Sufficient unto the day is the evil thereof." This is not only an exhortation not to burden ourselves with cares about our personal future material needs; in a more general sense, these words are also applicable to our moral activity for the good of our neighbor. The other side of this relation is that every objectively justified reform is a restoration and revival of a return to the normal, healthy, primordial, natural order of life. It goes without saying that this does not reduce history to a mere "running in place," an eternal repetition of one and the same thing. Since the conditions of human life and the concrete historical state of mankind change continuously, at every given historical moment creative efforts of thought and will are necessary in order to find a new, appropriate, concrete expression for the moral equilibrium and stability of life, i.e., for the incarnation of the unshakeable general foundations of the world's being. The genuine, absolute restoration of the historical past is inconceivable. Lost equilibrium is always restored on a *new* level (see Chapter V, 5 on the essence of natural law). The element of change and development of being must be taken into account here equally with the element of the indestructibleness and unshakeableness of the general foundations of being. As we have pointed out, conservatism and "progressism" (if we may use this term) are in essence not two opposing tendencies, but correlative elements of social-moral creativity. The improvement of life through the creation of new forms of life, corresponding to its changed inner and outer conditions, is also the restoration of the disrupted old, unchanging essence of life and is genuinely justified only as such.

Understood in this way, the task of the positive perfecting of life in the sense of the augmentation of the absolute quantity of the good in life is, of course, wholly legitimate. It is true, as we have pointed out, that this task cannot be the only task of moral activity, but must be secondary to the more essential task of the protection of the world from evil, the conservation of what has been attained in the world. The falsity and artificiality of the prevailing intellectual tendency of the last few centuries consist in the forgetting of this simple and evident truth. The general improvement of life, the absolute accumulation in life of good, happiness, dignified conditions of existence, is guaranteed neither by the sober observation of life nor by Christian faith. On the contrary, Christ predicted that the world will be spiritually unprepared to the very moment of its end and completion (Matthew 24: 38–39; Luke 18: 8). The idea of this general improvement of the world is only an uneliminable dream of the human heart, a postulate of our moral consciousness. Here, the words of the poet are valid: *"Du musst hoffen, du musst wagen, denn die Götter leihn kein Pfand"* ("You must hope, you must dare, for the gods do not give guarantees"). Faith in the success of our battle against evil, faith in the possibility that good will gradually, step by step, vanquish evil and take over the field of battle is a constant hope of the human heart; this faith is legitimate as long as it does not weaken our will with dreamy optimism, does not distract our attention from our responsibility for the simple protection of the world from evil.

But another thing also follows from the above. Even under the condition, never in fact attainable, of the complete success of this activity of the positive institution of good in the world, this activity can never (as we have indicated) lead to absolute perfection and remains separated from perfection by an insuperable abyss, for this activity remains the activity of the perfecting of an *essentially imperfect* world. In other words, the perfecting of the world does not coincide with its "salvation"; and wherever these two concepts, these two tasks, are confused, we are faced with the fatal error of utopianism (which we have sufficiently clarified), which leads in practice not to the improvement but to the significant *worsening* of the state of the world. The perfecting of the world cannot be its salvation, for the latter is that final triumph of the kingdom of God by which evil will be conclusively overcome and the world will be transfigured into a new creation, illuminated throughout by God's truth and power. This must be that "end" when Christ will "put all enemies under his feet" and deliver up "the kingdom to God, even the Father" (1 Cor. 15: 24, 25). According to Apostle Paul's profound thought, the distinctly visible, external sign of this salvation of the world as a genuine *ontological revolution in creation* will be the end of the metaphysical evil of death: "The last enemy that shall be destroyed is death" (1 Cor. 15: 25). For it is utterly evident that as long as death is master, the tragedy and imperfection of life cannot be overcome.

From this it is clear that not only the protection of the world from evil, but all human perfecting of the world is separated by an insuperable abyss from the genuine, essential salvation of the world—however much the human heart (and precisely the heart full of compassion for the woes of the world) tends to confuse these two tasks. If, following the Gospel tradition, we conceive salvation as a kind of healing, then the distinction between the salvation and the perfecting of the world will roughly correspond to the distinction between the radical healing of a sickness and palliative treatment that only moderates suffering and gives strength to the sick person. In regard to the sickness of the world, the former is a work that surpasses all human powers and is accessible only to the all-powerfulness of God. The latter is the work of human activity, only fortified by the powers of grace. Here, without overcoming the world as such, the perfecting of the world necessarily occurs in categorial forms of the habitual being of the world, that is, it is reduced to a relative improvement of life in the world—within the limits of the general ontological imperfection of the world, i.e., under conditions of the world's being determined by the fundamental fact of *sin*, which cannot be eliminated by human efforts. As Kant aptly says in his meditation on world history: "Out of the crooked timber of humanity no straight thing can ever be made." Whoever in his blindness and pride does not take into account this fundamental fact not only can never attain his goal, but, instead of perfecting human life, ruins and destroys it. All "saviors" of mankind have in fact been its destroyers; no criminals have caused so much evil and suffering in the world, have brought so much disorder into life, as people who have thought themselves called and able to save the world.

4. The Meaning of History

Everything said above and particularly our critique of the faith in progress, in the predetermined continuous perfecting of life, naturally arouses one objection or doubt: namely, if all this is so, does it not follow that the world's history lacks all meaning, is meaningless motion or turbulence without any definite direction, is (to use Dostoevsky's apt phrase) "a vaudeville of devils"? But the human heart and, consequently, the human mind cannot be satisfied with such a negative, destructive conclusion. For then the personal life of each of us would lose all meaning, for this life, being inextricably interwoven with universally human life, would inevitably have to share the meaninglessness of the latter. If the life-achievements of each of us are not points of departure or reference for the further achievements of our children and future generations; if all we have achieved can disappear without a trace, without being of use to anyone, then it is meaningless to care about or concern ourselves with anything at all. And there would be nothing left but to indulge in that wisdom of despair which is expressed in the cynical slogan *carpe diem*. Does not our argument drive us into the dead end of that very same cynical unfaith from which it sought a way out?

The general answer to this objection or doubt was already contained in the considerations of our introductory meditation, which disclosed the ground of our faith in Divine Providence. We saw that we have the right, first of all, to affirm the active participation of higher, Divine powers in human and worldly life; and, second, to believe in a mysterious meaning of life that is inaccessible to our understanding, a mysterious meaning determined by the ascendancy of Divine Providence over all of being. The religious man can doubt that the world's history has some higher meaning (though a meaning that is inaccessible to him), that it has some higher purpose—as little as he can doubt that his personal life is not a linkage of meaningless accidents, but is called to something, is guided by the will of our heavenly Father. The only question that can be put here is: To what extent are we able to understand this meaning, to penetrate into the mystery of Divine Providence?

In regard to our personal life, each of us has at least a chance to understand its meaning, to find out why we have been sent into the world, what is the rational plan that gives meaning to the sequence of outwardly random peripeteias, the connection of separate epochs and events of our earthly existence. This chance is given to us at the moment of dying, when the picture of our life is wholly present before our spiritual gaze. As we have already pointed out in our Introduction, to understand anything at all, it is necessary to have the possibility of surveying it as a whole in all its fullness. The understanding of life is like the understanding of a work of art, particularly a work of drama; the inner connection of separate episodes, the idea that dominates all the episodes, becomes clear when the drama ends and the curtain descends for the final time. Of course, not every personal life is a finished, harmonious, perfect work of art; this is rather a rare exception. Insofar as we create our life, we are unskillful artists, and very often do things that confuse and distort the artistic unity of the whole. But the plan of the whole can nevertheless appear through all these distortions and errors. And becoming aware of this plan, we can often understand what higher meaning (a meaning we did not understand before) even our errors have.

The situation is completely different in regard to the history of mankind or the world. We are always in the center of this history and we are not able to see its end. We are forced to leave the theater before the curtain descends; and not knowing what will happen after we leave, we are not in a position to see the world's drama as a whole and to understand its meaning. Furthermore, we are not present in the theater from the beginning of the drama; we enter in the middle of the action and are present for only part of the drama, without seeing the beginning or the end. And although we have the opportunity to find out (though never fully) what occurred before our arrival (this is what constitutes historical knowledge), the center of our attention must be the fragment of the drama which we see, i.e., that which historians call "our age." We judge the past and guess the future only on the basis of "our age." This inevitably creates an artificial, truncated perspective.

Hence, all attempts to rationally understand the drama of the world's history, to find out its meaning, its determining goal, are doomed to be essentially impotent and vain. Such attempts are made by the so-called philosophy of history, the most problematic and least achievable of all the strivings to attain a generalizing understanding of life, represented by "philosophy." From the first attempt, made by St. Augustine, to make sense of the world's history to Hegel's classic "philosophy of history" (the model for all subsequent attempts of this kind), human thought, guided by the general belief in the existence of a general plan of world history, by some form of faith in Providence—has attempted to penetrate the mystery of this plan. All such attempts not only age comparatively quickly and lose the interest they excited in their own time in the further course of history and with the further development of historical self-awareness, but they are also essentially doomed to failure, are inadequate to their object. Here, every construction is arbitrary, and is determined by two distorting errors, without which it would be impossible in general. Not knowing anything about the future, not being in a position even to imagine its content (at least the content of the more distant future), we involuntarily view *our* age, the epoch of the "present," as the culmination of the whole historical process, i.e., as its end, or at least the approach to the end. But on the other hand this present stands at the center of our attention, and our interest in the past, as well as the possibility of understanding the past, decreases with distance from us. Millennia of the remote past seem less significant to us than centuries of the more recent past or decades of that proximal past that has occurred before our eyes. And although there is reason to think that history really is (at least in some respects) a process of ever-accelerating motion, it is utterly evident that such an assessment is, in the overwhelming majority of cases, simply an error of perspective, determined by our purely subjective interest in the present. With some exaggeration, we can say that all philosophies of history are constructed according to the following scheme of division: (1) from Adam to my grandfather; (2) from my grandfather to me; and (3) I, my epoch, and all that comes out of my epoch. The arbitrariness of this perspective immediately strikes any unprejudiced mind. But what can be expressed here with a legitimate claim to genuinely objective significance?

I think that the only positive judgment we can make about the meaning of history is that history is *the process of the education of mankind.* Education, most proximally, is not identical at all with "progress," with continuous, successive improvement (as it was understood by Lessing, who first expressed this idea). The idea of education expresses only that the past does not pass in vain, that it somehow participates in the present and is utilized by the present, i.e., that some sort of process of accumulation, enrichment occurs here. I deliberately say "some sort of process," for the concept of accumulation or enrichment must be understood here only in the most general form, which does not pre-decide its concrete content. This concept means only that the history of mankind, like the history of an individual life, is a process in which *the past is conserved in the present,* a process in which every successive step or stage is really a continuation of the preceding step or stage: all that comes after is connected to what has come before, is accumulated on top of and supported by what has come before, and contains the latter. In other words, history is inconceivable without memory. Nothing is lost, nothing vanishes without a trace; all the achievements of the past, all great cultures, even those that at first sight appear to have been swept off the face of the earth and forgotten, leave a deep trace and are often reborn in a new form, as was the case, for example, with the classical Greek culture, which, after nearly a millennium of apparently complete oblivion, flowed into (through Arabic philosophy, Thomas Aquinas, and the Renaissance) the European consciousness and determined the culture of the modern period. Before our eyes the great ancient cultures of Asia, India, and China, are beginning to influence the spiritual world of the West. But even where this influence is not noticeable, even where in the perspective of historical judgment the life of the past has vanished (the historians speak, for example, of the vanishing of the Mayan culture in Central America), there is reason to assume that the traces of this life continue to act in the unconscious, in the blood and soul of the descendants. Psychology teaches that absolute forgetting does not exist, that all that has apparently been forgotten completely and forever can be remembered under certain conditions—which is evidence of its indestructible potential conservation in our soul. And this general affirmation is applicable to collective life not less than to individual life. In the last analysis, this is based on the universal ontological fact that the very concept of time, of the temporal process, as a continuous flux in which the past flows into the present and the future, is inconceivable (as Bergson justly pointed out) without the presence of something like a cosmic memory, for time and memory are correlative concepts. *Faithfulness to the past*, the conservation of the past in the present, and the action of the past in the present, are the very essence of what we call consciousness or life; and mankind in this sense, according to Pascal's profound and true thought, is one large man. All temporal life, all transition, motion, change, is embraced, permeated, and conserved by the unity of eternity. History has meaning precisely because it is the development, unfolding, disclosure, and incarnation of the eternal power of being. And on the other hand, eternity is not a fixed, dead unity, but the unity of eternal life, which is expressed only in the dynamism of continuous, successive incarnation. But for the Christian, believing in the absolute meaning of the incarnation of God and the sacrifice of Christ, the possibility of an even more concrete understanding of the meaning of history is revealed. For the Christian, history is a Divine-human process. The incarnation of the powers of eternal life in the concreteness of history must from this point of view be understood as the incarnation in history of the light of Christ's truth or as the continuous creative action in history of the Holy Spirit sent down to us to continue Christ's work. Most proximally, this does not at all mean that in this form we return to the idea of continuous progress which we had rejected above. On the contrary, mankind in this regard follows its predetermined path just as an individual man follows his: through epochs of rise and fall, advance and retreat, moments of creative energy and moments of fatigue, decline, regression—through moments of the faithful service of the truth and moments when the truth is forgotten and betrayed. Being a Divine-human process, history reflects all the imperfection and inconstancy of sinful mankind. In its tragedy, in its empirical meaninglessness, history most proximally is, according to Pascal's profound thought, Christ's *agony*, lasting until the end of the world. On the other hand, observing how slowly and only gradually in the course of centuries mankind has really assimilated the meaning of Christ's revelation; how late, for instance, Christ's revelation of the Godsonhood of man, of the dignity of the human person, was understood and began to attain practical realization, we have the right to believe that history is in fact—despite all its deviations and betrayals—the process of the gradual incarnation of Christ's revelation in the reality of man and the world. The paths and peripeteias of this incarnation are unknown to us; in our conjectures about them, we must beware thoughtless optimism, which would only be an expression of our self-satisfaction and pride. The incarnation of Christ's revelation, of Christ's truth, on earth is realized in the battle against darkness and the inertia of the human heart. Nevertheless the promise that the Divine light cannot be overcome gives us the right to believe that—often retreating into the invisible depths, chased by the powers of this world—the mustard seed planted by Christ continues to develop, grow, and mature into a gigantic tree, that a small leaven gradually, invisibly causes all the dough to rise. In this indefinite form, which fundamentally takes into account the unfathomableness of Divine Providence, we have *the only justified form of faith in "progress"*—faith in the approach of the world, by complex and mysterious ways, to its ultimate goal, faith in a kind of inner ripening of the world, preparatory to its ultimate illumination and transfiguration.

As a Divine-human process, the world's history is based on the interaction between the Divine power of the light that has streamed into the world's life and the reception of the light by man, or, contrarily, the resistance of man and the world to the light. Thus, two aspects must be distinguished in the makeup of the world's history: the action of the Divine power of the light which helps man and the world to defeat the darkness; and the purely human aspect of this history. The perfecting of the world can therefore be dual: Either it is the penetration of the Divine light, i.e., Christ's truth, into the human soul, and, as such, it is essential moral and spiritual perfecting. Or it is a purely human perfecting, the accumulation of human powers as tools that serve the good; in this sense it is technical perfecting in the general, broad sense of the word "technical"; or more precisely it is intellectual perfecting. Let us first examine this type of perfecting.

5. Intellectual Progress. The Technical and Organizational Perfecting of the World

Of all possible types of progress, the successive perfecting (from generation to generation) of life, the most unquestionable is purely intellectual progress, the gradual accumulation of knowledge and consequent practical skills. Of course, even this type of progress is not continuous. In the history of intellectual progress, facts bear witness to the possibility of periods when development is halted as well as (perhaps even more frequently) periods of decline and loss of the knowledge acquired by preceding generations. Specialists say that for thousands of years China possessed a large store of scientific knowledge, which later was completely forgotten. After having attained a certain level of astronomical and mathematical knowledge, the ancient East, Babylonia and Egypt, "froze" at this level for many centuries, perhaps for millennia. But when ancient Greece became acquainted with this knowledge, it advanced it with astonishing speed, and in the course of two or more centuries created a grandiose system of scientific knowledge. This turbulent period of scientific flowering was followed by a fall, which lasted more than a millennium and a half. Beginning with the Renaissance and especially the seventeenth century, European mankind finds itself in an epoch of astonishingly rapid scientific progress, which has advanced to our own age. There is no reason to think that this time the progress will not cease. Furthermore, it is necessary to point out that intellectual progress occurs comparatively

211

easily and stably only in such domains as mathematics and the natural sciences. In the humanitarian sciences and especially in philosophy, it is much more difficult to rely on the continuous accumulation of knowledge in the course of many generations. Since the conservation of this latter type of knowledge is impossible in the form of the simple mechanical transmission of its results from one generation to the next, but demands a continuous concentration of the intellectual gaze and, to some extent, a concentration of all the spiritual powers—what has been attained here can easily be lost in the succession of generations. In philosophy, for instance, phenomena of "progress," of continuous perfecting, are rather rare fortunate exceptions, as though separate brief bursts of intellectual light, succeeded by long periods of decline and stagnation. Mankind appears to tire easily from the concentration of intellectual and spiritual energy required for the progress of philosophical knowledge.

With all these qualifications, it is nonetheless necessary to admit that if we set aside extraneous causes, external and internal (the former include the destruction of culture by wars and sociopolitical revolts, while the latter include general moral-spiritual decline and degeneration)—the purely intellectual attainments of human thought, easily transmitted and assimilated from generation to generation, have, as a general rule, the tendency to multiply and be perfected in the course of time; subsequent generations build new stories of knowledge on the foundation raised by the preceding generations.

But in regard to our overall theme, we are interested not in the topic of scientific or intellectual progress as such, but only in the development of knowledge in its significance for the general perfecting of life. Just comparatively recently the question of the practical significance of the development of knowledge for the improvement and perfecting of life was never even raised, so indisputable seemed the answer to it. The growth of knowledge is the growth of the skill and power of man; this truth, proclaimed by Bacon, has firmly entered the modern consciousness. And to this truth has been added a second premise, which appears to be as self-evident as the first: the conviction that the growth of skill and power in itself guarantees a greater chance of a happy, healthy, rational life, i.e., leads to a general perfecting. For the age of Auguste Comte, Spencer, and Buckle, intellectual progress simply coincided with the progress of "civilization," and the latter coincided with the general perfecting of life.

But now, through bitter life-experience, we have learned the simple truth that intellectual progress in itself guarantees only the growth of the external skill and power of man, or what can be called the technical and organizational perfecting of life. But the latter signifies only perfecting in the use of *means* for the attainment of set goals; whether this leads to a *general* improvement of the conditions of human life or to their worsening depends on precisely what goals are attained by this perfecting of means. The growth of human power through progress in the skill with which the forces of nature are exploited can, depending on the direction of human will, be used either for the good or for the harm of man. A powerful benefactor is more beneficial than a powerless one, but a powerful tyrant is more harmful and dangerous than a powerless one. It happens even more frequently that the growth of man's power is useful for general perfecting in one respect but harmful for it in another respect, so that the overall balance of credits and debits can tilt to one side or the other.

This is a simple, evident truth, but bitter experience has been necessary for people to become convinced of it. The first disappointment for mankind resulted from experience with the invention of mechanized production. If already Aristotle dreamed that by compelling the powers of nature to work for him man would free himself from the curse of the necessity of hard labor to maintain his life, experience has shown that mechanized production, although reducing the cost and multiplying the quantity of consumer goods, has enslaved the working part of mankind, has doomed it to a labor more exhausting in terms of strain and monotony than the former manual labor, and has led to the impoverishment and enslavement of the formerly independent class of craftsman, and to the misery of industrial crises and unemployment. Special efforts of social reformers, a special intensity of moral will, were necessary to counteract these unexpected fatal consequences of technical progress. But the possibility of the use of technical progress for purposes of evil, for the harm and perhaps the total destruction of mankind, was disclosed to an especial degree in our own age through the application of this progress to military technology, i.e., to the art of destroying human lives. Thus, for example, the invention of powered flight, this apparently great and glorious triumph of human thought over the weakness of the human body—a triumph in which was realized the primal dream of mankind, expressed in the myth of Icarus and inspiring the scientific reveries of the great Leonardo da Vinci—did indeed partly turn out to be beneficial for life by speeding up transportation and mail delivery. But what is the significance of this improvement compared with the unprecedented horrors of destruction brought about by the military application of this invention? Now it is evident for everyone that if mankind could completely negate this invention, could utterly forget it, this would be a true boon. Another example: the successive inventions of a number of explosive materials, gunpowder, dynamite, and still more powerful materials of destruction, did indeed help mankind (e.g., in mining); but what is the significance of this help compared with the horrors of the military destruction brought about by these inventions? And is not mankind prepared to curse the day when scientific thought penetrated the atomic structure of matter and learned how to split the atom, a discovery that virtually promised to transform life into paradise through the industrial exploitation of the boundless free energy of nature, but now threatens the world with the apocalyptic horror of atomic bombs? And bacteriology, perhaps the most beneficial discovery of the nineteenth century— does this discovery not threaten mankind with mass destruction if it is used in war (something which till now has been avoided only by chance)? But war, which in its essence always was and is a medium of destruction, of the unchaining of blind demonic powers of killing and cruelty, is scarcely the only domain in which intellectual progress and the consequent development of technology can have fatal consequences. The improvement of weaponry, and the improvement of the means of transportation and telecommunication, can turn out to be fatal in even so normal a function of society as state power. For such improvements create unprecedented possibilities of despotic rule and the suppression of all resistance to established rule. The most unlimited despotism in primitive conditions of life was moderate and shaky compared with the all-encompassing and invincible power of tyrannical despotism in contemporary "totalitarian" states. It is sufficient for the contemporary state power to have a monopoly on tanks, airplanes, and radio communication; it is sufficient for the state to train a small group of obedient janissaries who manage these technical means to guarantee once and for all the slavish obedience of the subject population. Now a wholly special foresight is necessary to prevent the

214

degeneration of human societies into a state of permanent slavish dullness. How far we are now from the so-recent faith that for mankind is predetermined easy, unfettered progress on the road to freedom!

Thus, contrary to notions that were widespread till but recently, it now becomes clear that in the domain of the technology of the conquest of the powers of nature, the progress of knowledge can serve the genuine improvement of the conditions of human life only in combination with good moral will. In the contrary case, this progress serves only the powers of hell, dooming mankind to unprecedented suffering and perhaps total self-destruction. At the present moment, mankind stands under the threat of complete destruction as a result of the unexpected, almost miraculous triumph of its scientific thought, its power over nature. Everyone now begins to understand that to equip a being as stupid and evil as man still is for the most part with enormous, almost supernatural power can have terrible, possibly fatal consequences.

Before examining the concept, possibilities, and forms of moral perfecting, we must consider yet another domain of technology in the broad sense: i.e., the ability to control the powers of earthly being and to subordinate them to our will. Technology is usually understood to mean only the ability to control the powers of nature that are external to man. It is often not remarked that a technology of the control of the powers of human nature itself is also necessary. The performance of tasks that man sets in relation to society also demands a correct, purposeful functioning of some apparatus of means. These means consist of powers that motivate human will and determine behavior. Politics as the art of controlling and ruling society consists not only in moral guidance, i.e., in the ability to find the true goals of communal life and to convince people of these goals. Here an error is often committed that is directly opposite to the error in the evaluation of technical domination over the powers of nature. If the importance and beneficialness of technical control over nature are usually exaggerated, the necessity and significance of the technical control and guidance of social life are underrated or even not noticed. The majority of people (whose opinion has a decisive significance in democracies) does not take into account this side of social life at all; and only professional politicians and specialists learn of its existence from their experience. Public opinion usually judges political and social orders and their reforms only by the justice or beneficialness of the principles and ideals which they are called to realize; but public opinion forgets that this realization demands a certain know-how, namely, a rational choice of means. The goals of social life are realized by a certain apparatus, a certain system of means, which can be purposeful, operating successfully and with a minimum of friction, or unsuccessful and unsuitable. This system of means consists in able action on human will. Given the imperfection and irrationality of human nature, the task of the construction of such an apparatus of social life is far from easy and simple. Like technology for the control of physical nature, this apparatus presupposes a sober scientific knowledge, knowledge of human nature and the laws of the motivation of human will. Only such knowledge can lead to the ability to direct human will in such a way that the results of its action are maximally beneficial for the rational and just ordering of human life. Here it is disclosed at every step of the way that the order that is most just in the abstract can in practice turn out to be unsuitable, i.e., incapable of directing human will in such a way as to realize the desired result; thus, the abstractly just order often leads not to the improvement but to the worsening of the conditions of life.

The idea of natural laws that govern the motivation of human will and of the necessity of taking into account these laws has gained general acceptance in the domain of economic life and in plans for the reform of economic life. But here too, perhaps as a reaction to rather exaggerated ideas of the unchangeableness and precision of the laws that were dominant in the so-called classical school of political economy with its faith in "natural laws"—here too, we have observed, during the last several decades, the growth of the bold belief that human will can fundamentally transform the economic order without taking into account the reality of human nature. This has led to the widespread belief that radical reforms can be achieved easily; an example of such reforms is the all-encompassing nationalization of the economy for the purpose of the just distribution of goods. But experience shows how easily such measures, paralyzing economic will, lead to the impoverishment and disordering of the apparatus of economic life. Even more widespread is the inattention to the technical conditions of social life or their complete rejection, which always leads to the collapse of the corresponding plan. From a multitude of existing examples, let us take two at random. The recent attempt at Prohibition in the United States was completely unsuccessful and led only to an increase in alcoholism and crime associated with bootlegging. Consider another example: the electoral system that is most just in the abstract, i.e., the system of proportional elections, can lead in practice—by promoting the particularism of political ideas and the resultant party fragmentation—to the impossibility (as experience has shown) of forming an effective, stable government.

This technical-organizational aspect of human life must be taken into account in two respects. On the one hand, all plans of political and social reform must simply take into account certain unchangeable laws of human nature, in the same way that all technology based on natural science takes into account the unchanging laws of nature, and any invention that does not take into account these laws is doomed to failure from the start. The fundamental structure of the world sets a limit here to every striving—even if morally justified—of human will. And to human nature are applicable Bacon's words: "*natura parendo vincitur*": "we can conquer nature only by submitting to it." On the other hand, an understanding of this aspect of human life makes clear that it is possible (and therefore obligatory for our will) to have a perfecting which consists simply in the perfecting of organization, the apparatus of the functioning of social life—in the perfecting of a system of means for the attainment of a definite goal. Again consider an example: the elimination or prevention of unemployment and the struggle against the economic anarchy that is expressed, for instance, in the fact that some countries suffer from hunger and need while in other countries products are destroyed because there is an oversupply of them—are purely technical-organizational tasks. For the successful solution (far from simple and easy) of these problems, it is extremely important to clearly distinguish them from the moral task of establishing a more just order of economic life, the former task differing from the latter one as means differ from the goal. The problem of socialism would receive necessary clarity if the task of the just distribution of economic goods and hardships were clearly distinguished from a wholly different problem that is purely technical-organizational in nature: namely, to what degree is state control of the economy purposeful and fruitful for the functioning of the apparatus of economic life?

It follows from the foregoing that such a technical-organizational perfecting of life is not in itself a genuine perfecting of life in the sense of the introduction into life of good and the destruction of evil. This perfecting is only the functional perfecting of life, the

217

improvement of the *means* of battle against evil, the protection of life from evil, and the utilization of the forces of the already-present good. In this kind of perfecting, man attempts to adjust the economy (in the broad sense of the word) of his life by means of the powers that are already present in nature. This functional perfecting is fundamentally different from *the moral perfecting of life.*

6. The Moral Perfecting of the World. The Tasks and Essence of Christian Politics

In the introductory considerations of this chapter it was pointed out that the moral perfecting of life can be dual in character: either *essential moral perfecting* in the sense of the introduction of good into human souls, their moral education, or *the perfecting of the order of life*, the norms and institutions effective in life.

When striving to attain some goal, man tends, at the outset, to employ simple, easily accessible, outwardly acting means, and to avoid as much as possible means that are more difficult and less accessible, that act more invisibly and out of the depths. Man tends therefore to exaggerate the significance of the former and to neglect the significance of the latter. Life-experience only gradually teaches him that those means are usually genuinely more effective which are more difficult to acquire and which act inwardly. The belief that life is improved most simply and easily by the improvement of its outward orders and structure emanates, most proximally, from this general tendency of human thought.

This prejudice has intensified and become particularly widespread during the past few centuries in connection with a basic error or heresy of modern times, according to which human nature in itself has no need of improvement, for it is rational and good in its essence. According to this idea, the evil in life can flow from only one source: the incorrect ordering of human life (although it remains incomprehensible here how perfect man could till now have such an evil, ineffective, imperfect order of life). Beginning at least with the second half of the 18th century, contemporary man firmly believes that the perfecting of life simply coincides with the perfecting of its political and social structure, with sociopolitical reforms. Meanwhile, the task of the inner moral and spiritual reformation of people recedes to the background, is considered, at best, a secondary, less significant task; great hopes are not placed on it in the work of the general improvement of life.

The unprejudiced observation of life as well as an attentive attitude to the significance of the inner powers acting in life, that is, to the spiritual element of human being, easily discloses the superficiality and falsity of this dominant intellectual tendency, a tendency which, moreover, contradicts the very essence of the Christian moral position. We have already touched upon this theme in our discussion of natural law as an inevitably imperfect expression of Christian truth, and of the meaning of Christian realism (see Chapter V, 5). Let us now examine in detail the relationship between these two forms of perfecting.

Christian moral activity in its fundamental permanent essence is the pouring down of the gracious power of love into the world, the introduction of good into human souls, and, hence, into direct personal relations between people. Although here the Christian moral consciousness does not set for itself the deliberate task of improving the general state of life, but is satisfied with concrete assistance to concrete people in their everyday spiritual and material need—this position is connected with the consciousness that precisely this kind of activity of love is the main, fundamental path to the general perfecting of life that determines everything else. In connection with what was said in Chapter V, 5, it is necessary to point out that the early Christian church did not in general pose the problem of changing the general *order* of life and the legal norms and institutions operating in life, but rather taught a humble toleration of the order as it is—including even such an essentially anti-Christian institution as slavery. The early church taught its followers to introduce into all the orders of life and relations between people the spirit of love, a brotherly relation to one's neighbor, attention to his needs, respect for the dignity of every person as the image and likeness of God, as a valuable co-member of one gracious organism of Christ's church (classical evidence for this spiritual position can be found in St. Paul's Epistles: 1 Cor. 7: 20-24, Ephesians 6: 1-9, Collosians 3: 12-25, and 4:1, in 1 Timothy 6: 102, and in the Epistle to Philemon). Slavery was not only moderated precisely on this path but even gradually died out by itself long before the institution of slavery was legally revoked.

Before clarifying all the significance of this path of the inner moral perfecting of life, let us examine and attempt a moral evaluation of the second path: the perfecting of the general orders of life.

From the general moral principle according to which every man (owing to the total unity of spiritual-moral being) is responsible for the fate of all people, for all the evil that reigns in the world, and has the obligation to struggle actively against evil and to promote good—from this principle it follows that the Christian consciousness as such, i.e., in its collectivity as the Christian church or Christianity, taken as a unity and as a unity that encompasses all its historical development, also has the obligation, as one of its secondary, derivative tasks, to *creatively christianize* the general conditions of life, to reform these conditions in the direction of their maximal agreement with the Christian truth. In brief, Christianity must implement *Christian politics.* If the early Christian church ignored and even rejected this task, we must have sufficient spiritual freedom to understand that this rejection was due to certain special factors, which lost their significance later; and that therefore, despite all the exemplary fullness and intensity in general of the Christian consciousness of the early church, the early church cannot be an absolute model for us in this regard. This was due partly to the early church's position as an insignificant and persecuted minority in the society of that day (owing to which it was wholly occupied with the simple protection of the spiritual treasure entrusted to it against the hostile powers of the world) and partly to its faith in the imminent end of the world, which made inessential all work toward the improvement of the earthly structure of life. Under different conditions, i.e., in the epoch of the decline of the ancient world and the invasion of the barbarians, the church became the leader in the task of ordering, healing, and perfecting the world. We now live in an epoch that is analogous to the epoch of the collapse of the ancient world and, therefore, it is completely natural that the Christian consciousness again faces the task of the moral revival and perfecting of the general orders of earthly human life.

Above, in another connection (see Chapter IV, 5), we rejected the teaching, distorted by spiritual provincialism, according to which the life of society and the state, or the general orders of the earthly life of man, are excluded in general from the Christian consciousness, from the concern about a moral and righteous life. We pointed out then that it is impossible to draw a strict, distinct boundary between the so-called personal or private life of man and social life; and that society or the state, like every human collective, is—for the responsible moral consciousness—something like a great human family, for the life and order of which we are responsi-

220

ble, just as we are responsible for the life and order of our small family in the precise, narrow sense of this concept. In connection with our present discussion, this relationship can be clarified now more precisely in another aspect, which directs us toward an understanding of the relation between the two forms considered here of the moral perfecting of life.

As we have seen, the distinction between these two forms is determined by the distinction between the sphere of the inner state of souls and personal relations (flowing from this sphere) between people—and the sphere of the *general orders* which normalize life, the sphere of the general external conditions of life. We must now supplement this idea by clarifying the other, correlative aspect of the problem. These two domains have an inner connection, formed by that stratum of human life which can be called the domain of mores, customs, moral habits. Thus, for example, between the sphere of the personal erotic life of a man (the personal moral level of his behavior in this domain) and the sphere of general laws or effective orders normalizing relations between the sexes—there stands as a connecting link the domain of mores, moral habits, prevailing moral concepts and evaluations, concerning erotic life. Between the personal relation of a man to the material need of his neighbor, the intensity of attention to this need, the degree of self-renunciation and active beneficence, on the one hand, and social law-giving, determining compulsorily the general order of relations between those who have and those who have not, on the other hand—there stands, as an intermediate link, the sphere of customs, hospitality, rules, and habits accepted by social opinion, general customs of courtesy, kindness, compassion, prevailing in a given nation, or contrarily, habits of coldness, reserve, indifference, and so on. The same sort of intermediate link between these two domains is the totality of voluntary collectives and, hence, organized efforts to assist the needy, carried out by all kinds of ecclesiastical and secular associations in the work of philanthropy (in the most general and broadest sense of this word, including all kinds of improvements of the social conditions of life). Through this intermediate sphere, the general legal order normalizing the general structure of collective human life is, in the final analysis, an expression and product of the personal spiritual life of the members of society, the degree of their moral perfection or imperfection.

The opposite situation is also possible. A general legal order, instituted by a law-giver or political reformer, can educate people, accustoming them to higher and more demanding moral concepts, stricter moral behavior. Or, on the contrary, it can lower the moral level of people and corrupt them (let us recall the influence of legal norms determined by ideas of religious intolerance, class struggle, or racial hatred).

This determines the meaning and nature of the moral perfecting of the general order of human life. This perfecting is, in essence, *the collective self-education of mankind*, the result of the collective efforts of the Christianization of life, i.e., the attempt to approximate the general orders and conditions of human life to the commandments of Christian truth. Furthermore, contrary to the widespread tendencies of all political fanaticisms and all onesided politicism in general, the path to the most effective and solid results here is the path *from inside outward*, the path from personal life to social life, the path of the perfecting of general relations through *the moral education of the individual*. This is the fundamental, royal road of the genuine Christian perfecting of life, on which, through the preaching of love, compassion, respect for man, the restraint of dark, selfish, chaotic desires, through appropriate education, through pedagogical and missionary activity—the solid foundations are laid of a better, juster social order, a social order more permeated by love and respect for man. That which is justly called the Christian culture of Europe was founded precisely on this road. On this road, the institution of slavery, for example, had been gradually dying out by itself before it was legally abolished. And on this road, among the still rather primitive tribes of Europe that were just converted to Christianity, the foundations of international law were laid, and faithfulness to agreements made on oath was observed; that is, there existed as a solid reality what appears to many in our epoch a naive and comical illusion.

This clarifies one highly significant relation, constantly forgotten by political reformers to the great detriment of human life. The above-mentioned necessity to take into account in the social reformation of life the "technology" that is determined by the general properties of human nature has another, profounder aspect. Social reforms are fruitful and lead to the good only insofar as they take into account *the given moral level* of the people for whom they are intended. Thus, for example, the degree of the relative severity or mildness of criminal punishment, the amount of freedom and self-rule granted individual citizens or groups and communities, the amount of freedom of the press, and so on, are wholly determined

222

by the moral state of the people for whom they are intended. It is evident to every pedagogue that the pedagogical standards applicable to little children are different from those applicable to young adults, that, for example, the freedom to choose a course of study, natural in the university, would be fatal in elementary school. But people tend to forget that a similar situation holds for the orders of social life in general. The best intentions of social and political reforms not only are fruitless, but can even lead to fatal results if they do not have support in a definite, suitable human material. As Spencer remarked justly: "That political alchemy has not yet been invented which can construct a golden building from rough bricks."*

It is possible to formulate a general proposition here: in the plane of stable, enduring being, *the level of the social order is a function of the moral level of the people who make up the order.* It is true that external legal reforms can, in their turn, influence the moral (as well as intellectual) education of people. In this connection, we must remember that such reforms can have a solid, fruitful effect only when they create conditions favorable to the elevation of the level of human nature, to the improvement of moral habits and concepts. Examples of this in social life are the role of legislation concerning schools, the education of youths outside of school, legislation concerning the family, measures concerning the protection of mothers and children, measures concerning the creation of favorable conditions of work, and so on. In these cases, improvement, coming from outside, from the outer layer of being, from the domain of external normalization, does not merely attempt to mechanically, compulsorily regulate life in order to improve it, but, educating the will, the deep spiritual root of being, attempts to improve the conditions of life by means of powers that spring from this root of being. Compared with legislative reforms of this type, the external legislative normalization of relations between people, which attempts to improve the conditions of life *immediately from outside,* signifies as a general rule only the above-clarified improvement of the technology and organization of social life, i.e., its external *protection from evil* and not at all the essential moral perfecting of social life. The distinction here is like that between police measures which protect life from crime and educational measures which in-

---

* Back-translation from the Russian.—Translator.

223

wardly overcome the criminal will through the moral improvement of man.

One must never forget that *direct* legislative measures against evil, e.g., against vices (alcoholism, debauchery, or gambling) or against the manifestation of cruelty, egotism, exploitation, and injustice, are prohibitions or, in any case, *compulsions* in the fundamental mode of their action. These are always measures that externally restrain human will, either by preventing this will from acting upon life or by forcing it to a definite mode of action. Mocking liberal socioeconomic politics, Lassalle once said that this politics reduces the state to the role of a "night watchman." This critique is completely legitimate insofar as it is the obligation of the state not only to protect the security of its citizens, but also to positively promote their well-being, their health, education, and so on. But if the state is something other than a "night watchman," one must not forget that the executor of all the compulsory norms of the state is, in the final analysis, the *police*, and that, therefore, when the state attempts to normalize and direct all human life in the interests of the social good (like the socialist state, for example), it fatally becomes an *absolute police state*. In essence, the activity of the police is reduced to the function of compulsion; but the action of the police does not fundamentally eliminate evil will or urges that are harmful to society, but only restrains their manifestations, pushes them aside as it were. *But there are certain immanent limits to the effectiveness of this kind of compulsion—limits which are thus the limits to all automatic perfecting of life by means of state power or the law.* Compulsion is necessary for the restraint of sinful human will, for the protection of life from the harmful consequences of this will. However, the attempt to direct all of life by compulsion leads not only to slavery, but also to the inevitable revolt of evil power, which always find new, unexpected paths of manifestation. Moreover, even purely *moral* compulsion (i.e., compulsion that does not call for the physical force of the agents of power), when it acts upon the will from outside as the pressure of public opinion, can be experienced as an intolerable tyranny and can in essence be a tyranny. This purely moral compulsion often leads either to the inner poisoning of moral life by lies and pharisaical hypocrisy or to reaction in the form of the explosion of moral licentiousness.

These considerations determine the Christian attitude toward plans of social reform by means of legislative measures and state normalization and control, and, in particular, the Christian attitude

224

toward the problem that, at the present time, is at the center of social attention, namely the problem of the legislative reform of social relations. A Christian must in principle approve of legislative measures that, in the interests of a just and rational order of human life, limit human egotism and willfulness or counteract the chaos that arises from the unopposed action of elemental human urges and desires. But he must also be aware of the inexorable limits to the beneficial action of such measures of the external restraint of the will, and of the necessity of another, deeper foundation for a just and rational order. Thus, for example, a Christian can and must sympathize with state control over economic life when this control really protects social life from disorder and injustice, but he will object to the attempt of the state to rule all of economic life, i.e., he will object to the intention of using state power to *force* people to act rationally and altruistically. To this intention he will oppose the task of the individual and collective education of human will toward its moral perfecting. Or, insofar as it is a question of legislative reforms, a Christian, accepting the necessity of a certain minimum of social security in the form of the automatic operation of the law, will insist on reforms that can educate the human will. In brief, although aware of his Christian responsibility for collective, organized, compulsory measures relating to the concern about the destiny of his neighbors, *he will reject all political and social fanaticism*, all faith in the possibility and even desirability of the use of external, mechanical measures to attain the fullness of the good in human relations. To this faith he will oppose Christ's words: "My kingdom is not of this world." But this does not mean that the kingdom "not of this world" is not intended for the world. On the contrary, the powers of the kingdom "not of this world" must more and more deeply penetrate into and heal the world. But this means that the genuine, *essential* perfection of the world is attainable precisely only through these superworldly powers, that this perfection flows from the spiritual depths in which man is rooted in the kingdom of God. To all political and social fanaticism the Christian must therefore oppose the fundamental path of *the Christianization of life, the path from inside outward.*

This path from the deep layer of the moral being of the person through the layer of personal relations of man to man, and, further, through the layer of collective habits and efforts directed at helping one's neighbors, to the external general conditions and orders of social life—this path is the path from the spiritual depths in which the human soul can directly receive the saving powers of grace, can live in God, can participate in the kingdom of God, to the imperfection of the world, to the kingdom of the "law," which in its essence does not attain the fullness and perfection of Christian truth. Every step on this path from the depths to the surface, from the uniquely personal to the universal for all, from freedom to compulsion, leads us away more and more from the fullness of gracious being, from the true essence of the concrete Christian truth, to the imperfect kingdom of the impersonal "law" (see Chapter IV, 5). Repeating and supplementing what was said above, particularly about the concept of natural law, we can say that insofar as Christian life (in the absolute sense of this concept) is taken to mean life that is genuinely saved, immanently permeated and illuminated by the powers of grace—the concept of *the Christian order of life is essentially impossible*, a contradiction in terms. In this sense, there is no and can be no Christian family, for the simple reason that in the kingdom of God, in the superworldly stratum of gracious redeemed life, there is no state, no social relations, no economic life, and even no family. What there is, according to Christ, is life as the life of "the angels which are in heaven." But in a relative sense, it is possible— under the conditions of the imperfect, earthly nature of man—to attain earthly orders which more and more closely approach the ideal of Christian truth, the commandment of respect for the person of every man and active love for one's neighbor; it is possible to have a Christian state, a Christian economic and social order, a Christian attitude toward property, and especially a Christian family. Furthermore, it is possible to have an infinite number of degrees of closeness to the goal of the Christianization of life, though this goal is never actually attained.

Let us return to the original idea of our discussion of this problem. As Christian politics (the striving for the Christianization of the general conditions and orders of life), the moral perfecting of the world is the penetration of the gracious powers of love, through human activity, into the general order of human life. In contradistinction to technical-organizational perfecting, moral perfecting is not a purely human process, but a Divine-human one. The root of the effective power here lies in that depth of the human soul where the purely human naturally touches upon gracious Divine powers, where freedom is not of human devising, not human willfulness, but the obedient assimilation by man of the higher, gracious reality. The closer we come to this root, the stronger and more natural becomes the action of this higher, superhuman power. But the farther we go away from it, the closer we come to purely earthly worldly being, the greater the role played by the purely human application of this power, and the smaller the gracious influence of the Divine principle when it is refracted and reflected in the imperfection of human nature; and the more mechanized and rationalized becomes the life-giving, formative power acting out of the depths. One must always keep this in mind. And since nothing living, strong, and truly fruitful is possible without nourishment by this inner life-giving power, which penetrates into human life through the element of the freedom of inner personal life and personal love for concrete people, it follows that a truly fruitful Christian politics must be conducted in forms which assure the possibility of the maximal participation of this inner, essentially Divine-human sphere.

This clarifies a highly significant feature of the necessary general sociopolitical ordering of life. This ordering is most normal and fruitful when it consists of the harmonious coordination of many small unions and social groups, the way a biological organism consists of the mutual connection and interdependence of many living cells and tissues. For precisely in such small unions the social order can have, to a maximal degree, the character of personal relations between concrete people and thus be determined by inner moral powers, whereas the all-powerfulness of larger unions and, in particular, of the state is inevitably based on soulless compulsion, on the impersonal action (an action which therefore never, in the final analysis, takes into account the concretely moral nature of the individual case) of the general law or on cold bureaucratism, indifferent to the concrete needs of life. The family, neighborhood organizations, professional cells and unions of all sorts, philanthropic organizations, local self-governments, are all channels through which the life-giving spirit of personal relations between people and, hence, personal moral life penetrate into the sphere of compulsory general orders and facilitate, to a maximal degree, the action of gracious powers of the inner Divine-human truth in these orders.

We must not forget that Christ's words, "without me ye can do nothing" (John 15: 5), have an everlasting and absolute force in politics as well as in all other domains of human life. Man is powerless and fated to err; his best intentions turn out to be vain and often fatal when he loses his living relation to God and God's truth, as they are revealed in the depths of the human soul. And in politics too, an attitude of prayer, humility before God, an ardent living love for man as the image of God—mean more than the boldest, cleverest plans of perfecting invented and willfully implemented by people.

The moral perfecting of the world stands midway as it were between two wholly heterogeneous tasks, clarified above: the task of the simple, external protection of the world from evil and the task of the essential overcoming of evil, which surpasses all human powers, i.e., the task of the salvation of the world. In moral perfecting, the light—in its tireless and unending struggle against the darkness—passes from simple defense to attack, forces the darkness to retreat, and dissipates it (but never entirely). Never attaining the goal of the salvation of the world (a goal that is essentially unattainable for man), man moves toward this goal in his striving for the moral perfecting of the world.

7. The Problem of the Perfecting of the World in the Present Historical Epoch

The task of the perfecting of the world, like all moral tasks in general, acquires a distinct concrete form only in connection with the completely concrete, given state of the world—a state in the midst of which and in relation to which this task is posed and is to be realized. What can we say about our epoch in this respect?

Compared to the relatively peaceful flow and stability of life in the nineteenth century, we are conscious that in the twentieth century the world finds itself in the grips of turbulent destructive motion, when all the moral habits of life and even the very physical existence of man are threatened with destruction. In such a state, the primary task is that of the salvation of the world from destruction, i.e., the simple protection of the elementary order that insures the very existence of the world. But on the other hand, pointing out the imperfection of the order that was unable to prevent disaster, and inducing the desire to reward oneself for one's suffering and sacrifices by the creation of something better than what existed before, the experience of the disasters of the twentieth century inspires one to dream of building the world anew, on completely new, better foundations. To all the difficulties of the conservation and establishment of a normal order of life in such threatening and

228

destructive epochs is added the inner conflict between these two essentially heterogeneous tasks.

This inevitable confusion of ideas is deepened by the ambiguity (already pointed out above) of the very concept or ideal of the perfecting of the world: it can mean the attainment of *the relatively best order of things under the given conditions of* life (even if this order is worse or no better than that which existed under more favorable conditions); or it can mean an *absolute improvement*, the attainment of an absolutely greater (compared with the past) amount of the good, justice, and happiness in human life. Despite the fact that they are obviously different and even opposed to each other, both tasks are in harmony to some degree and must be realized together: that is, in order to protect life from destruction, to cure the world of its destructive sickness, and to simply restore the elementary conditions of the world's preservation, it is necessary to somehow improve the foundation of the world, to correct that in the old order which led to these calamities or was powerless to prevent them. But such a legitimate and necessary improvement of the state of the world, coinciding with its maximal protection under the given concrete conditions, must be clearly distinguished from the striving, precisely in an epoch of troubles and all kinds of danger, to realize the ideal of the absolute perfecting of the world. In this respect, precisely our epoch makes especially urgent a critique of that prevailing dreamy optimism which forgets about the reality and power of evil (an attempt at such a critique has been an object of our book).

In a certain sense, there is a bitter irony in the very posing of the problem of the perfecting of the world at a moment when the world is in danger of falling into an abyss, of falling to the level of utter savagery and moral barbarism. This is like giving a man wise and morally elevating advice on how to raise his life to a higher moral level at the moment when, pulled off by a powerful wind, he is falling from a mountain into a chasm. Consider that during the last few decades, the elite of the European spirit, the subtlest and noblest minds of Europe, were occupied with the development of complex plans of political and social relations at a time when it was necessary to harness all available powers of mind and will to the extreme limit in order to prepare a simple defense of the most elementary foundations of European society against the attack of the powers of hell that were trying to destroy those foundations; further consider that this tendency is evident even today when the fire that engulfed the world has not yet been extinguished, but threatens to burst into flame again at any moment. One thus begins to understand that the striving for the moral perfecting of life can be a terrible, unforgivable sin when it is irresponsible, when it is based on dreamy inattention to the severe *real* conditions of life. In the last analysis, this is another version of utopianism, the fatal danger of which we discussed above. For utopianism in its harmful fatal essence is present not only in the perverse striving for absolute perfection under the conditions of earthly life. Utopianism occurs wherever the striving to attain the simple relative improvement of life, in itself legitimate and valuable, does not take into account the magnitude and intensity of the powers of evil that dominate the world precisely in the given concrete state of the world. Utopianism occurs wherever the moral will is afflicted by the vice of *irresponsible dreaminess*, wherever it is occupied with the building of air castles, wherever it is not based on responsible attention to that which it is necessary to do to promote good and counteract evil precisely now, in the given concrete, real situation. For the value of a moral act of will never lies in some general, abstract principle, but always only in its genuine correspondence to a real need of life.

The necessary intensity of the consciousness of the task of the simple salvation of the world from destruction, the protection of the world from the dangers that threaten it, presupposes a just evaluation of that which has already been attained in the past. Despite the inevitable imperfection of the existing "old," habitual order of European mankind, it must not be forgotten that this order is the fruit of heroic, stubborn, prolonged efforts of past generations to improve life. The intense Christian consciousness justly perceives the imperfection of this order, its remoteness from a more or less adequate realization of the commandments of Christ's truth. But despite all the legitimacy and usefulness of this consciousness, it must not degenerate into the irresponsible radicalism of the affirmation that European culture only appears to be a Christian culture. One must not forget the other side of the matter. Precisely now, in a troubled epoch when darkness has gathered over the world, when the fundamental moral achievements of European culture are threatened with destruction, one must be distinctly aware that such achievements as, for example, the abolition of slavery, the abolition of torture, freedom of thought and faith, the affirmation of the monogamous family and the equality of the sexes, the political

230

inviolability of the individual, legal guarantees against the arbitrariness of power, the equality of all people without distinction as to class or race, the acceptance of the principle of the responsibility of society for the fate of its members—are all achievements on the path of the Christianization of life, the approach of the orders and norms of life to the ideal of Christ's truth. That which has eternal value in the ideals of democracy and socialism—not as specific sociopolitical systems but as the general intent of the effective incarnation in life of the principles of the freedom and equality of all people, the holiness of the person as the "image" and "child" of God, and the brotherly solidarity of responsibility of all for the fate of all—is precisely the realization of certain orders and the recognition of certain obligations that indirectly and approximately express (through the evil and imperfection of the world's being and in the derivative plane of law and order) a new moral consciousness of mankind illuminated by the light of Christ's truth.

This does not mean, of course, that our conscience has the right to be satisfied with these achievements. This would contradict the fundamental essence of moral life as the tireless striving for perfection. If our first and most essential task in the present troubled epoch consists in the intense sacrificial protection of these great achievements from the hostile powers that are attacking them, nevertheless we must remember that, along with these positive achievements, in our life there are many habitual, generally accepted phenomena and orders that sharply contradict Christian faith in the holiness of the human person, the Christian commandment of love for one's neighbor, the responsibility of all for the fate of all. It is sufficient here to point out, only as an example, the existence in the Christian world of such a blasphemy (in the capacity of an institution of law) in regard to the holiness of the human person as capital punishment (which future generations— if the world is destined to undergo further Christianization—will come to view the way we now view the institution of torture). Further, it is sufficient to point out how little European mankind has learned to accept, even in principle, the subordination of international relations to principles of truth and law, and how widespread yet is the conviction that national egotism is legitimate. And finally, one must consider wholly legitimate and encourage in all ways the growing awareness (forming the moral truth of socialist striving, wholly irrespective of the usefulness or desirability of a socialist world order) that the principle of Christian love for one's neighbor must be more effectively applied to social relations through the responsibility of all members of society for the fate of the needy and unfortunate, the right of all people to equal conditions of physical health, leisure, and education. The Christian principles of the holiness of the human person, equality, and the brotherly responsibility of all for all must be put to greater, more consistent use.

Correctly understood, all such strivings for the further perfecting of life do not overturn that which exists, do not attempt to replace it with something absolutely new. Despite the novelty, compared to the habitual past, of that at which they are directed, they are nothing else but strivings for the solidification and deepening of the old foundations of European life and culture, namely, the Christian concepts and ideals on which European life has been based for eighteen centuries already. It must not be forgotten that, even though Nazism and Fascism have been overcome, those new powers, which in our epoch have entered into battle with the commandments of Christian truth, have not yet been overcome.

The epoch of the world into which we have entered during the past few decades is not, as it is frequently said to be, the epoch of the lordship of the "new paganism." It is something wholly other and *much worse*. Paganism—at least in its classical forms and partly even in its most primal forms—basically accepted the obligation of man to submit to the Divine will, knew the difference between good and evil, the necessity for man to temper his chaotic desires. In its own way, though imperfectly, paganism knew and recognized Divine truth, the Divine norm of being. But the contemporary world—being a deliberate revolt against Christ and His truth (which truth was previously, in principle, the object of reverent faith, despite the actual sinfulness of man)—is a *fundamental rejection* of the will and truth of God, the cult of self-sufficient human willfulness, which in essence is tantamount to the worship of Satan, "the prince of this world." We repeat, under such conditions, it is essential to remind people of the necessity of being guided in all of their life—including in social life, in the general order of their being—by the ideal of Christian truth; to remind them of the necessity of improving the world through the observance and protection of the eternal, unshakeable moral foundations of being. This constitutes the special significance, precisely in our epoch, of the task of the Christian perfecting of the world.

8. Conclusion

If in concluding this analysis of the problem of the perfecting of the world, we ask, What ontological relationship is the ground of the possibility of the perfecting of the world and of the moral obligation to strive for this perfection?—we would have to say the following (which will be a brief summary of the foregoing discussion). The possibility and moral postulate of the perfecting of the world are ontologically grounded in *the relation between God and the world.* Until the end and conclusive transfiguration of the world, God is *transcendent* in relation to the world; therefore, the kingdom of God is essentially "not of this world," does not fit into the limits of this world. Thus, God in the world (in the present aeon of the world) is not "all in all"; or (what is the same thing, as we have seen) God is not all-powerful in the sense of externally visible and tangible triumphalness. Rather, He is only invisibly and ideally all-powerful, and within the limits of the world He acts like the light, which, illuminating all that is around it, nonetheless remains surrounded by a dense wall of darkness and shines only in darkness. This determines the immanent imperfection of the world, which cannot be eliminated by any human, worldly forces, but abides until the end of the world and ends only with the miraculous transfiguration (surpassing all human and earthly forces) of the world. On the other hand, God is not only transcendent, but also *immanent* in relation to the world: He is present and acts immanently in creation itself. Furthermore, being the image of God, the reflection of God's light and glory, and in their primordial nature originating from God—man and the world are not a being that is directly opposed to the gracious power of the Light, but are potentially akin to and permeated by the Light. In its primordial ground, creation itself is *light*, though only reflected light. Therefore, through man and his spiritual, intellectual, and moral creativity, the gracious power of the Light reveals its action also in creation itself.

"The light shineth in darkness." As we have seen, this is indirectly applicable to the makeup of creation itself. "The true Light, which lighteth every man that cometh into the world," the light of Logos through which the world itself came into being—this light not only pours down from above its gracious powers into the world, but also continues to shine in the depths of the world's being, in the primordial depths of the human soul. More precisely, this light pours down its gracious powers precisely through the human heart which it penetrates and through the participation of the human moral will which this light awakens. And this light, in its being that is immanent to the world, also shines in darkness, finds itself in a continuous struggle against darkness, and therefore *really* shines only with a dim, twilight glow, like a small distant flame (what Meister Eckhart called "*Fünkchen*," a spark) breaking through a thick layer of darkness and sometimes barely visible. But if the final victory of the light over the darkness within the limits of the world is impossible in the present aeon of the world and it is fated to remain the light that shines in darkness, nevertheless this light can sometimes flare up more strongly and more brightly illuminate the kingdom of darkness than at other times, while sometimes it can be faint and very dim. Therefore, it is our obligation as "children of God," as children of the light, not only to strive to live in the superworldly element of this Divine light, and not only to protect man and the world as creatural incarnations of the light from the destructive powers of evil, but also to be the bearers of the light within the limits of the world itself, to strive ceaselessly to a state within the world itself in which the light is not faint but flares up as brightly as possible and illuminates as strongly as possible the world with its life-giving rays. Not only did Christ invisibly overcome the world, having taken upon Himself the world's sins and having been crucified in the midst of this dark, sinful world, and not only is He to triumph one day over the world, transforming it into a new creation, where God will be all in all; but, abiding now and forever together with us within this world itself, within our earthly life, He can—in proportion to the intensity of our will that prepares the ways of the Lord—penetrate more and more deeply with His light-bearing, life-giving Truth into our common human life.

This determines the duty and meaning of *Christian activity* in the world. The general tendency of our book can easily encounter the objection that, delineating the boundaries of human striving for truth and the good in the world, exposing as unrealizable and fatal illusions certain beloved hopes of the human heart, we weaken the impulse to moral activity and facilitate the propagation of the position of moral passivity. This objection is based, however, on the dangerous erroneous conviction that it is necessary to believe in the possibility of the impossible in order to have a moral motive for the realization of the possible, that it is necessary to set goals that surpass human powers in order to sustain the impulse of moral activity in regard to the perfecting of life. This appears to be the hidden volitional motive that lies at the base of secular humanism's faith in the all-powerfulness of the principles of good and reason in human nature, at the base of secular humanism's disinclination to see the reality of sin and evil and to recognize the imperfection of man. But however widespread this intellectual tendency, such an artificial spurring-on of the moral will is evidence of a certain morbid spiritual state of contemporary mankind. Such a striving for the impossible, for what contradicts the very ontological makeup of being, can in practice lead to only two things: either to an impotent dreamy state, to a preaching of moral activity that actually conceals passivity, to the sloth of a "wicked servant"; or to a feverish, morbidly excited, and blind activity, strong only in destruction and utterly powerless to create—to self-sufficient "dynamism" (so glorified nowadays), intoxicated with its own meaninglessness. In both cases, this is a position of moral *irresponsibility*, which always coincides with inner, spiritual passivity.

On the contrary, genuine activity, flowing from inner, *spiritual* activity, is always *seeing* activity—activity that takes account of the makeup of the reality at which it is directed. Therefore, genuine, healthy activity is not only compatible with sober realism but requires it. And precisely for this reason, the Christian realism of which we spoke above does not weaken Christian activity, but is its necessary condition and natural, healthy stimulus. Christian realism not only does not lead to passivity, but requires *maximal intensity of moral activity*. Only when we do not weaken our will by the politics of the ostrich, but courageously confront the dangers and difficulties of our life, are distinctly aware of the goals of our activity and the forms in which they can be realized in practice—do we possess a genuine moral foundation for intense, energetic activity. Moral power is acquired here not from inevitably shaky illusions, not from the false painting of empirical reality in a rosy color, but from the genuinely inexhaustible, everlasting source of superwordly Truth, in which we participate—from the Supreme power, genuinely all-powerful within the limits of our spirit, though, in its empirically human manifestation and within the limits of the world, forced to struggle against the hostile powers of "this world." Such is genuinely healthy moral activity, combining the inexhaustible power of faith with a reasonable account of reality—the activity, courageous both inwardly and outwardly, of a servant of the God of love, who has no need to become a Don Quixote in order to

235

be a fearless and tireless knight of the Holy Spirit in the world. In its essence, Christian activity is *heroic* activity. It is the activity of the sons of light in the kingdom of darkness, combining an unshakeable faith in their higher calling with a clear consciousness of the power of evil in the world—the power of the prince of this world. It is to battle against the prince of this world that they are called, with a humble and sober consciousness of their own imperfection.

"The light shineth in darkness." This means not only that it shines precisely *in darkness*, which does not receive it but resists it, so that it is not able to disperse or illuminate the darkness conclusively. This also means that it *shines* in darkness, that the darkness does not have the power to overcome it. Living in darkness, not only can we be consoled by the fact that the light abides in the superwordly Divine element, but we can also place our hopes upon its creative, illuminating power in the world itself. For this reason, we are obliged to watch over this light and to take measures that allow it to shine as brightly as possible in the world.

Index: General

Angelus Silesius, 39
Arago, François, 45
Aristotle, 104, 115, 213
Augustine, Saint, 37, 67, 96, 114, 207
Aquinas, Thomas, xxi, 16, 40, 109, 184, 209

Bacon, Francis, 212, 217
Belinsky, Vissarion, xii, 168–69
Berdiaev, Nikolai, xi, xiv
Bergson, Henri, 41n, 209
Bolshevism, xxii, 27
Bridget, Saint, 132n
Bruno, Giordano, 21
Buckle, Henry Thomas, 212
Bulgakov, Sergei, xi, xiv

Caesar, kingdom of, 86–91, 146
Calvin, John, 114
Catherine of Siena, Saint, 132n
Cato, 32
Celestine V, Pope, 131n–132n
Chernyshevsky, Nikolai, xii
Christ, xv, xix, 12, 51–52, 54, 55, 57–58, 60–63, 65, 71–73, 76, 77–78, 81–82, 84–87, 91–92, 95–96, 98–101, 104–6, 110, 113–15, 119–21, 133, 140–42, 147, 152, 155, 158, 160–61, 164, 204, 209–11, 226, 231, 234; Ser-

mon on the Mount, 53, 134–35, 156; the significance of the person of, 67–68, 70; His victory over the world, 79–80
Christian politics, 193, 220, 226–27
Christian realism, 179–81, 219, 235
Christianization of life, 222, 225–26, 231
Church, the, xx, xxi, 52, 73, 89–91, 142–45, 156–57, 192, 219, 220; as communion of saints, 74, 141
Churchill, Winston, 48
Communism, 14, 90, 167, 168
Comte, Auguste, 212
Condorcet, 17

Dante, 17, 132n
Darkness, 1, 5–7, 11, 27, 30, 50, 74, 91, 101, 105, 111–12, 116, 119, 121, 126, 145, 153–54, 158, 162, 182, 184–87, 198, 210, 211, 233, 234, 236; resistance of, 2–4, 9; overcome by the light, 8; as evil, 9; self-condemnation of, 10; power of, 12, 15, 18–20, 28, 31, 45; as the outer shell of the world, 183, 188
Darwin, Charles, 24, 93
Darwinism, 22–23, 163, 196
Demonic utopianism, 27–31
Descartes, Rene, 21

238

Index: Biblical

A Note about the Translator

Boris Jakim is Chief Abstractor at Technical Information Service, American Institute of Aeronautics and Astronautics. He has previously translated two other books by S. L. Frank, *The Unknowable* and *The Spiritual Foundations of Society*, both published by Ohio University Press.